MW00800634

KEVIN BALL

HEART

OF A

STUNTMAN

FROM HOLLYWOOD TO HUMANITY

ARMINLEAR

Heart of a Stuntman: From Hollywood to Humanity
Copyright © 2022 by Kevin Ball
All rights reserved under the Pan-American and International Copyright
Conventions. This book may not be reproduced in whole or in part, except for
brief quotations embodied in critical articles or reviews, in any form or by any
means, electronic or mechanical, including photocopying, recording, or by any
information storage and retrieval system now known or hereinafter invented,
without written permission of the publisher, Armin Lear Press.

Library of Congress Control Number: 2022947297

ISBN (paperback): 978-1-956450-56-9
(eBook): 978-1-956450-57-6

 Armin Lear Press Inc
215 W Riverside Drive, #4362
Estes Park, CO 80517

KEVIN BALL

HEART

OF A

STUNTMAN

FROM HOLLYWOOD TO HUMANITY

FOREWORD BY CINDY MCCAIN

ARMINLEAR

To the four most influential and important women in my life.

TO MIA HAMWEY
Through a single phone call, you trusted me enough to accept my authenticity, allowing me into your life and to take my first steps into the unknown. My journey into humanity began with you and the wonderful women of "Freedom Fields".

TO CINDY MCCAIN
We met on my first mission to the landmine fields in Cambodia and you saw something inside of me that I had yet to understand. Your guidance, nurturing and your offers to take John and I around the globe many times forged my empathetic soul and made me realize that I could actually help those less fortunate in the world.

TO MY WIFE – ASHLEY KITZMAN-ORTIZ BALL
Ashley, you have always said "Go, do it, live your life" without fear of me not returning. You accept me for who I am and have never asked me to be anything different. I love you baby.

TO MY MOTHER – PATRICIANN MARIE BALL
I put your full name down because I want everyone to know who you are. It took some time for me to realize it but its because of you that I received the heart of a humanitarian. It was born into me and it came from you. No matter how rebellious and sometimes unkind I was, you always loved me and saw goodness. I can never thank you enough mom.

CONTENTS

FOREWORD: CINDY MCCAIN 1

PREFACE 3
From Hollywood to Humanity: The group that started it all

CAMBODIA – JANUARY 2007 16
Freedom Fields USA

VIETNAM, JULY 2007 67
Operation Smile

KENYA, NOVEMBER 2007 94
World Journey of Smiles

KOSOVO, MARCH 2008 123
The HALO Trust

PERU, JUNE 2008 190
International Health Emissaries

ASIA TOUR, JUNE 2008 232
Cindy McCain / Campaign

ASIA TOUR, VIETNAM, 2008 236
Operation Smile

ASIA TOUR, THAILAND, 2008 .... **254**
World Food Program

ASIA TOUR, CAMBODIA, 2008 .... **267**
World Food Program

GUATEMALA, NOVEMBER 2008 .... **299**
International Health Emissaries

DUBAI, JULY 2009 .... **343**
International Health Emissaries

GUWAHATI INDIA, JULY 2009 .... **364**
Operation Smile

LAST THOUGHTS **407**

EPILOGUE **409**

FOREWORD
CINDY MCCAIN

STEPPING INTO A LANDMINE FIELD for the first time is enough to make you freeze in your tracks, but that's where I met Kevin and John, cameras in hand. Deep in the heart of a landmine zone near the border between Cambodia and Thailand, I was impressed with their passion for humanity and entertained by their daring stories of being professional Hollywood stuntmen. After a week of watching them film in harsh and deadly conditions, I invited the pair to accompany me to Vietnam to document a medical mission with the international children's organization Operation Smile. As a board member of both The HALO Trust and Op-Smile, I know just how important it is to get the true stories and images out from the field and into the public eye; that's exactly what they were doing. From there our friendships grew, and within a short time Kevin and John were accompanying me around the world as my personal documentary team, including during the 2007 campaign trail where my husband, Senator John McCain, was running for the office of the President of the United States.

Country by country, cause by cause, the men learned, taught, and engendered smiles wherever they went. The knowledge they received along the way has allowed them to give back to many humanitarian organizations—and you always know that it's going to be a fun trip when you see their faces show up at the start of a mission. Kevin chose to put his thoughts and experiences into words and has created a work that you will not only find fun and entertaining, but also packed with years of personal experiences that can teach others how to open their hearts to humanity.

Kevin has spent decades in front of and behind the camera on many Hollywood movies and TV shows, it has gifted him with an eye to tell the stories of those he comes across, and a voice to get his message heard. His goal is not only to introduce people to the true definition of the word *humanity* but also to invite them to step through the doors that life opens and to bravely see the world through others' eyes. As with my own experiences while traveling and helping to advocate for a number of these NGOs that Kevin writes about such as The HALO Trust and Operation Smile, I am happy to know that my actions have led others to seek out their own platforms to spread the word of those doing amazing work to help those in need.

PREFACE

THE FIFTY CALIBER SHOTS RANG OUT as the sniper perched on the radar arch of the old freighter let loose a barrage of ground cover from behind us. In the darkness, muzzles flashed everywhere, silhouetted by the dust kicked up from all the purposeful, yet panicked, foot movement of everyone involved in the firefight. It was turning into a real war zone. If you have ever twisted a roll of bubble wrap to the point where each pop overlaps the next, then you know what I was hearing—the bubble wrap sound replaced by the noise of pressurized gasses exploding from heated rifle barrels. I squeezed off a burst from the fully automatic forty-five caliber assault rifle I had been handed earlier and then ducked behind the white Cadillac Escalade, narrowly missing the shrapnel that flew from the vehicles hood. "Don't waste all your rounds. Watch your aim. Listen for the lull in the shots before you fire again." All these thoughts ran through my mind. The guy to my right went down grasping his leg. I wanted to help him, but after witnessing a round from the fifty-caliber shoot through the entire body of a Dodge Charger in front of me I was more worried about self-preservation. The explosions in the car blew the body in the driver's seat apart. Then, just as I thought this scene of mayhem would never end, I heard a voice over the electrified volume of a bullhorn shout, "Cut!! Okay, that's good. Let's check the playback." and Michael Mann emerged from under a protective sound blanket and handed the camera perched on his shoulder to one of the many assistants who followed him everywhere. I removed my earplugs, carefully returned my weapon to the props guy waiting just off set, went back to my stunt bag, found a place to sit down and waited. Miami in March was hot and muggy. Even on the all-night shoots there was no let up from the humidity and the onslaught of biting insects that thrived in the brackish air of our location on the Miami River. This was the second time we had shot the ending scene for the soon to be finished Michael Mann not-so-much blockbuster, *Miami Vice*. Not the second time we shot it there that night, but the second scripted and full location change. We had shot the first ending, one that culminated in a huge meth lab explosion, two weeks earlier at a trailer park. The studio bought out an entire neighborhood for a week and the families were put up in a nice hotel during that time. Because of Mr. Mann's reputation for changing everything at the drop of a hat, the stunt coordinator decided it would be a great idea to bring in a stunt double for every actor on set each night. It didn't matter if we were used or not, as long as we were there. I was the stunt double for one of the Aryan Brotherhood guys; the only one with long hair and a long beard—neither of which I had. This meant that each night I sat for hours having my hair twisted into pin curls to keep the wig from flying off my head as I dove around dodging imaginary bullets. To further match my actor, a handmade beard was glued to my face whisker by whisker, creating full nights of itching, poking, skin pulling fun. Add to that the moisture and heat and I was miserable. When they were done with me, I looked like the singer Rob Zombie. My only relief from the discomfort was knowing that I could rip the beard off at the end of each night, (or early morning). My stunt friend Chris also had an application of facial hair, though much less than mine, and made a game of seeing how many times he could eat away his fake mustache each night and have the makeup girls re-apply it. Four, I believe, was his record. Take after take, adjustment after adjustment until finally the visions in Michael Mann's head matched the ones we had filmed. By the last evening I was told that we'd spent $1.3 million a night filming— part of the reason the film cost over one hundred million dollars to make.

This was the catalyst that sent me over the edge and caused me to make some huge changes in my life. Don't get me wrong. I love the film industry and I will always be a professional stuntman. I fought long and hard to get where I am, but my sense of reward was diminishing and witnessing that much money go to waste made me realize that I needed to do something. The timing for my epiphany was perfect because, while looking for an emotional escape, I had started volunteering with a nonprofit that helped with the growing population of homeless people in downtown Orlando. One day I worked with the haves, the next I helped the have-nots and, after a while, the faces and stories seemed to blend. I could see how the producer who made millions could easily find himself penniless and on the street. I could also see how a person living on the streets, if given the right chances, could quickly rise to power and fortune. It was all a matter of being in the right or wrong place, making good or bad decisions, having a bit of luck, and allowing the universe to unfold as it chooses.

So, my decision was made. Armed with my years in front of and behind the camera, the knowledge I had gained from the people on the streets, and a stuntman's need for adventure, I set off to make a change. I yearned to help humanity find a voice that would be loud enough to overpower greed and negative energy, so I decided to document the groups and the people around the globe who were making a difference. I would use whatever outlets I could find to tell their stories to the world. It ended up being the most amazing ride I have ever taken, and I refuse to let it stop.

FROM HOLLYWOOD TO HUMANITY- THE GROUP THAT STARTED IT ALL

My remarkable journey began with a group that I ran across while surfing the Internet. Freedom Fields USA is a non-governmental organization (NGO) based in Carmel, California and they had a story that needed to be told.

It was the story that first attracted me. "What an original scenario to document," I thought. "*It would make an amazing documentary. A group of women, stuck in the mundane, turn their book club into an international humanitarian landmine removal organization.*" I would learn that the intriguing stories and individual passions behind their NGO's mission was much more than just a set of surface images and, along the way, Mia Hamwey, the founder of FFUSA, became an amazing friend of mine. I owe her more than she will ever know because without her open trust and belief in me who knows where I might be.

Mia and her friends had a book club in Carmel, where once a week they met and did what book clubs do. They discuss the latest great read over a glass of wine, debated topics about raising their children and socialized. Things changed for them after they read a book by Loung Ung called *First They Killed My Father*, which follows the life of a young girl growing up in Cambodia as the Khmer Rouge was brutally taking over. The story resonated with Mia who realized she needed more. She was feeling a bit lost and bored with life, so she decided to use her sister Kara as a sounding board to see if Kara could help her find ways to alleviate her doldrums. Kara worked at Armitage International in Washington, DC. Her field was weapons abatement and removal—which included landmines. She suggested that Mia involved some way; maybe she could throw a fundraiser in Carmel. Mia ran with the suggestion and raced to make a huge suggestion to the members of the book club. She proposed that they turn the club into a nonprofit organization that helped with humanitarian landmine removal. To her surprise, the idea not only met with no resistance, but was greeted enthusiastically, and with this new passion, Freedom Fields was born. Aided by some of Kara's DC connections, the women started to hold very successful local fundraisers and funneled the donations to an international NGO named The HALO Trust." HALO is an acronym for *Hazardous Area Life Support Organization,* and they do the dirty work—the actual removal of deadly landmines, I will have much information on them in a later chapter.

After a few emails to some contact names I found on the Freedom Fields website and a phone call placed to the only number I could locate, I received a response back. It was Mia calling me and we hit it off from our first words. Our conversation started my destiny. I spent much of that phone call talking about the homeless people I had been helping in Orlando and elaborating about my filming credentials (but making it up with much Hollywood stuntman talk.) In my emails I had stated something to the effect that I was a documentary filmmaker and that I thought their story would make an amazing topic for my next documentary. "Next Documentary? Like there was a first one?" The amusing fact here is that I was not really experienced in the world of documenting stuff. I had once documented my pug running around the back yard, but not much more than that. Still, how hard could it be? I had years of television and film experience, even if it was mostly getting thrown off stuff, beaten up and lit on fire as a professional stuntman. Speaking with a bit of pompousness, I told Mia that I felt my many years on camera made me ready to start my career as a documentary producer, video operator, audio mixer, editor and a host of other hats that I thought I could handle wearing. Truth be told, as a stuntman and stunt coordinator you do get the chance to review scenes and to analyze the shots with the director to make suggestions and adjustments that help perfect the overall stunt segment. As the years went by, I discovered that I have a very keen eye and an artistic judgment of how shots should play out. However, creating a full documentary would be a bit of a stretch. At this point I don't think that I knew how to turn on the new video camera I had just bought, not to mention how to use the microphone equipment; the assortment of cables, clips and lenses; and the one fuzzy microphone cover that came with its own brush and resembled a phallic Muppet with no eyes. So here I was, loaded up with shiny new gear and trying to talk my way into an invitation to fly to Carmel, California, where I'd meet the group of women with whom I hoped to travel to Cambodia and shoot a masterpiece that would make the film festival circuit gasp and award me high honors. Somebody needed to slap me and tell me just how much in over my head I was!

Like any good adventurer, I wasn't going to walk into the

unknown all by myself. Hell no! I was dragging my best friend John with me, although he didn't quite know it yet.

This would be a good time to introduce John. John Evanko was a good friend of mine then; now he is an amazing friend. The timing was perfect for all this documentary and travel talk because we both had taken jobs at Universal Studios working as stunt riggers in the *Fear Factor Live* show, and within a short period John had been offered the position of stage manager. This position only lasted for a few weeks, during which time he gave himself the title mis-manager. Like me with my documentary fantasies, John was in way over his head, both with the management job and with a new house that he had bought to flip. These two huge stress bombs were continuously looming over him.

What better time for me to step in and try to persuade him to drop everything and buy a plane ticket to Cambodia. I mean, who wouldn't want to go to Cambodia, live in a tent and try to film ten or so women touring landmine fields near the Thailand border? To my wonderment when I mentioned it to him the first time, he didn't think I was crazy. He wasn't persuaded to go with me yet, but fate would soon give him a push in my direction.

The *Fear Factor Live* show was forced to close down for the annual Halloween holiday season. This was so the park could use our stage for another show, one that featured scantily dressed parodies of b-list celebrities dancing provocatively to top 40 music hits. John and I were forced to take other jobs in the park until the *Fear Factor Live* show started back up in November. *Halloween Horror Nights* at the Universal Orlando Resort is the largest ongoing professional Halloween attraction in the United States of America. The park is filled to capacity every night and people make the pilgrimage to see this event from all corners of the globe. Why am I telling you this? Well, mis-manager John, was given the job of mis-managing the scare zones in the streets around the entire Universal Orlando theme park complex. This was a huge responsibility. John had never even considered attending a *Halloween Horror Nights* event as a guest, much less imagined himself in charge of managing this huge division of it. If it wasn't high enough before, John's stress level now went through the roof. He was working over 70 hours a week, he'd stopped sleeping and he was becoming mentally unstable.

On the other hand, I spent most of September helping to build haunted houses and then, during the actual *Halloween Horror Nights* event, I was in charge of some bungee jumping vampires. Stick with me here; this information might not seem that exciting but it will give you an idea of our emotional states and what we were doing at this time of our lives.

My communications with Mia continued and we agreed that I should come out and meet the women of Freedom Fields, pitch my ideas to them and to see how receptive they were to being filmed for ten or so days.

"Before you come out here," Mia said, "there is one person that I want you to speak with on the phone. She is a member of the group and I value her opinion tremendously. Her name is Dina Eastwood." I paused, pondered my knowledge of the Carmel, California area and said, "Eastwood, as in Clint Eastwood's wife?"

"Yes," Mia said, "She is a dear friend; here is the Eastwoods' home phone number. Clint rarely answers the phone but if he does, just ask to speak to Dina." This would be the first of many speechless moments throughout the next six years that left me motionless, thoughtless and blankly staring at the phone in my hand. Like most stunt guys, I am a huge fan of Clint Eastwood and his movies. Now I was instructed to call his house and ask to speak to his wife. It took about two weeks to make this phone call happen and I was on a vacation, in Las Vegas of all places – another first because I had never traveled to Sin City before. I was sitting in my room at the soon-to-be finished Planet Hollywood hotel. At the time it was still transitioning from its former life as the Aladdin Hotel, leaving a strange combination of Hollywood bric-a-brac mixed with Ali Baba décor. Anxiously I stayed in my room waiting for two o'clock, the agreed upon time for my call to the Eastwood household. Palms sweating, I picked up my phone and dialed the number that Mia had given me. A female voice answered,

"Hello, this is Dina."

"Hi, Dina, it's Kevin Ball." There is a long pause, followed by an almost frantic voice that caught me a bit off guard.

"Oh my God, Kevin. I dropped my laptop and I don't know what to do. It has all my family photos and work on it." That was our introduction: Clint Eastwood's wife, in our first conversation, confided in me about a possible family emergency and asked me about computers. This was so down to earth that it reminded me of the recurring tech talks I had with my own mother. My heart rate steadied and I went into help mode.

"What type of laptop is it?"

"It's a Mac," she said. That was our connecting point, the simple word "Mac." I calmed her down a bit and told her the information on the hard drive was fine and to take it to the local Apple store and they could retrieve everything. I totally forgot I was going to talk to her about filming a documentary on her group until she said, "I get a good feeling about you, Kevin, and I think it's great that you want to help out the group. I can't wait to meet you in Carmel when you come to visit us next month." That was it; no stress and not the Spanish Inquisition that I was expecting.

After I returned home from my Vegas vacation I pushed the

trip on John again and told him that Mia and I had set a date for me to fly out and meet the group. I filled him in on the amazing phone call with Dina Eastwood, and how the documentary idea was moving forward and the wonderful support that I was getting from everyone. I let him know the dates of my trip and again told him that I would love to have him come with me to Cambodia on this adventure and help me film. I could see the gears turning in his head. With each bit of new information, I could tell he was getting more interested.

I'll skip forward a week or so, to the point at which John hit his maximum stress level with the supervisor position. I pulled him away from his duties to help me move some tractors that were used to tow parade floats. It was brainless, almost relaxing, work and John needed to relax. So it was perfect. As few of the tractors were broken down and would not run under their own power, we decided to use a rope and tow them around the perimeter road that encircled the park. John steered the nonworking ones as I drove the tractor towing him. *This is such an important time in our story.* It's the moment that John let go of what he thought he was supposed to do, and let the universe take over and guide his direction. As I was pulling him down the back roads of the park he started to smile, then he started to laugh and then he yelled,

"I am having fun right now! I just had an epiphany: I hate my job! I am coming to Cambodia with you to film this thing!" So fate, karma and stress forged our new filming partnership that we named Karma180 Productions. People always ask, "Why didn't you name it Karma 360? That would be a full circle and things would come back to you." My response is that this is not the way karma works. You can't give something away with the hope of getting something back in return. That's not karma: that's greed, and it's the worst type of greed because it's disguised as a favor or a kind gesture. For karma to be true karma you must give away at 180 degrees, not wanting anything back in return. This is the only way to find true karma. It's a strange thought; to get something good back from the universe, I have to give away and not expect or want anything back in return. Trust me, it's a puzzle of logic and it takes much meditation and deep questioning to truly get a grasp on it.

Sometime in mid-November of 2006 I made the first trip to Carmel to meet Mia and the group. On the plane, I couldn't help asking, "What am I getting myself into?" At the same time, I kept thinking how amazing it felt to do something a bit outrageous, to finally step – or, more appropriately, to leap—out of my box, my comfort zone. When I landed in San Jose, California, Mia was waiting to pick me up and drive us back to Carmel, about an hour away. Neither of us knew what to expect. We had only spoken twice on the phone and communicated mostly through emails. But what could have been a long, awkwardly silent drive from the airport turned instead into something quite the opposite. After we both came clean about our fears of running into an axe murderer, we chatted as if we were old friends. We talked about our love of humanity and quizzed each other on our life stories. A quote from a book that I had been reading came up:

Listen to your heart. It knows all things,
because it came from the Soul of the World.

I'm not sure how one simple quote from a book could bond two people forever, but it did. The book was *The Alchemist* by Paulo Coehlo, and it turned out that Mia's daughter had just finished reading it in school.

The book is all about finding your own personal journey, and that is just what I was doing. I was starting my own personal journey—one that just happened to lead me to a landmine field in one of the poorest places in the world by way of Carmel, California, one of the most comfortable places in the United States. Carmel-by-the-Sea, the city's full name, is as close to a fairytale land as you will ever find.

Kris Howard, one of the Freedom Field members, had graciously offered her guesthouse to me for the visit. Over the past few years John and I have grown to call her guesthouse our Carmel home. The house is nestled among the pines on a hillside overlooking Carmel beach and the rocky coastline of Lobo's Point Park. Sitting on her back deck in the morning, as the fog burns off the shoreline, is like living a coffee commercial. So there I sat on my first morning in Carmel, relaxing and drinking a wonderful cup of Fog Lifter coffee in a fantasyland and thinking about meeting the group for a dinner in my honor at Mia's house later that evening. I still had no idea what I was getting into but I knew that, whatever it was, I liked it.

About seven o'clock Mia drove down to Kris's to pick me up and take me the mile or so back up the hillside to her house. Some of the ladies had already arrived and were awaiting us, the rest casually showed up in within the hour. So many new faces—housewives, teachers, business owners and realtors. Some were in their thirties; some were a bit older. As we mingled and chatted about what I wanted to accomplish with my documentary, a fashionably late Dina Eastwood arrived sporting a very well-aged bottle of Tequila. She greeted me with a perfect smile and a hug. I was hugging Clint Eastwood's wife, who was holding bottle of Tequila, in a room full of lovely women with whom I was going to fly halfway around the world. John probably thought I was losing my mind, given all the random text messages that I sent him that night. Most started with phrases like, "Holy crap, dude!" or, "You are not going to believe this…"The one message that I remember exactly read, "I am now holding a landmine, John. Mia just handed it to me." Of course, it was not live; it was just an inert shell that was sent to her piece by piece to be used as a prop to show people just what they were taking out of the ground in Cambodia. Inert or not, when someone hands you an item that is used to blow off people's limbs you take a deep breath and think about how not so bad your life is.

As the night flowed on, so did the drinks. Everyone knows how spiritual you get when you drink and I for one was feeling really spiritual! At one point, Dina Eastwood and I drank Tequila straight from the bottle as we talked about topics for the documentary. I agreed with all of her suggestions and frequently added, "Yeah, I was thinking that too." All while I'm thinking, "This is Clint Eastwood's wife! Please don't do or say anything stupid, Kevin!"

I can be a sensitive guy if the right Hallmark moment comes up, and all of us were filled with humanitarian passion as we discussed this fantastic documentary that was going to tell the world the story of the book club turned humanitarian landmine removers. Maybe it was the moment, or maybe it was all the energy in the room, but we all hugged, shed a few tears and laughed a little. If there had been any lingering apprehensions among the women about inviting two strange men travel to around the globe with them and film their adventures, they were now gone.

CAMBODIA – JANUARY 2007
FREEDOM FIELDS USA

FROM CARMEL TO CAMBODIA

I HAD EXCITING STORIES TO TELL JOHN when I returned from Carmel, and it only took a couple of days for us to cough up the thirteen hundred dollars per ticket to fly to Cambodia. There were probably cheaper ways to get to Cambodia but this was the flight that the group had chosen. Since we were telling their story, it only seemed reasonable that we travel with them. To begin our journey John and I would spend a week in Carmel filming the women in their everyday lives. We figured that this footage would work great to show the stark contrast between their ordinary lifestyles and the extremes of life in Cambodia.

It turned out to be a great idea that we took this extra week. At the beginning of the week, John took a picture of me sitting on the couch in Kris's guesthouse, wrapped in a blanket and holding the video camera like I didn't know which end to look through. I did, of course, know which end to look through but I had no clue what most of the buttons on my new toy did. So, in addition to getting tons of useful footage of the women living their normal lives in Carmel, I used the week to figure out what to do and what not to do while filming with my new Sony FX 1 High-Definition

Video Camera. It would be really useful to know all this *before* I flew to the other side of the world to walk through live landmine fields.

LET'S TALK TRAVEL

I have become a very impressive luggage packer over the last six years. I know just what to bring with me; what I won't need; and just how to pack for the most efficiency and space. I have collected the lightest travel clothes, socks and shoes, and even underwear that states right on the package you can take only one pair on a three-month trip (The underwear works, by the way.) However, at the time of our first Cambodia trip, neither John nor I had a clue about how to travel efficiently. Instead of packing light, we did the complete opposite. I took my largest bag—one that was designed to carry SCUBA diving gear. It transformed into a backpack and I thought this was quite clever. It was so large that if you walked behind me, all you could see were half of my arms and my legs from the knee down. The camera gear was in a carry-on size Pelican case, which I was very proud of because I had cut spots out of the case's foam insert for all the batteries, chargers, microphones and other electronic trinkets. Since it was made of impact resistant plastic the case also made a great seat—something I thought might come in handy somewhere, in some random country that lacked seats. It was a unique looking case but, now that I think about it, I realize that it screamed, "Steal me! There must be something worth taking in here!" This is really not the image you want to project while you are walking around in developing countries.

John's bag of choice was an old, generic-looking suitcase with a Stunts Unlimited patch on it, a zipper whose life expectancy had expired a few hundred zips ago and a bad wheel that caused the bag to wander off to the right while he pulled it along. The new backpack he carried, which had been shipped to Mia's house in Carmel, contained his laptop, electronic gear, camera stuff and whatever else he could cram into the side pockets. Its makers at Oakley had lovingly named it the Kitchen Sink; this alone should give you an idea of its size. On this first international trip, other than a couple of travel shirts that I had bought, most of our clothing was what we would wear on a normal day back in Florida—jeans, T-shirts, sneakers and such. Now, many years later, we are mean, lean, travel packing machines.

CLEAN CLOTHES POINTER

Here are a couple of pointers I have learned from experience. Pack as much synthetic, moisture wicking material as possible. This goes for shirts, pants, socks and underwear. The underwear and socks should also be antibacterial. You only need two or three outfits, which you will rotate through on your trip. At the end of a long, hot, sweaty day simply hop in the shower with all your clothes on and soap everything up. Then, take off all your clothes, scrub them together and rinse. Don't forget to do the same to yourself. When you're finished, wring everything to get as much water out as possible and then do what is called a burrito stomp. That is, find a cotton towel—even in the most primitive areas, I have found at least a few cotton towels. Lay the towel out on the ground and then lay your cloths flat on the towel. Starting at one end, roll the towel and your clothes up like a burrito and then stomp on the roll. This will only work with synthetic clothing because the material will not hold moisture and the cotton towel will absorb most of the liquid. Hang them up and within a couple hours you will have fresh, dry clothes. Gold Bond powder is also something that I won't travel without. It and a good deodorant stick can lengthen the wearing time of almost any clothing, even if you are a trapped for few days in a place without running water. Like a landmine field at the border of Cambodia and Thailand. These are just a few pointers that I know work. I have tested them in some pretty harsh real-life situations.

CAMBODIA HERE WE COME, MOST OF US

After a few more days of filming, practicing with the gear and exploring the stunning coastline roads to Big Sur the day to embark on my first international humanitarian trip finally came. Everyone met at Mia's house for a family and friends send off. Husbands chatted with us about what we planned to film, champagne flowed freely and children cried at the idea of being separated from their moms for over ten days.

Eventually, the chauffeured vans that would take us all to San Francisco International airport arrived. Wasting no time, we loaded up our gear and we were off—John, over a dozen women and me. San Francisco is not too far north of Carmel, so we arrived at the international branch of the airport after only a few hours. Our flock unloaded the vans and ventured inside to start the journey of a lifetime. Almost immediately we had our first back out. We had barely passed through the terminal doors when one of the women—who had never been away from her family and kids before, let alone ventured anywhere near where we were going – got cold feet. As gently as possible, other women tried to convince her that this was something she needed to experience; that she should fight her fears and go with the group. But she just couldn't go through with it and called her husband to pick her up. She simply wasn't ready.

This made me realize just how many people in the US never venture outside their comfort zones. On one of our later trips, John said a few words during a dinner that will stay lodged in my memory forever. We were going around the table answering the question, "What's the one thing you would tell others about your experiences from this trip?" I believe we were in Ecuador on a dental mission.

When his turn came John said, "I wish everyone in the United States would get a passport and just leave; go somewhere they never thought that they would go and just experience life." Our journeys have taken us in and out of many developing countries and I can say for a fact that when it comes to the world, we, the people born in the United States, are the minority. Most people on this planet don't live the way we do and no matter how bad you may think you have it, trust me you don't. There are grocery stores with food in them here and all you have to do is work a job, earn money and buy the things you need. The government doesn't change overnight, so you probably won't wake up one morning and discover that half the country is trying to kill you because your tribal leader was overthrown. Children here can walk to school without fearing they will step on an abandoned landmine. You can drink the water right from the faucet. You don't have to scrounge for scraps of cardboard in the winter to fill the holes in your shack in some shanty town. Your first childhood memory isn't of the white UN planes that dropped bags of food from the sky. You don't have to remember the fights that broke out when many of the bags broke on impact and children as small as you were had to fight for nourishment. We in the USA live in an environment that much of the world will never see or understand. That's why it's so important to get out and see things—not to dwell on the suffering and poverty in the world, but to look at your own life in an entirely new light. For the first few days that I am back home from a mission, I forget that I can put my face into the showerhead and take a mouthful of water. I always find myself keeping my lips pressed tight together as I wash my hair and rinse my face. Then it hits me: I can open my mouth and drink. I remember that a few days ago, I could not have done this simple thing because the water where I was would have caused me to get sick from bacteria or pollution. Everyone should experience these differences in the world. How else can you really know balance in life?

The flight to Cambodia was the longest that I had ever taken. I believe it was close to twenty hours from San Francisco to Cambodia, with a quick stop in Taiwan to change planes, and most of it was at night because we were flying east, away from the sun. That can seriously play havoc with your brain. The airline the women had chosen was amazing. The cabin had extra wide seats with fully programmable video systems in the seat back, loads of leg room and food that made you think you were in a five-star restaurant. We made this happy discovery when we boarded and it made our twenty hours in coach seats so much more comfortable than we had expected them to be. Daylight finally decided to show itself as we landed. Looking out the window at Phnom Pehn below us I remember thinking, "We really aren't in Kansas anymore!" I just stared through the glass, looking at the vast green landscape that went on as far as I could see. Clusters of tall palm trees surrounding what looked like small, temple-shaped buildings dotted the land. My mind was foggy after the long flight and everything seemed a bit surreal. But one thing was clear: I was in Cambodia.

Before we landed, Mia made sure to tell us not to declare anything and not to say we were part of a humanitarian mission. The governments in these areas sometimes frown on that and might detain us. It's better to just play it safe. John and I continue to follow this practice on all our trips. Stating that you are a tourist and staying in a local hotel can save you hours of questioning by an immigration official who is mostly likely just looking for a little cash bribe or a small sampling of anything you might be bringing into the country.

After a quick stop to change to a much smaller airplane we continued to our destination, Siem Reap. There, some representatives from The HALO Trust would meet up with us, take us to our hotel and formally welcome us. They would brief the group on the events that were to unfold over the next ten days.

When we landed at Siem Rep International airport, the plane rolled to a stop and a member of the flight crew opened the door. Even from the back of the cabin I could feel the heat as it entered the plan. It carried a smell that is uniquely Cambodian. Very early each morning people, people from households and businesses alike sweep the fallen leaves, sticks and rubbish that have accumulated during the night to the edge of the street and light the small piles on fire. The result is an almost incense-like smell that takes over the air and lingers throughout the day. It may sound like a foul smell, but somehow these random ingredients combine to create a pleasant aroma that is hard to forget. It's a memory triggering odor and, to this day, smelling something remotely close will take me back to the streets of Siem Reap.

We walked down the stairs and crossed the runway to a small, well-used airport immigration building. We got our passports stamped, retrieved our bags, then walked out of the other side of the building to greet our local contacts from The HALO Trust . What waited outside turned me into a giddy child: it was the most amazing white British Land Rover I had ever seen. It screamed adventure with its boxy look high sides, thin off-road tires with exposed leaf springs and this huge antenna, as thick as your arm, mounted to the front bumper. On each side door was a blue oval sticker with the letters HALO printed on it. Below that was a red diamond sticker with a white skull and crossbones, and the words "Danger Mines." This single moment started my love affair with the Rover. I have spent much time in them and, much like the smell of Cambodia, you never forget the first time you saw one of these majestic four-by-fours. Wasting no time, we loaded all our bags into the Rover and piled into a couple of vans that accompanied it. Next stop, the hotel where we would stay while we were in the Siem Reap.

As in most Southeast Asian towns, the roadways were over-crowded with families using a moped or scooter as their only means of transportation. This was the first time that I had person-ally witnessed this sight— a young woman, holding an infant in her arms, sitting sidesaddle on the seat of a scooter, her husband driving from a position almost centered over the handlebars and a six-year old sandwiched between the two parents. I stared out the window with amazement as we passed family after family riding this way, swerving in and out of traffic without a bit of fear. I alternated between trying to film the women as they pointed out the windows at what they saw and trying to take it all in myself. Talk about a brain overload. Hell, I was still trying to grasp the fact that I was actually in Cambodia and more than just a tourist. I was totally clueless and blithely attempting to make a documentary. Even though we had just begun the journey I felt high on life. I knew this would become my life's addiction. This is what I want to do for the rest of my time on earth. Though I didn't know it yet, the universe wanted this too.

The closer we got to our hotel, the tighter and more congested the roads became. People crowded the sidewalks, markets sprouted up everywhere and a new vehicle, distinctive to Cambodian streets, showed itself to me for the first time. This unique mode of transportation was a hybrid creation called a Tuk-tuk. The Tuk-tuk received its name because of the peculiar sound the motor makes as it weaves through traffic. It was really nothing more than a small scooter, 50 cubic inch motor at the most, with a two-wheeled covered wagon attached to the back of the scooter by a single round bar. Most would hold up to four people quite comfortably. This mode of Cambodia transit is cheap and extremely fun. but at the same time leaves you with a feeling of impending doom. Your sense of immediate peril will depend on the size and condition of the roadway, the amount of booze you've consumed and, the volume of traffic engulfing you.

Evening was approaching but we still had enough daylight to see just how beautiful the Angkor Village Hotel was as we checked in to our traditional, Cambodian styled room. But it only took a few seconds for John and me to notice that something didn't look right. There was only one bed in the room, and not a very large one at that. We looked at each other, then at the bed, then back at each other. This was the first of many comical, awkward moments of silence we would share. We had never been to Cambodia before. We had no idea of what the customs were or what a typical hotel room was even supposed to look like. How were we to know that the hotel had rooms with twin beds in them?

Well, this was Southeast Asia for God's sake; maybe they did things differently here. John and I agreed that we would make this work by facing opposite directions, back-to-back. We'd go to bed fully dressed and pray that our butts did not touch during some delusional, time zone induced dream. I believe that we would have gone through with it too, had we not overheard two of the women talking about switching beds in their room because one was too close to the window that overlooked the street . We rectified the bedding problem in Siem Reap but, for some reason, it would follow us to other countries. This would eventually include a Mr. and Mrs. Kevin Ball room in London, complete with his and her slippers, and a room in Vietnam that we had to completely disassemble and rearrange, rewiring the lamps between the newly separated twin beds in the process, to avoid the Cambodian sleeping situation. Call it a macho guy thing, call it what you want. I like John; I just really don't want to accidentally snuggle up to him as I seek warmth during a good night's sleep in some far away land.

That night the group had a relaxing meeting in the hotel's open lounge, The drinks flowed and Nigel Robinson, our HALO Trust guide, gave us the week's itinerary. I had met Nigel once before when I was visiting the group in Carmel. He is a very charming, very knowledgeable individual, with a past in the British Military. When it comes to the topic of mine removal, he knows his shit. The women lovingly called him their very own British Brad Pitt, and graciously accepted his offer to tag along to the children's hospital, our first stop of the next day.

LOST CHILDREN OF THE TEMPLES

After I woke up from my first good sleep in quite a few days (in my own personal bed, might I add), I ventured out in search of some coffee and to see what the hotel restaurant had to offer for breakfast. One by one the rest of the group followed, wandering over the bridge that spanned the small pond separating the open-air dining pavilion from the rest of the hotel. Mia sat with John and me and tried help us wrap our minds around the fact that we were actually eating breakfast in Cambodia, on the first morning of a trip that was going to permanently change us forever. According to Nigel's schedule, our first stop of the day would be the Angkor Hospital for Children.

While taking photos of the temples around Angkor Watt, a Japanese photographer named Kenro Izu became appalled at the numbers of homeless children he saw who were in desperate need of medical attention. Many of the children had fallen victim to the abandoned landmines laid around the temples and were missing limbs. These children touched him so much that a new purpose took over his life and he founded an all-volunteer hospital, which sees up to five hundred children per day.

I grabbed my camera gear, John picked up a big red duffle bag full of donated medical supplies that we had brought from Carmel and we started off to the hospital. It was situated a short distance from the hotel, just off the highway. As we entered the main gates, we met the Cambodian girl who would give us a tour of the facilities and I ran into my first sea of parents and children patiently waiting to be seen in a Third World hospital setting. I find it amazing how the brain can clearly remember specific images and how it's impossible to forget some of the things that you have seen. As I approached the hospital's front door, I saw an old green plastic laundry basket tied to a hanging produce scale. This was used to weigh the children in the outside screening area. Next to the makeshift scale was a dry erase board with the number 350 written on it. This was the number of children they had screened so far that day—three hundred and fifty children by eleven o'clock in the morning. A doctor in the US might see twenty patients per day on average, so the thought of a nonprofit hospital seeing up to 500 children per day is insane by our standards. But they do it, every day.

This was it. For the first time ever we were going to film something important— something life changing, something that we would be adding to our masterpiece documentary. Then it hit me: Sound. I needed to record some usable audio. I realized that every time our guide turned away from the camera to lead us down another hallway, the only sounds I could hear were footsteps and the echoing cries of Cambodian children. Logic was seeping into my mind: "Ah... this is called acoustics." I was about to make a rookie mistake by using the shotgun microphone mounted on the camera to record the sound. If I didn't adapt to this run and gun style of filming I would have nothing to listen to when I replayed the tape. When you film humanitarian groups, you quickly find out that something emotional can happen at any time, and there are no cuts or reshoots when it comes to real life emotions. They comes and go fast, and you have to be prepared. So I chose to interrupt the tour for a moment and pull out a different weapon in my audio arsenal, the wireless microphone.

Our very cute and shy tour guide gave me permission to put my lavaliere microphone on her blouse. It was an uncomfortable moment. She blushed, I blushed and I did my best not to make eye contact. This was the first time that I had used it on someone other than John and I was desperately trying not to accidentally run my hand over her breast while reaching down her shirt to pull the small microphone up to her lapel from the waist pack. Unlike the camera, the microphone only had one button on it— mostly because I could only afford a really cheap one at the time. But it was a piece of sensitive equipment and, as with most of my newly bought equipment, I had very little idea of what the hell I was doing with it. So the hospital provided us with a very valuable lesson about using highly sensitive audio equipment near crying children. From Cambodia to Africa to India to Guatemala to Peru to Ecuador to Vietnam, frightened children all scream at the same ear-splitting pitch. It's a sound that will make your right eye cross while the left rolls toward the back of your brain looking for shelter. The only thing that took my mind off the ear-splitting volume was what I was seeing. This was the first time either John or I had been in a Third World hospital and, as Third World countries go, Cambodia is one of the poorest on the planet. Tattered mattresses that looked like weathered trampolines were held to bed frames by rusty springs that protruded from the edges of frames. The beds themselves were held together with tape and twine. The overcrowded rooms were in no way sterile healing environments. The floors were filthy and the only airflow was from open windows, which also let in the hazards of the environment. Items that would be discarded after one use in a US hospital were cherished and used until they fell apart and could no longer be held together with wire or duct tape. But the hospital functioned and no one, doctor or patient, complained. This is reality of life here and it is not going to change. They all feel lucky to have this much.

Of all the places we visited on the trip, I believe this was one of the most emotional for the group. All but a few of the women were mothers and seeing injured children in these conditions was overwhelming. Even John and I, two hardened stuntmen, were devastated. Hell, we were in culture shock and a little disoriented from just being in Cambodia. Imagine yourself in this state when a tiny, dirty, very malnourished six-year old looks up at you with an old, crusty feeding tube taped in his nose and starvation in his eyes. Even the strongest will succumb to basic emotions.

Children will always be children though, and their curiosity about our cameras and us kept us smiling, and them dancing around and playing like children should. It was at that point I learned that a camera could distract a child from an unfortunate environment and provide, if only for a brief moment, the sense of wonder and excitement that should belong to every child.

Another first for us, and one we found ever so amusing—as any global travel virgin might, were these signs posted all over the place. They showed an outline of a man squatting and two small Snickers Bar shaped objects falling from his ass. There seemed to be a serious problem with random public pooping in the area. "Oh, the lessons we are going to learn," I thought, "as our global humanitarian schooling begins."

That night, back at the hotel, our group was quieter and more self-reflective than we'd been. We were still excited about what we were doing and eagerly anticipated events to come, but the experience had taken its toll. The women, as mothers, had taken in a lot on our first day and the emotional roller coaster was far from over.

The next day would prove to be as physically demanding as the day at the hospital had been emotional. Shortly after our peaceful breakfast, The HALO Trust vehicles arrived to pick us up and take us to their base camp near the outskirts of Siem Rep. Here we would have our first real briefing on unexploded ordinance, and then drive into the minefields in the provinces bordering Thailand. After a short trip through the city's center to a more rural area, we pulled off the main two-lane road and continued through a secured fence into one of The HALO Trust's outposts. We exited our vehicles and were given a few minutes to stretch our legs and wander around a bit. I went in search of coffee while John located the communication center. This was well before the time of the smartphone, and he wanted to find an Internet signal so we could send out a few emails before we headed deep into the border regions of the countryside.

Directly across the courtyard from the radio room where

John and I sent our messages, was a room set up for group lectures. Here we received our instructions on how to act and what to expect when we arrived at the minefield. We also got a brief history of the K-5 mine belt, one of the densest concentrations of mines on the planet. We learned why the mines are there, who laid them in the ground, the types of landmines we would come across and just how catastrophically the K-5 mine belt had affected the lives of the people living in and around it. The lecture room looked like something out of a black and white World War II movie. I would not have been surprised in the least if John Wayne, dressed in a Flying Tigers pilot uniform, had walked in and sat down next to me. All around the room, from floor to ceiling, were maps of the minefields. Like in a war museum, there were handmade display cases containing an assortment of inert landmines, grenades, bombs and other explosive devices—all of which you could pick up for closer examination. John and I found that especially cool.

During the briefing we also learned from Nigel that, in Cambodia, the issue of landmines turns out to be a very long and confusing subject. Without getting into excessive detail, I will try to explain a bit.

DEADLY STEPS

When I thought of landmines, I pictured the Vietnam War and soldiers walking through rice paddies probing the ground with their bayonets, or a bombed out-building in a town like Warsaw during WWII, complete with tanks rolling through the crumbled streets and the thunderous rumble of artillery shells. I had even had a GI-Joe action figure with a backpack full of landmines that snapped together and a small plastic metal detector. The situation here was very different, the way reality often is.

The mines in this area had been laid in the ground as recently as 1993. The huge mine belt called the Kapeia 5, meaning "protect 5 province," or K-5, runs for over 450 miles along the border between Cambodia and Thailand. No one knows the exact numbers of mines in the ground but, at one time, it was estimated that there were over a million. The reason the numbers are so high is because the border between the two countries has changed many times. The Cambodian military, the Khmer Rouge, the Thai government and the Vietnamese forces that helped fight off the Khmer all laid minefields in overlapping patterns at various times during the conflicts. As recently as 1998, the government of Cambodia would not let the landmines be taken out of the ground because they felt that their presence would stop possible invasions from Thailand.

What the mine belt really did was stop transit between the two countries – the transit that brings in vital goods and services to some of the poorest people in the world. As I have seen over the past six years, this pattern is repeated in many countries around the globe. Major cities grow larger and, as they expand outward, the poorest are forced to move farther away from the advancing cities and closer to the inexpensive border regions where these minefields are located. Many countries have this problem, but Cambodia is one of the most heavily mined countries in the world. Very little government assistance is available, so humanitarian organizations remove most of the landmines. HALO Trust is one of the largest of these organizations.

No one kept good records of just where the mines were laid during the conflicts. If there were any maps of minefields at all, no one has been able to locate them. Unfortunately, this often means that the location of these minefield stays a mystery until some poor Cambodian, living or working in the area, steps on a mine. NGOs mostly rely on the villagers as a first line of notification.

Animals often venture into the mined locations first. After an animal trail becomes visible, the locals know that this spot is free of mines and that it's safe to follow. Greater use of the trails inevitably creates a wider path, often leading to a surprising wrong step and contact with a buried landmine. Those who venture off the trails to harvest wood or use the land to plant crops take their lives into their own hands. But they do it to survive. Consider that a man from the inner city can make $1.50 (US currency) a day by harvesting rice during the wet season. This is enough money to make a trip through potentially dangerous minefields worth the risk.

We heard the story of a father and daughter who farmed the land around a minefield because it was the only place available to them. Their survival depended on whatever they could grow. Any extra was sold at market, which involved journeying through yet more minefields. While raking the land one day, the father stepped on a landmine, destroying his leg from the knee down. He recovered from this trauma and later went back to farming the same plot of land, where he stepped on another landmine. Luckily this explosion only destroyed the prosthetic leg that had been fitted for him after the first accident. The farmer managed to crawl from the field without striking another mine but his daughter had to go in to retrieve their gardening tools. Without them they couldn't farm. They would starve. During her retrieval attempt she also stepped on a buried landmine. It blew her foot off.

As they told us this story, the HALO staff showed us a recent photo of the pair. They are minus two legs, but smiling because they still farm the same plot of land which, thanks to HALO, is now free of mines

This is how desperate the people in these areas are and the story gives you an idea of the impact that removing landmines can have on a person, village, or a country. The sobering truth is that, on average, it costs about one hundred US dollars to remove one landmine from the ground, but only about five dollars to put one in the ground. The price created an incentive for governments to continue using these weapons; that and the fact that, from a military perspective, they work. So economics contributed to a problem that not only touches farmers and commerce, but also extends to children trying to walk to local schools. Mines block access to clean well water and impede proper medical support to thousands of families that live around minefields. There are even areas in which parents tether their children to their huts, so they do not walk too far out into their own yards, where buried mines may well be present. What type of life is this for a child?

Land being cleared of mines is so valuable that local villagers are always hot on the heels of the HALO demining teams as they clear. Sometimes people follow a team right up to the edge of the danger zone. They start moving in and cultivating the land less than one hundred yards behind the live minefield actively being cleared. This quickly leads to the creation of more small villages and even more people trying to find their way safely through a maze of hidden landmines.

I sat in the back of the room during the briefing and tried to film while my brain processed all of this new information. I realized that I had stepped into something much larger than I ever thought existed. I would be struck by this realization many times over the next six plus years. With each NGO mission we accompanied, with my mind expanded to take in more of what is really going on in the world.

A short time after the briefing started, a second caravan of vehicles pulled up alongside our building. Through the open door, I watched them unload and start to head our way. On a visual timeline of my life, this would be one of those life-changing events marked with a picture and a story. This is when John and I met Cindy McCain for the first time. I truly believe that, at that very moment, God applauded vigorously and yelled out, "Yes, here we go!" Until that time, all I knew about Cindy was that she was the wife of Arizona Senator John McCain, that she had something to do with beer (which made John and I love her from the start) and that she sat on the board of directors of The HALO Trust. She and her small entourage entered the briefing and the lecture came to a stop as she was introduced to the women of Freedom Fields. I had no idea that she would become such a principal part of my life in the years to come. Had someone told me then, I probably would have just shrugged it off.

Cindy McCain is one of the most amazing individuals I have ever had the privilege of meeting, and I am honored to call her my good friend. Her stories rival those of any great adventurer and her heart is open wide to the world. She became involved with The HALO Trust after the conflict in Kuwait. From 1988 to 1995 she founded and ran the NGO American Voluntary Medical Team. Her group organized trips by medical personnel to disaster-struck or war-torn Third World areas. Cindy and the team were doing work in the Gulf area when she witnessed children becoming victims of landmines that had been buried in and near local playgrounds by the invading Iraqi forces and became a passionate advocate for the removal of abandoned landmines and UXO (unexploded ordinance) around the world. As an active board member of HALO Trust, she had come to tour the minefields they were currently clearing in this area of Cambodia. Luck was on our side as her visit and the Freedom Fields trip coincided and the groups merged into one large traveling unit.

When the briefing was over and everyone had met, John and I packed up our gear, took one last restroom break and climbed back into one the vehicles for the five-hour drive to Battambang Province. This is the border region of Cambodia and Thailand.

The first leg of the journey was easy going. The road was paved and jumped between two and four lanes as we drove through small settlements. Most of the vehicles we came across were large trucks transporting goods between villages, markets and bordering countries—much like you would see on any US highway. But that's where the similarities ended. Scooters, mopeds and bicycles were everywhere and many homemade, gas-powered things, that looked anything but street worthy, clung to the outside edges of the roads, desperately trying to avoid being blown over by the passing trucks. I never would have imagined that you could use a scooter as a transport vehicle, but I now know that it is fully possible to strap two very large pigs, fed large amounts of Cannabis, across the seat of one and drive to market at full speed. If you can imagine it, we saw it carried on a scooter. Sometimes the load was tied down, as with the pigs, but most of the time the items rested in the lap of a passenger who straddled the rear tire, poised to bail off and run when the driver lost control of the unbalanced bike and rocketed off the road into a water buffalo grazing in a muddy ditch. (True story; I witnessed it.)

As time passed, the road gradually turned from pockmarked asphalt into dusty orange clay, bumpy washboard and then to kidney pounding trails.

I had been told that there are only two seasons in Cambodia—wet, tropical green and dust. We were in the dust season, but this dust was like nothing I have ever seen. If you can imagine something ten times lighter then talcum powder, your image is heading in the right direction. The farther off the highway we drove, the dustier and more inhospitable the road conditions became. Each time we turned down the next unnamed road, buildings became smaller, farther apart and more primitive. Eventually we just drove through a dusty jungle, the occasional herd of cows or inquisitive gang of young people taking the place of motorized traffic. After one last turn, we made it to our first destination and our encampment for the night. The HALO compound rose surprisingly out of nowhere, even though its white-walled perimeter fence blended with nothing around it. I would have missed it entirely, had it not been for the large blue oval with the letters H, A, L, O painted on the gate. As the razor wire topped gate slid open, it felt more like we were entering a prison camp than the home of an international NGO. But once inside the gate, it was as if I'd stepped back in time and into a black and white war movie. The compound gave John and me an amazing testosterone hit.

To the right of the entry gate was the motor pool that contained a number of mismatched surplus military transport trucks – all originally from different countries. There was a water tanker, a bulldozer and a front-end loader, all the type you would see on construction sites in the states. Here they were painted white and sported the blue HALO oval. Red, diamond-shaped "Danger Mines" signs, with the skull and crossbones, finished out the look. All of these vehicles help remove landmines, clear land, build roadways and perform an assortment of other jobs. HALO staff find it more efficient to buy existing items and convert them to fit their needs instead of trying to build heavy demining equipment from the ground up. Surplus lots turn out to be one of their favorite places to shop. To the left of the gate was the main office, the map and briefing rooms, the kitchen and sleeping quarters. Toward the rear of the compound was the explosives dump. Next was the outhouse containing the squatty potties. Sandwiched in among all of this was the repair area for both mechanical and electronic equipment.

Our caravan pulled up and parked in front of the main office area. With much excitement we exited the Land Rovers and gazed in awe at the environment in which we now stood. After a few brief instructions, we dispersed to our appropriate sleeping and unloaded our bags. The women stayed in the upstairs quarters while John and I were shown the barracks where the rest of the male HALO team members slept. They had set up a table as a power spot, so we could charge our camera batteries. The rest of the room was filled with cots topped with bamboo mattresses and surrounded by mosquito netting. A few wobbly ceiling fans kept the balmy air moving around, giving the illusion of a small breeze, and if you picked a cot directly underneath one of the fans, you could almost get a decent night's sleep. And I can't leave out the room's doorway; it was ten inches too low for an average human to walk through. Within an hour of our arrival, we had hit our heads on it often enough to pad it with some duct tape and an old pillow. In hindsight, this was a good idea. Finding your way to the facilities in the dark, in this strange compound, surrounded by all the night-time sounds of Cambodia was challenge enough without adding the need to remember to duck upon exit or entrance. But the cooler filled with ice-cold beer that John and I discovered seemed like more than adequate compensation for any inconvenience.

That night, some of the local village women served an amazing dinner in our honor. It included the best fried chicken that I have ever put into my mouth and an assortment of other local dishes. I believe this is where my love of eating strange foods from around the world was born. It was an evening to savor, but it came after a long day. We were physically drained from the long drive and the excitement of just being where we were. Now, with very full stomach's, we were ready for bed. After a round of good nights that rivaled the iconic closing to *The Waltons*, we crashed hard.

As dawn's light crept through the barrack windows I opened my eyes like a child on Christmas morning. Nothing had changed during the night. I had not been dreaming; I could reach out and touch the mosquito netting. "I am now somewhere deep within Cambodia," I thought, almost in disbelief. I lay on my bamboo cot for a bit, drowsing in the balmy air, and reflected on the day to come.

Most of the women were already up by the time John and I crawled from our cots, and they were ready to explore the local streets before breakfast. So we slammed a couple cups of instant coffee, grabbed our cameras and headed down the road after them. The sounds of the morning echoed in the stillness as we ventured out of the front gate. Roosters crowed and children talked in a local dialect as they made their way past the compound, en route to school. In the distance, we could hear a haunting Khmer song broadcasting over crackling speakers. We later learned this was a call to announce the wedding season and it played at first light each day. As we walked along, the smell of breakfast being prepared over small cooking fires hung in the dry morning air. Mia and the women ventured down the narrow streets, waving and doing their best to communicate with the children they met—fundamentally acting as friendly goodwill ambassadors from America. This they all did effortlessly. On the other hand, John and I would run ahead of the group, then fall back, trying to get the microphone aimed at a good conversation. At one point, we jumped a ditch to chase down two women who were trying to approach a baby water buffalo. We did our best to film everything but trying to capture ten women moving in ten different directions proved difficult and kept us on our toes. Chalk up another new experience for the novice documentary filmmakers.

THE SCHOOL IN A MINEFIELD

After a quick breakfast back at the compound, we loaded up in the Rovers and hit the dusty roads to make our way to the border where the K-5 mine belt was located. But the first stop on the day's agenda was a visit to a local school located in an area that, thanks to donations raised by Freedom Fields US, had previously been cleared of landmines. About an hour's drive away from the HALO compound, we turned off the dusty, two lane road onto what can only be called an ox cart trail. This trail was exactly that; *a trail*—sometimes widening just enough to allow the Land Rovers to stagger in line and sometimes so tight that tree branches would slap you in the face if you rolled down your window for air. This was one of the most difficult trips that we would encounter on our trek and it lasted for about two hours. The dust clouds thrown up by our vehicles were so thick and hung in the air for so long that visibility sometimes stopped at the windshield. At times it almost seemed as if we had left the trail and were flying through the clouds, but the kidney bruising condition of the terrain reminded us otherwise. The only understandable words repeated by our Cambodian driver, who spoke little-to-no English were, "OH SHRIT," which I interpreted to mean "Oh shit. This is rough." Each time he said it, he glanced at me in the passenger seat, smiled a toothless grin and laughed nervously. John and I joined in with his nervous laughter from the back seat, then went back to singing along with the 80s mix tape that was playing in the cassette player. At one point we had to go around some frisky water buffalo in a field because the trail became impassable, even for the four-wheel drive Land Rovers, and, at another spot, the trail stopped at a small body of water. After a short radio debate, we rolled up the windows and plowed through. It got deep and, as the brown water splashed over the windshield, I think even our driver had his fingers crossed that our convoy had made the appropriate decision. Of course, coming from a stunt background John and I couldn't stop giggling as we tried to film through the sloshing *Adventureland* ride. All of our Rovers successfully forded the river and continued back onto the trail and into the dust—which found a lovely new home on our now river-water coated vehicles.

A short time after the crossing we slowed to a stop and I was told that the school was up ahead. As we slowed, I hopped from my Rover and ran past the others to jump into one of the lead vehicles so I could get into the schoolyard first. I hoped this would give me the opportunity to film the rest of the group as they approached and entered the school yard. This is what the term "run and gun" means: when you are documenting a group on a trip like this, you have to be ready to jump out at any time to get the good shots. Movie stunts trained me well for my new career as a humanitarian documentary cinematographer. Catching up with it, I transferred into a lead Land Rover leaving John farther back in the line so he could film from a different angle. As we pulled up to the front of the schoolyard, children started running out from the small schoolhouse. With military precision they formed two perfect lines on either side of the entrance driveway. There had to be over 150 kids of all ages making their way out to line up. I bolted to the head of the line, camera in hand, and started filming as Mia and the rest of the group drove up, exited their vehicle and, one by one, walked down the drive flanked by two lines of applauding children. This humble gesture from the children brought tears many of the women to tears. They knew how important this visit was to the school children. Likewise, the children knew that, without the generous donations from Freedom Fields, they would still be attending school in the center of an active landmine field. I think this was the first time I had personally witnessed what giving to an international charity can achieve. I could see where the donations and the hard work ended up—in the hands of people in need It was changing their lives and it inspired me.

I am often asked "Why go to the other side of the world to give? Why not just keep all your charitable aid within the United States?" I have never seen this as a choice: I give my time and donations to my country as well. But need in the developing world is staggering and the gratitude and kindness with which help is received make your heart swell with love.

I vividly remember hearing the story of a farmer in the American Midwest who would open his fields to those in need after the harvest was over. There is usually produce remaining after the harvest crews have left, and he invited poor families to freely pick and take away as much as they could carry. Eventually, though, he had to stop doing this. He had been sued too often to continue. Once a lawyer filed suit on behalf of an individual who sprained an ankle in his field, and there were other complaints pretty obviously devised to bring fast money to an unscrupulous person. Unfortunately, in my eyes, our legal system seems to favor situations like this—situations that allow unprincipled lawyers to make a paycheck at the expense of good people.

In countries like Cambodia, no one wants to sue you or do anything malicious towards what you're giving. They look into your eyes with sincerity, grasp your hand and say thank you. They know that all you're really trying to do is help them, even if the gift is as little as a pair of used shoes or a few school supplies. On medical missions we have filmed I have seen parents who have never seen the inside of a hospital before hand over a child to unknown strangers from different countries. They do this with full trust – not in the medical degrees of the doctors and nurses, but in the compassion of one human being for another. On dental missions, people open their mouths and allow a person with whom they can barely communicate to remove their teeth a in make-shift clinic. They need help and a stranger is willing to give it. No questions are asked, nor is anything wanted in return. They receive heartfelt help and return their heartfelt trust. This is why we love to help those around the world. In doing so we get back so much more then we could ever give. It really is an addictive force.

After the initial greeting from the children was over, one of the local HALO guides, familiar with this particular school. started yelling to the children in a local Khmer dialect and with, the same military precision, the children lined up in rows of about ten deep, stretching out nearly the width of the schoolyard. With help on an interpreter, Mary, one of the Freedom Fields members who was a schoolteacher back in Carmel, introduced herself. She told the children where Freedom Fields was from, that she was a teacher back in the states and that she could only dream that someday her students would be as well-mannered as these children were. Then Mary got the privilege of surprising the sea of kids with the announcement that she had gifts for all of them. The waiting children watched eagerly as two large, overflowing cardboard boxes were removed from the rear door of one of the

Land Rovers. Mary and the other women then presented each child with a brand-new backpack, courtesy of donations raised back in Carmel and shopping help from the local HALO team. Each backpack contained a pencil box, two pencils, pencil sharpener, ruler, pad of paper and a rubber. (Rubber turns out to be what the British call an eraser and the immature kid in me found this very humorous! I laughed each time I glanced at the list of school items we were handing out to the Cambodian school children.)

With the children and women occupied, John and I decided this would be an opportune time to interview Nigel. He was the perfect person to speak about the small school in the minefield and the children who used it. From my research I knew that Cambodia was one of the poorest nations in the world but, until our interview with Nigel, I didn't know the reality behind the statistics. Nigel told us that most of these children had probably never received a gift in their lifetimes. Imagine being ten years old and so poor that you had never received a gift given in kindness. He said that these children would cherish these school supplies. They would carefully sharpen each pencil to the nub, ever so slowly, to make it last as long as they could.

Children in Cambodia, as in many in developing countries, long for an education because it is their only way to gain the knowledge that will help them escape poverty. Along with reading and writing, most of the lessons taught in these countries are life and survival skills: they learn why they shouldn't drink unclean water and how to avoid diseases like malaria, bird flu and diarrhea. All of these are huge killers of children in this area. In this particular location, avoiding landmines was still an importance subject. The school yard itself had recently been in the middle of a live mine field and, even as we spoke with Nigel, we could hear in the distance explosions caused by Halo crews demining nearby fields. Education is the key to existence for these children.

Emma McCune, a British aid worker in the Sudan, has said that some children, facing starvation and genocide from rebel armies, would flee across hundreds of miles of open desert to get to refugee camps. Upon reaching safety, instead of asking for food or water they would ask for paper, books and a pencil so they could get an education and avoid the fate of those they left behind. Here in Cambodia the war was long gone, but the children's quest for an education by the children was the same.

For the next hour or so, the women of Freedom Fields and Cindy Mc Cain passed out the backpacks. They fitted one on each child and truly enjoyed the peaceful smile and amazing politeness as the child placed their hands together in front of their face and bowed, saying "*awkunh,*" the Khmer word for thank you. During a *happy*, emotionally crying breakdown, Mia told me that this was the most meaningful part of the whole trip to Cambodia. She said, "I have kids, and coming from where we lice, I couldn't have imagined how something as inexpensive and simple as a backpack could change a child's life." A bit later, while filming around school, I saw Kris, another Freedom Fields member, sitting in the dirt and leaning back against the two-room schoolhouse, which was nothing more than random boards nailed together to form a rough shack. She had snuck away from the rest of the group for a few minutes and, as I approached her and raised my camera. I could see that this trip had mentally exhausted her. With a tearful half laugh, half cry, she looked up at me and said, "I just want to give it all right now, everything I have! I just want to give it all."

As I write this now, I can still see her eyes as she spoke. I realize that it's one of the many moments permanently imbedded in my mind, and why I will continue to preach that through selfless actions you receive back so much more then you could ever give away.

If this group of unlikely heroes from Carmel, California, one of the most beautiful and coveted locations in the United States, can travel to the other side of the earth to visit and help people in need, then anyone who puts their mind to it can accomplish the same. Physically and mentally drained from our experiences, we drove away from the school to the sound of the children chanting "Freedom Fields, Freedom Fields," over and over in their best-English sounding voices. These children may not know exactly why these light skinned strangers from another land visited, and, when they walk through mine free school yard, they may not stop and think about the women who raised the money to clear it. But each time they put on their backpacks or sharpen their new pencils, they will remember the generosity and warmth of the people who visited them that day.

TO THE MINEFIELD; MORE BUMPS AND EVEN MORE DUST

The drive from the school to the landmine field was more of the same—dust, bumps, more bumps and even more dust. About an hour out from the school it became so rough that the caravan had to pull off the trail onto a small strip of flatter ground so that we could get out, stand up and free ourselves of the kidney punches that the trail kept offering. I got out of the Land Cruiser, stood up and, when my feet hit the ground, my kidneys screamed to my bladder and my bladder yelled up to my brain. Half expecting to pee blood because of the severity of the drive, I stepped away from the vehicle to find a more private nearby tree to relieve myself. As I took my first step toward the nearby tree line Nigel made an announcement to the group:

"Please ladies and gentlemen, do not wander away from the vehicles because we are surrounded by uncleared landmine fields!"

He followed that up with a warning that were we to walk even a few feet into the woods, there was a chance that we could step on a buried landmine. This would be bad because we were so far away from the facilities that housed the medical teams.

I stood there trying to keep my body as close to the Rover as possible while still maintaining my coolness. My urge to urinate had left me and my body replaced it with a slight weak-kneed sensation, I remember glancing at my feet and thinking how attached I had grown to them. Let me tell you that even though I am used to fire and explosions in the stunt industry, I always knew exactly where they are and which way to jump to avoid injury. This was a completely new feeling. I just kept staring off into the woods thinking, "How far would I get before I found a mine? Or would I find one? Maybe *I* would make it and the person behind me would step on one by placing their foot only inches from where I had just placed my foot." I was experiencing what the prospect of a landmine does to your mental state. Where do you go? Where do you step? How many are in the ground around me? What's worse? One hundred landmines in an area the size of a football field, or just one? The ground all looks the same, *but it's not.* One wrong or unlucky step and you lose a leg, or worse, *you die.* Landmines are at least as much psychological weapons as they are explosives. Standing at the edge of the trail I felt this effect in my own mind, and, to tell the truth, it was a hell of an adrenalin rush!

Because of the location of our stop, our leg stretching session was brief. We loaded back up and took off in hopes of making it to our destination by early afternoon. Finally, after many more miles of trail, we turned one last corner and came to a large white sign with a lot of Khmer writing on it, the blue HALO oval and a section of black writing that read, "Sponsored by Freedom Fields USA." We had finally made it! John and I were both nervous, excited and utterly amazed that we were here, in a minefield, in the K-5 mine belt, somewhere in the untamed jungles of Cambodia. We were about to step into a live minefield for the first time It was surreal to remember that only weeks before, we were sitting in the *Fear Factor* break room back in Orlando.

As we drove into the field, the first thing I noticed were the hundreds of white stakes hammered in the ground—each with lettering on it, all about waist high. Some were on their own, some grouped together and some seemed to make up a kind of staggered pattern across the cleared ground right up to the live mine fields. The white stakes marked the locations where landmines had been previously unearthed and destroyed. The lettering on each stake described what type of mine had been found. There were also large red and white striped stakes at the edges of the field that marked the boundary between cleared and uncleared ground. No fences or guards. Not even a sign. Just a red and white striped stake the size of a broom handle to keep you from getting blown to bits. We pulled up and parked next to a large, white canvas tent with open walls. Here I could see yet another stake in the ground. This one was much smaller, painted blue and marked the only place in the entire minefield area where you did not have to wear the protective Kevlar bib that would be handed out to us shortly.

Before we were allowed anywhere near the danger zone, the Cambodian gentleman who supervised the minefield and the general area gave us a safety briefing. Before the lecture started, we were given a few minutes to stretch out our cramped body parts, have some water and to finally use the facilities. These facilities were your basic hole dug in the ground with a small tent over it. The design was expected; the location was a different story all together. The chosen place was located about seventy-five yards away from the briefing tent, in what was once a live minefield— although the ground was now clear and safe. To get to the crapper we had to weave our way through a maze of white stakes that marked where landmines had once lived. Just staring across to the toilet you could get a good idea of what the minefield had once looked like. Had you attempted to cross the field a month ago, chances are you would not have made it. This was my first *visual*, ever, of what the layout of a landmine field would have looked like, were the mines still buried in the ground. I'm not going to lie; it was pretty fucking disturbing. The *idea* alone had been enough to make me pee on a tree close to the Rovers and hold everything else for back at the compound. When John came marching back from using the toilet, he told me that even though he knew the mines had been removed from the ground in this area, just walking through the stakes left him with an uneasy feeling. This was a remainder of war, of genocide, of people trying and succeeding to kill each other. Who knows how many poor souls, not as fortunate as we were, lie dead in this very ground?

The briefing was basic and focused on safety. The superintendent explained the colored stakes and the layout of the field. The last thing said was, "In the event of an uncontrolled explosion, *stand still*. Check to see if you are unhurt and wait for further instructions." That pretty much summed up our situation. This was no safe tour through a theme park.

The briefing completed, it was time we were introduced to the outfits that might save our life. At the far end of our briefing tent some HALO deminers began pulling safety gear from bags and inspecting it. Each bag contained a Kevlar apron, about same size as an apron you would use in a kitchen, But this apron would help to keep all of your organs intact and easy to find if you got too close and accidentally detonated a mine. There was also a polycarbonate face shield created to protect you from flying debris. Its curved shape would help redirect the blast to the sides. All the protective gear was designed to protect miners from the front and at close range while they were on their knees digging in the ground to expose a landmine that would be marked for later detonation.

John and I donned our Kevlar and filmed the women getting suited up. Then our new guide, Tim, called, "Alright, then. Let's be off." We followed Tim, while Cindy McCain's group went with Nigel, and, just like that, we left the safety of the blue stake and walked into the danger zone. From holding the clean mine in my hand at Mia's house in Carmel, to my first steps into a live minefield in Cambodia—I had planned and accomplished this. Now John and I were experiencing this highpoint and seeing the passion that drives these NGOs. I couldn't have been more high on life than I was at that moment.

The minefield was sectioned off into squares much like a chessboard. Within each square, the areas known to contain live landmines were marked off by red stakes about three feet tall and placed every four feet to mark each section's perimeter. In each square, one deminer with a metal detector worked from the outer edge in, reducing the area to search by four feet with each pass, until the point at which the entire square was cleared of any explosive mines. Ahead of the guy with the metal detector in each square was a person with a basic weed whacker who cut down the taller grasses. Behind him came a guy with a garden rake who carefully cleared out what was cut down so that the metal detectors could get closer to the soil for better readings.

Simple right?

As we approached a deminer working an area of ground, Tim explained the equipment and the procedure each HALO trained deminer used. A German company called Ebinger specially created the metal detector that HALO Trust uses in Cambodia's nonferrous soil. Nonferrous means there are very few natural iron deposits in the soil, so these metal detectors can be calibrated to go off at the slightest hint of metal. The most abundant type of the landmine found in this particular area is the Russian made PMN mine. The main body of this style of mine is made from a substance called Bakelite, an early form of polymer plastic. While Bakelite is invisible to metal detectors, the sensitive equipment can easily detect the springs and the firing pin inside the mine. This results in a very strong audible sound when the dinner plate sized head of the detector gets anywhere close to a buried landmine. This was the only high-tech piece of equipment in each deminer's arsenal. The rest of the tools used to expose the mines were just basic gardening tools and an occasional piece of equipment handcrafted by an individual to get the job done easier. Tim said that, at HALO, they believe manual mine clearance provides the best results with the least damage to the soil. As this was very fertile ground, much needed for farming by the locals after the mines were removed, heavy equipment was out of the question. In addition, by training the locals deminers, HALO, had also stimulated the economy of the surrounding towns.

As we made our way even closer to the man with the metal detector, we could see just how simple the procedure was. The first step was to start at one edge of the square and move in a clockwise or counterclockwise pattern. The deminer used a board about four feet long, one inch thick and six inches wide. He would lay the board on the ground in an area the was previously cleared from landmines to provide a base from which to safely start. Then he would run the metal detector back and forth over the board, about a foot in front of the board and on the sides into the uncleared ground. If he heard no sound from the detector, the deminer would simply move the board forward by its own width of six inches into the area that he now knew was clear. With aid of a simple measuring device, he would pound a new red perimeter stick into the group every four feet he progressed. He would continue this pattern over and over until he received a signal from the metal detector that let him know something was in the ground and it needed further investigation.

When a deminer found what he thought might be a landmine, he would pound two red stakes into the ground on either side of his large board. This way he knew where he had left off and where it was safe. He would remove the board and lay down a thinner piece of wood between his newly planted red stakes. Knowing where his safe zone was and where the mine might be located, he would move back about a foot and start to dig a hole about a foot deep. When he felt he had dug down far enough, he would switch from his small spade to a tool made for scraping the dirt from the far side of the hole—the side closest to the possible landmine. Here's where it gets a bit nerve racking: the deminer would continue scraping forward until he found the side of the landmine. Tim told us that it was fine to come into contact the side of a landmine. As long as there was no downward pressure on the top plate or any pressure from below which would pry the mine upward, there would be no explosion. However, during this entire time, the deminer would still frequently check the ground with his metal detector to make sure he always knew where the mine was. To me this seemed ridiculously simple, and insanely dangerous. Here we were—John, me and the women from Freedom Fields—all standing eight feet from a Cambodian guy digging in the ground to expose a live landmine with only a fancy metal detector and three dollars' worth of gardening tools. The danger level was off the charts and we all loved it.

But this was just the first step of the protocol to destroy a landmine. Once he had unearthed the mine, the deminer marked the hole with a red sign that read "Danger Mine" in white letters just below a white skull and crossbones. As an added precaution, he placed a small red and white wooden triangle, about the size of an adult's hand, inside the hole and pointed it at exposed portion of the landmine. Even if he knew nothing about the procedure and its intent, any passing person would be clearly warned to stay clear of the hole. After this was done, the deminer would relocate to another square and start his hunt all over again.

So we have a bunch of guys digging with garden tools and leaving holes all over the place with half exposed landmines in them: now it gets really exciting. Every forty-five minutes an alarm went off—an alarm that is loud enough to be heard over any activity going on in the minefield. At this point the deminers would stop what they were doing, put down their tools and walk out of the field to the big tent or to someplace safe to take a smoke. During this break time, another group of specialists would head into the minefield armed with some pretty heavy explosive charges that HALO buys locally. Each charge was one hundred grams of explosive putty, usually dug out of old artillery shells and then packed into four-inch sections of PVC pipe. One end was capped off and a small hole, called a detonation well or det-well for short, was drilled into the other end. The hole was just large enough to insert a military-grade blasting cap – these were about the same size as a pencil snapped in half. The specialist would measure a slow burning fuse to the appropriate length for the time needed, then attach it to the wires coming from the blasting cap he'd inserted into the PVC charge. He then placed the device in the hole, rested it against the exposed side of the landmine, and banked dirt up against it to hold the charge in place and to help direct the explosion into the landmine. Once lit, the time delayed fuses allowed the team ample time to casually walk from the field, get to a safe distance, turn around and watch colorful explosions bloom from the red, dusty earth. For our group, they switched from the slow burning fuses to handheld wind-up detonators. This allowed each member of the group to have the hands-on experience of blowing up a landmine. This was the moment many of the women had been waiting for. All their hard work of raising donation to help rid Cambodia of landmines was coming to a finale – one that they were now controlling.

John and I continued filming. Hour after hour we kept going back into the minefield, following each small group of Freedom Field members around the field and doing our best to capture everything that happened. To the women from Carmel, the heat and humidity seemed close to unbearable, but to John and I it seemed no worse than an average summer day in Orlando. I think that Mia thought we were superhuman for standing out in the fields for so long, and that we were extremely committed to filming our documentary. We were committed to the filming, but we were also having so much fun just being in and around that much danger that, even without the cameras, you would have been hard pressed to get us to come out before nightfall. Especially on our second day in the minefields, when Tim asked us if we would like to get real up close and personal to a mine dig-up. Hell yeah! Of course we did. So that afternoon, Tim, John and I ventured deep into the minefield in search of the perfect shot. It didn't take long before one of the deminers had a strong audio hit on his metal detector. Tim heard it and, followed closely by us, made a careful beeline across the field to the location of the sound. Trying not to startle the deminer, who was actively waving his detector back and forth over a patch of soil, we approached carefully. Tim gestured to the man to let him know that we would be standing very close and filming while he was unearthing the mine. I settled in at a safe distance and began to film. To my surprise, Tim kept pushing us to move closer. When he finally said, "I think that's good, lads," I was no more than three feet from the mine. I got down on my knees so I could capture the best angle and, for the next hour, I sat motionless in that position, totally engrossed by the image I was viewing through my camera. While I held my ground, John moved carefully around, getting other angles of the dig. Finally, I began to inch my way closer while Tim narrated the entire process as it happened. When the mine was completely uncovered, I could have reached out and touched it with only a slight lean forward. As if all that wasn't cool enough, while still narrating his every move, Tim wet his finger and cleaned the caked dirt from the side of the *still live* landmine to show us the Bakelite housing and to point out that this mine sat only about two millimeters beneath the surface of the soil.

Had anyone or anything applied even a tiny bit of pressure to the ground just two feet in front of me, my face would instantly have relocated to another time zone. Call me insane, but I didn't want it to end. All of the danger that I face on a regular basis in the movie industry is planned. Yes, we get hurt sometimes but, ultimately, what we do is faked for people's viewing enjoyment. This was real. This was history. This was the consequence of war and what these humanitarians do changes the lives of those who call places like this their home.

We didn't stay at the HALO compound that night. We

chose to drive back to Siem Rep. The long, brutal drive back from the border regions included a river crossing right out of an Indiana Jones movie, but we still had a couple of stops to make that day. For the first, we drove through the streets of a small village, handing out clothes we'd brought from the states and flip-flops the group had purchased at a market back in Siem Reap. I could barely keep up with the women as they leapt from the vehicles and ran down the streets handing out gifts to the groups of children and families that were lining up to see what was causing all the commotion. I can't imagine it's a common occurrence to encounter a bunch of white women, bounding from a convoy of Land Rovers and thrusting T-shirts at anyone whose curiosity caused them to pause for a moment. It was very amusing to watch them. One by one, they would return to the rear door of one of the Land Rovers that was loaded with the goods, grab as much as they could carry and then, like excited children, bounce off each other as they ran back down the dirt road to deliver the loot. It reminded me of one of those family game shows in which you had to perform silly stunts for prizes and what made it even more comical was that the caravan of Rovers was trying to keep pace with the women without running over them. John and I, caught up in the midst of the frenzy, tried desperately to film the scene without losing our footing on the uneven trail. I have hours of footage of my feet running down the village roads then, for a few minutes, the camera would pan up to capture the faces around me—the smiles and emotions of the women as they distributed their goods. Then, it's back to my feet again as I tried to catch the next wave of charity givers. At first, I tried to run and film at the same time—not an idea I recommend unless you like finding every pothole in the ground.

This surge of goodwill lasted until the trail ended at a river too deep to drive through at the bottom of a gorge. On one side of the road was a footbridge made of old planks, a couple of nails, and some tree limbs tied together that had been turned into handrails. This provided the illusion of safety, but the handrails acted more like a directional guide than something to trust with one's body weight. On this foot bridge, you could walk across the gorge from about ten feet up. Some of the members chose this path, while others stayed in the vehicles to look for an even more adventurous way across.

The clay road ended at the water's edge, near the bottom of the red rock and clay gorge. However, an extension of the road had been laid down that spanned the river at only about five inches over the surface of the water. This makeshift auto bridge was handcrafted from full-length sections of felled palm tree lashed together with hemp cord. Laid across this substructure were the same type of hand cut planks used to manufacture the nearby footbridge. The bridge was about the same width as a Land Rover's wheelbase and it flexed tremendously because of its age and its waterlogged condition. From the driver's seat, it looked as if you were driving on the water, and, without spotters, it was all too easy to drive right off the bridge and into the river below. When the crossing was completed, we were met with an equally challenging climb out of the gorge. All four tires on the four-wheel drive Land Rovers spun as they bit and clawed their way back to the bumpy trail that led in the direction of Siem Reap.

Our last stop was a quick visit to a HALO medical training camp where we were able to see the mock minefield disaster training area. Here, deminers who were also training as medical personnel could run practice drills for what they hoped would never happen—an accidental detonation of a landmine during the unearthing process. HALO has an amazing reputation for safety but when doing something as dangerous as hand digging landmines from the ground, you can never be too prepared for an accidental explosion. This is why there are plenty of medically trained personnel in the minefields. Given the great distance most people live from an actual hospital, this medical training also makes the individuals who have it much more valuable in their own village areas. In addition, they get a pay bonus added to the substantial salaries that HALO offers them.

The last planned visit of the day now over, we were all ready to get back to some creature comforts at our hotel in Siem Reap. By this point, the road was getting smoother, which made the drive more relaxing, but it was still extremely dusty and hot. Also, this final leg of our trip was much longer because it was not broken by stops as it had been on the way in. Now it was just hours of trails. Our bodies more hardened to the driving conditions, John and I had no problem nodding off, but we were periodically jolted back awake by an encounter with a bit of really nasty road. At one point, though, I woke because our momentum had changed and the vehicles were slowing down. This usually meant there was something interesting to see. John sensed it too and, with his eyes still closed, asked what was going on,

"I'm not sure, but people seem to be getting out of the Rovers up front," I said. Cindy McCain had spotted something in an approaching roadside hut. These huts were a kind of Cambodian convenience store where you could get fuel—fuel siphoned by mouth out of a barrel and sold in old plastic soda bottles. It was ideal for the scooters that drove up and down the trail. Fuel stops meant that we were closing in on civilization. This particular convenience hut also had some fruit flavored drinks, water none of us were desperate enough to try, a full-sized pool table, complete with game in progress, under a palm-frond roof and the item that had made Cindy stop the parade of vehicles—ice cold beer. This was not just any beer though; it was the coldest Asahi Super Dry Japanese beer that I had ever tasted. Cindy McCain became our new hero when she bought every last beer that the guys had at this roadside hut. She walked over to our Land Rover, two beers in each hand, and poked them through the window at us. Then she smiled and went back for more. John and I had enjoyed a few conversations with her and her assistant, Wendy, throughout the trip, but we had mostly focused on our group from Freedom Fields and the documentary we were making. What we didn't know was that she and Wendy had been watching us film on those long, sweltering days in the minefields and I guess we made an impact with the few conversations that we had as well.

ANGKOR WATT AND OUR NEW FRIEND CINDY MCCAIN

On our second to last day in Cambodia John and I decided to venture out to see and film the famous Angkor Watt temple in Siem Rep. We thought that footage of the temple and some of the surrounding areas would make good landscape shots, adding to the documentary, giving it a bit of history. Not to mention that we were dying to see where Laura Croft fought off all the statue gods in *Tomb Raider*.

Nursing a bit of a hangover from a late-night trip to "Pub Road" and a belly rumble due to some fine dining at a street side food vendor John and I got up, found some coffee and hailed our favorite tuk-tuk driver. We gave him enough cash to take us around for the day. This normally cost about five dollars US, but we gave him twenty so he would treat us extra special and act as a makeshift guide if the need arose. It was a half-hour drive from the hotel to the temples and we hit the road very early, when it was still dark. Our plan was to get the sun rising behind Angkor Watt. This was supposed to be an amazing sight and we wanted it for our video archives. As it was our first time in Cambodia, John and I had never seen the temples in the daylight so we had no idea what to expect. After paying our fee to enter the temple grounds we walked over the stone bridge, past the manmade lakes (featured in the second *Tomb Raider* movie) and through the smaller temple gate entrance to a football field sized courtyard. Somewhere in the darkness, on the other side of the courtyard, sat the Angkor Watt temple complex. The first thing I noticed was that quite a few other people seemed to think that this particular morning would be perfect to get the sunrise over the temple shot, so we had to search for a secluded quiet spot to set up our cameras and avoid getting anyone else in the video.

Mosquitos also gathered in the early morning darkness. Their job was to feast on all the tourists awaiting the sunrise. With my trusty travel size bottle of 100% DEET in hand, I was ready for them. This was our maiden adventure to a developing country and I didn't want to go back to the states with some strange form of malaria. After I covered myself with the liquid insect armor, I left John on the rock wall where we had set up the tripod and cameras, and walked into the nearby woods with the audio equipment. My goal was to record some early morning darkness atmospheric sounds—bugs, animals, the breeze blowing through the trees and any other nocturnal audio clips I could find. Using a highly sensitive microphone I could hear everything. Then, from the quiet darkness, in the direction of the temple area, came an unrecognizable sound: it was an almost human scream, as if someone were writhing in pain, and it bellowed through the silent morning air. This grabbed my attention. Using the microphone as a guide, I followed the scream to try and locate its source, which seemed to take me closer and closer to the location on the wall where I had left John. The sky was starting to lighten and although it was still somewhat dark, I could make out the image of John still sitting on the rock wall where I left him. His right hand covered his right eye and he held my small bottle of 100% DEET in his left hand. As I got closer, I realized exactly what had happened and I laughed, hard, like any great friend would, knowing his buddy had just accidentally done something dumb.

All John could muster up was, "My eyeball. DEET. Can't see." I kept laughing and said, "John, what did you do?" He looked up at me, his hand still covering his right eye, and painfully mumbled, "I had the damn nozzle the wrong way. It was dark. I couldn't see and I squirted DEET onto my eyeball."

It is one of those things that is probably much funnier when you are there, but it sets the scene for our morning rather nicely. So here we sat, Mr. Hangover and One Eye John, at dawn, waiting for the sun to come up behind the famous Angkor Watt temple complex so we could get mind-blowing shots to add to our soon-to-be award-winning documentary. Slowly it happened: the sky lightened enough for us to lay our eyes on the outline of the massive temple complex for the first time. It was a spiritual vision, and it was much farther away than I thought it was. Also, what I thought was a large courtyard appeared to be something else entirely. Whatever it was, the ground seemed to be moving. The more the sun outlined the temple, the more the ground swayed. Then the ground began to pulsate with small, moving lights flashing in random patterns. What the hell was this? From the silence we could make out sounds—human sounds, voices, all speaking Japanese! It seems that we had chosen to visit Cambodia during the annual Japanese tourist photography pilgrimage. Half the population of Japan now stood between the temple of Angkor Watt and us.

This is a problem I've found at most of the famous historic

sites and temples around the world. Wherever there is an interesting spot for tourists to visit, there is a place for commerce. Hotels and markets spring up everywhere, competing for the visiting travelers' dollars. Scam artists selling fake relics and people begging for money persistently approach you on every street corner. Ancient places of worship that are still used by local families are overrun by tourists and their cameras. Money speaks loudly! There is very little concern for the people worshipping at the site or trying to connect with their own history. Worse, tourism can sometimes bring in billions of dollars in revenue to the townships and countries that house these mysterious icons, forcing the poor local families who lived in the area to move elsewhere. Wealthy tourists spending thousands of dollars to stay in a five-star hotels with a view of an ancient temple don't want see a homeless family cooking dinner over an open fire next door to the million-dollar resort pool. Of course, the local government often lends its hand in persuading the poor to move away, sometimes using less then friendly persuasion techniques. This means that, to find a more comfortable life in post war locations like Cambodia, families relocate to the border regions of the country, where they are met with leftover refuse of war—like abandoned landmines—and possible future border conflicts.

The things got better as the day moved on. The temple was incredible and the morning rush for sunrise shots died down to a point where we could film uninterrupted. When we'd had our fill of filming Angkor Watt, we casually meandered back to the temple entrance to search for our tuk-tuk driver.

Fate has the most amazing way of dropping great things in your lap if you are willing to accept the gifts. The timing could not have been more perfect because out in front of the temple, waiting for their car to be brought around, were Cindy McCain and her assistant Wendy. They too had gone on a last-minute tour of the temples before they headed to the airport. This was no coincidence if you ask me: karma had John and I in its grips. We chatted with Cindy and Wendy about the trip and about how amazing the temples were. Then, their car pulled up and we said our goodbyes. Before she got in the car, Wendy pulled me aside and said that Cindy was really impressed with the tenacity and dedication that John and I had shown during our filming and that there might be some stuff coming up in the future where our services might be needed. This was great!

Wendy and I exchanged information and we waved at their car as it drove away. We went back to our touring around the temples. At that moment we were just proud that someone was impressed by our work ethic and that we had made friends with a Senator's wife. The possibility of a future connection seemed appealing but not yet firm enough to consider. I still had a few things to learn about karma and coincidences.

Looking back now, I can see that the one, real truth in my life at that time is that I continued to step through the doors karma opened for me. Only slowly did I realize that there is no such thing in our universe as a coincidence. Whether or not you believe it, and you might be tired of people saying this, everything happens for a reason—even if that reason doesn't affect you personally at a particular moment in time. Everything I experienced on this journey, from coming up with the idea to create the documentary, to traveling to Carmel and then to Cambodia happened so that John and I would be in that exact spot at the temple complex, at that exact moment, to run into Cindy McCain and Wendy again.

THE MEANING OF LIFE AS I SEE IT

Caroline Myss, one of my favorite authors, wrote that we some-times refuse to move forward in life because it slows the speed of time. I thought about this for quite a while and realized that this can really happen. I can relate it to my time in the film industry. The life of a stuntman is not an easy existence. You're a salesman, and the product you sell is yourself. The highs of the roller coaster ride are equal to the lows. Rejection is a constant and, if you're lucky, you get one out of every ten jobs for which you apply. With the highs come a lucrative financial status, but the jobs can come on a month-by-month basis, leaving much downtime and a large deficit in your bank account. You never know just where or when your next job is coming from. When you do get the call for work, you drop everything and run! Finding a full-time job to supplement stunt work is out of the question if you are serious about a career in film industry. There is no way to get enough time off to go to castings or stunt gigs because of their short notice. Once you're a member of the Screen Actors Guild (SAG) you can qualify for medical benefits, and, after ten years in the guild, you are vested for the retirement plan. Every SAG stunt job, every dollar earned then goes toward your health insurance and your retirement. So, as you can see, it's very important to take all the film work you can get. This can even make it hard to hold on to part-time jobs. Most people in the film business, including John and me, choose to go on unemployment to supplement our income when there is no stunt work. The entire industry can play havoc on your mental and financial status. I love it though, and I will never leave it! There is an enormous mental and physical rush that starts from the first call of a stunt coordinator, then lasts through the filming, the parties and the premieres. It's addictive! The years in which I had a lot of work and traveled from state to state filming movies seem short in retrospect. Time flew past when I was busy. On the other hand, during the down years, when I was in and out of the Florida unemployment system, afraid to spend anything and extremely unhappy, time crept by at a snail's pace. Anyone can relate to this in their own life; time is relative to what is going on. When you are busy your mind stays occupied with ideas, times and places, and time truly seems to fly past.

The universe is a collection of doors that presents itself to us every day. What we choose to do with these doors is up to us. We can step through into the unknown and see where that takes us. But this means we give up control. Or, more precisely, it means that we give up some of the control we think we have over our own lives.

However, we also have the choice to not step through the doors that the universe opens. In doing this, we try to maintain control of our lives. When you make this choice, you say, *"No"* and hold yourself back. *"I choose not to move forward. I will settle for what I have right here and now. I will watch others move forward in life because I am too afraid to live it."* Even if a particular door isn't the right decision at that moment, it leads to many more doors that will continue to guide you forward in life. By giving up some of the control that you think you have, you open up space for the universe to interject its ideas and plans. Buddha called this elimination of suffering.

So, to my mind, the meaning of life is to move forward, to step through open doors without fear. Do this with curiosity and the understanding that the universe only conspires to do good for you, if you will let it. Life is meant to be lived. This is the simple meaning for which we all search. But we spend more time holding life back instead of just letting it flow the way it wants to go. We do this because we are afraid—of change, of the unknown, of finances or jobs – and we become unhappy, unsuccessful and depressed. John and I have accomplished so much in the past five years because we have not been afraid to walk through the doors that opened and see where they led.

VIETNAM, JULY 2007

OPERATION SMILE

OUR INVITATION TO VIETNAM
AND INTRODUCTION TO OPERATION SMILE

CAMBODIA WAS JUST A MEMORY NOW, but John and I were finding that we had run across the really difficult part of creating a documentary—editing it. We needed to make something from the eighteen hours of footage that we shot of the Freedom Fields group weeks before. I am proud to say that we did eventually finish the documentary, even with the huge learning curve to overcome, although we never got the chance to do anything with it.

A few things stood in our way. One, we had never used the new editing software we had recently bought. Two, we had to learn how to input and store all the massive gigabytes of high-definition video footage we had, and three, we had promised a documentary masterpiece and had no idea what we were doing. The cost kept growing and we continually discovered we needed more programs and equipment to achieve the look that we wanted for our project. Even though we would have loved to commit all our time to editing the documentary, we had to go back to work at the Universal Studios, back to our *Fear Factor Live* jobs and paychecks.

When you are a professional stuntman, jobs pop up very randomly. One day you're broke and the next day you get a phone call to go and work on the next million-dollar Hollywood block-buster film. John and I had been back in Orlando for a few months when I received one of those calls. A stunt coordinator friend of mine needed me to come to Shreveport, Louisiana and double an actor on a movie called *Mad Money*. It was only a few days' work but it would help to re-pad my bank account from the all the money spent on the documentary. I was told that I would be driving a motorcycle with Katie Holmes hanging on behind me. Pretty cool! Queen Latifa was also in the movie and I have had a star crush on her for years. So this sounded like a great job.

Three days later, as I sat in a hotel in Shreveport waiting for the rain to stop so that we could go film the motorcycle stuff, and an email popped up in the inbox on my Mac, which I just happened to be working on that very moment. It was from Wendy, Cindy McCain's assistant. She asked me to call her about a possible filming job in Vietnam. I reread the email a few times and excitedly forwarded a copy to John, just before dialing the number listed in the email. She answered the phone with a happy sounding voice and asked how things were. I told her that I was in Louisiana doing stunts on a movie. The stunt conversation always seems to help open doors because people have so many questions about the industry. We talked about the movie that I was working on, what I was doing and how John was. Was he with me also working on the movie? How was the flight back from Cambodia? We covered a host of other things before she casually said,

"Cindy would like to have you and John come to Vietnam to film an Operation Smile mission. Would you be interested?" I responded with the calmest, "Sure, that sounds fun," all the while trying not to pee with excitement in my uncomfortable wooden

Days Inn desk chair. Wendy said that Cindy was only going to be there for the last couple of days to see the surgical part of the Operation Smile mission, but she suggested that John and I go for the entire nine days at her expense. Because this would be our first mission with them, Cindy felt it would give us plenty of time to get a feel for how a typical Op-Smile mission runs. The extra days would also give us many opportunities to film the volunteers and the families who came to the screenings in hopes of having their child chosen as a surgery candidate. With a lot of nervous excitement on my part, our phone call continued and I was told I would be getting an email from Cindy's travel agent with all the logistics, dates, timetables, airlines information, etc.

"Look it over to see if it's all okay and get back to me," Wendy said. "Someone from Operation Smile would be contacting you soon with more information," she added.

Normally, volunteers for an Op-Smile surgical mission are required to attend a weeklong training class at their headquarters in Virginia Beach. Because we were coming along as Cindy McCain's personal video crew, we were being given red carpet treatment. I was familiar with the Operation Smile organization and at least the basics of what they do. Operation Smile is a nonprofit organization that sets up surgical missions in countries around the world, specifically to correct cleft palates, cleft lips and other childhood facial deformities. The missions are all volunteer run. The volunteers take time off from their regular jobs and pay their own expenses on the missions, and each is chosen from thousands of applicants. Tens of thousands of children have been helped by Operation Smile over the last twenty years, and, with their assistance and inspiration, permanent clinics have been set up by governments in certain countries such as Vietnam, Kenya, Panama, China and now India. Our destination on this trip was a small town about three hours north of Ho Chi Minh City called Bao Loc, and this time someone else was paying for our trip. My phone calls to John were loaded with excitement as you would expect. Cambodia and now Vietnam, both in the same year—both places that I would have never thought to go.

When I returned home from the stunt job in Louisiana, John and I got busy making sure that we were ready for this trip by going over our what not-to-do list from the Cambodia trip. We bought better travel clothing and went through all our gear, making sure that we packed light and had only what we needed this time. No extra crap would take up room in our luggage. The morning of our flight to Vietnam we decided it would be better if I met John at his house as it is much closer to the Orlando International Airport. I pulled up to see John trying to fit his full size, extended-cab, four-wheel drive Chevy pickup truck into his tiny, one car garage—a garage that was already loaded with stuff. The mirrors had to be folded back, and, even in that position, there were only about two inches on either side as they passed through the garage door opening. The rear bumper almost rested on the dryer door latch and the only way he accomplished this parking trick was to back the truck in so that the driver side door opened at the door leading into his kitchen. This gave him about two feet to squeeze out and enter the house. While John finished his game of truck Tetris, I entered the front door of his house to see our old friend, the large bag with the Stunts Unlimited patch sewn onto it, sitting on the floor. The zipper had almost made it around to close the bag, but this time even more stitches had popped and you could see where it was pulling apart. This bag contained all of his clothes, shoes and personal items. Of course, no trip would be complete if The Kitchen Sink backpack wasn't loaded up and ready for its next adventure. I seriously believe the sole design of this pack is to confuse the hell out of non-English speaking airport baggage screeners in foreign locations. The pack contains so many steel cables and clips that we are always met by a double take when the screener looks at the X-ray monitor as the backpack goes through. I have glanced up myself and, at the right angle it does look like a shit load of shrapnel hooked onto a crap load of electronics. So far, though, we've made it through with only slight delays.

John finally made it in through the kitchen door and then did his last looks around the house for anything that was left unpacked. Satisfied with his last inspection, he loaded the bags into my truck and were off. On international flights we usually give ourselves plenty of extra time to make it through check in and security, because we take so much camera gear in our carry-on bags. We often have to pull out half the stuff to demonstrate what it does. It's a crap shoot, really. I've received a full range of treatment from the TSA screeners—from a hand slap when I reached into the safe zone (whatever that is) to unzip my camera pack so nothing would fall out, to being ignored completely when I tried to offer verbal information on the content of the bag and the purpose of our trip. It's not just the TSA; security screens are very inconsistent on a global level. But if you have issues with someone who speaks a language that you understand sticking their hands in your personal items, I suggest you get over it before becoming an international traveler. Because when a smelly man with a very big machine gun and no understanding of personal space wants to poke his grimy hands through your stuff, you just smile and let him.

After making it through security and our traditional 7:00 AM tequila stop at the airport bar, John and I boarded the plane for our second Southeast Asia trip of the year. One neat thing about traveling on Operation Smile missions is watching the volunteer count increase as you get closer and closer to the final mission location. By this I mean that each time you change planes en route to the mission country, there are more volunteers on the plane, until, finally, the aircraft is loaded with more Operation Smile team members then regular passengers. Volunteers are easy to pick out because they proudly wear Op-Smile patches and shirts from previous missions, presenting them like war medals. Also, the big, florescent orange or green stickers Operation Smile gives out to put on your luggage make it easily locatable amidst the chaos of Third World airports.

HO CHI MINH CITY WE'RE HERE!

We stepped into chaos when we exited the plane and walked to the baggage carousel at the Tan Son Nhat International Airport in Ho Chi Minh City, formerly known as Saigon. It wasn't exactly a baggage carousel as much as a torn-up conveyer belt that went through a small hole in the wall of the terminal. The mission team was starting to get to know each other a bit and we all stood around laughing as we watched the torso and arms of a small Vietnamese man protrude through the hole and throw our bags onto the tattered belt, We then watch them run down the belt and abruptly just fall off onto the dirty asphalt tile floor. Fragile medical equipment and personal luggage crashed indiscriminately into a large, unorganized pile.

The airport was very empty at this time because we had landed right before it closed. It was a shock to me that an international airport would close at night. Our flight was actually the last arriving flight of the evening and you couldn't help but notice that the local employees were ready to go home. As each volunteer found their luggage, they were escorted to the immigration checkpoint and then directed to the bus that awaited us in front of the terminal. One by one the bags came out and one by one the volunteers walked away, until there were only three people waiting by the black, fraying, squeaky, conveyor belt—our Op-Smile contact Vonnie, John and myself. My bag was securely by my side but John's large bag with the mortally wounded zipper was nowhere to be found. We really started to worry when the lights inside the airport began to randomly turn off, hallway by hallway, the squeaky bag belt began to slow until it came to a gear grinding stop. We all looked at each other in disbelief and continued to stare at the hole in the wall like it was going to miraculously belch out one more bag—Johns bag. What we got instead was the man who had been handling our bags outside. He crawled through the hole and down the belt, then headed home. There was a door next to the hole in the wall from which the bags emerged, so, logically, we thought that would be a great place to start looking for John's missing luggage. Maybe it had fallen off the conveyor belt on the outside of the building? I walked over and, to my surprise, the door was unlocked. With an effortless turn of the handle and a gentle nudge of my shoulder I was through the door and staring at an empty airport runway. Empty except for one last plane that was still there and readying for takeoff. Not a bag in site.

Back inside we looked around and found that most of the airport employees had left work for the night, and now the lights in our section had been turned off as well. We were sitting in a dark baggage area that was void of any airport sounds, looking for a bag that was probably not even in the country. If zombies had started coming at us from the dark hallways, it would not have surprised me one bit. The environment was that weird. Then, just as we were about to concede defeat, a person wearing an airport looking uniform scurried past and we ran at him. I guess to him we might have looked like zombies—three people just off a twenty-hour trip in coach, dazed, confused and upset because of the missing bag, emerging from the shadows, yelling incoherent words in English to get his attention and all running toward him on legs that had been stuck in one uncomfortable position for nearly a day. I am surprised he didn't drop his clipboard and run away. Slightly out of breath from the run, we followed him to the nearest computer where, with his help, we managed to fill out some type of makeshift lost luggage form—all the while knowing there was absolutely no way we were ever going to see John's bag again. Of course, the bag contained all his clothes and toiletries. As drained as we all were, we decided to make the best of it, laughed to relieve our stress and boarded the bus for the hotel—which we had now delayed by over two hours. Fifteen minutes in Vietnam and the entire mission team knew who the two problem children were going to be on this trip. Good publicity, bad publicity; it's still publicity.

For some reason John and I always seem to land in foreign countries at night, leaving us with no idea what the landscape looks like. All we see are dark streets lit by an occasional roadside light. That was our initial experience of Ho Chi Minh City. As the roads became smaller and more cluttered with scooters and bicycles, I could make out that this was a very well used and overcrowded city. With each turn, the buildings seemed to get closer and closer together, until each block was just one continuous building. The businesses were street side and on the bottom floor, with the proprietors' dwellings stacked above and occupying floors two, three and up. The space on the sidewalk was littered with street vendors, street people and parked scooters. Lots of scooters. Hotels ranging in quality from zero to five stars squeezed themselves in among the businesses and scooters, along with some amazing restaurants in which a five dollar bill could get you a gourmet meal and a warm beer. The bus pulled up in front of one of the hotels and we all unloaded. This was our home for the first night and the next day while we waited for the rest of the mission volunteers to arrive. The rate at the hotel was a whopping thirty-five dollars per night for a double bed with a private bathroom. Of all the locations we have worked, Vietnam, in spite of its popularity, is still one of the cheapest. For thirty-five dollars this was a great room—cold A/C, hot showers and even a wireless Internet signal. And two beds, which made us very happy.

After a shower and despite the late start, most of the volunteers met in the lobby as we had planned dinner just a short walk from the hotel. It was a valiant effort, but I was not the only person who had a hard time not falling asleep in their bowl of warm soup. Things were better the next morning when John and I met the group in the lobby restaurant for breakfast and a quick briefing about our trip to the actual mission location later that day. For breakfast the Vietnamese traditionally eat Pho, which is a delicious rice noodle soup with some kind of meat, fresh basil and sprouts on the side. Trust me when I say, when in Vietnam, eat what the locals eat for breakfast. When you see how a Vietnamese cook can murder an American omelet you might prefer to go away hungry.

John and I weren't really sure where to start filming, We were primarily there to document Cindy McCain, but she wouldn't arrive for a few days. So, we grabbed random shots of the volunteers walking around, chatting with each other and then loading up their bags onto the bus when it showed up to take us to the mission location in Bao Loc. This was more practice than anything because we hadn't picked up our video gear since

Cambodia, which, if you remember, was the first time we used it at all. All our recent free time was still going into the Freedom Fields documentary edit.

The bus took us from the chaotic city of Ho Chi Minh to the peaceful farmlands of Bao Loc. The buildings were farther apart, there were not as many scooters on the road and our quiet hotel had a massage parlor in the rear. When the sun went down, the massages provided a happy, relaxing ending to the day. Still, there were a few things we needed to understand. One of the volunteers, who ventured in for a message on his aching back, explained the situation over breakfast the next morning. "For five dollars the massage is amazing," he said, "but, if they say; 'Boom Boom,' grab your towel and run."

The rooms were not as modern as the hotel in Ho Chi Minh City, but ours came with a breathtaking view of the mountains from the rear window. It also came with mosquito netting around the beds, which told me what type of environmental hazards we might be facing. However, the view was well worth the bugs and a couple of friendly geckos.

Now let's not forget that John was still wearing the clothes in which he had flown halfway across the world. That's all he had, with exception of the new, bright yellow Op-Smile Vietnam T-shirt we were all given to wear on clinic days. John is a full size larger than I am and my extra-large shirt fit very snugly. Unfortunately, extra-large was the biggest shirt they had, and John's made him look like a bright yellow balloon that was almost ready to pop. Paired with the slightly adjustable camouflage pants that I had lent him, it really made a fashion statement as he walked from the hotel to the hospital where the clinic was set up. Amazingly, we found out that John's bag had somehow ended up in Texas instead of Vietnam. It would make it to our location in about four day—halfway through our ten-day mission. This was an obvious and easy mistake to make, of course, as the words "Texas," and "Vietnam," look and sound so much alike.

We were very excited to begin filming the real meat and potatoes part of the mission—the hospital, the surgeries and the interactions with both the volunteers and the parents who came with their children in hope of giving them new, beautiful smiles. That night we both fell asleep listening to the haunting sound of the locusts singing as the sun fell behind the Dai Binh mountain range just west of the city.

We awoke early the next morning to the sounds emanating from the hotel's kitchen. Refreshed after a cold shower, we made our way down to the hotel's lobby restaurant. Breakfast there usually started after the hotel's owner removed his parked car from the center of the eating area, which doubled as his garage overnight. We would have quick meeting over Vietnamese coffee and Pho and then the bus would arrive to take us to the hospital a couple miles away. John and I quickly discovered that if you take the bus every day with the same people, you get the same people on film every day. So we chose to walk whenever the area was safe enough to allow that. This walk was a wonderful one. Each morning we filmed new sites and each morning the school children passing us would practice their English. "Hello and how are you," they would say and then giggle and walk away. They were no doubt laughing at John in his yellow shirt that was three sizes too small and exuberant Kevin who hollered, "hello," back to them in his best Vietnamese. Within a couple of days, we knew a few different routes to the hospital and we would leave breakfast early to walk the streets.

The first day was spent setting up the Op-Smile equipment, creating the screening area and reconfiguring the operating rooms. These operating areas lacked much of the modern surgical equipment that I was used to seeing. In Cambodia we had gotten our first look at a Third World hospital but we did not get the chance to see an actual operating theater. The hospital's surgery tables were rusted and antiquate, and some of the equipment I would almost have called barbaric, But remember, this was a small town far from Ho Chi Minh City.. The local doctors were still using the US Army surplus cauterizing machine that was left over from the Vietnam War. One electric cauterizing unit fascinated me. It was drab green and sat in a green wooden box with control handles the size of doorknobs. It was plugged into the wall by a frayed, black electrical cord and it still used glass tubes circuits. The floor of the clinic was covered with the same dirty asphalt tiles we had seen in the airport and there was a small window A/C unit in the far wall that had been sealed with duct tape to keep out the flies. Nothing in these operating rooms was sterile at all. In order to enter the areas the hospital considered sterile, all you had to do was to leave your shoes in a rack at the entrance of the nearest hallway, and put on a pair of old, dirty, lime green, close-toed sandals and some hand-me-down scrubs. Then you were free to enter the operating rooms during procedures. Facial surgeries are not as susceptible as other surgeries to staph infections from outside bacteria or germs because of the face's normal openness to the environment, and this allows for some leeway in the sterile zones for these procedures, but this was sobering.

While investigating the hospital on our own, John and I came across a man who had been brought in with a bloody, mangled leg tied to a piece of weathered wood that looked as if it had been pulled off a construction site. It was secured on with the torn strips of a T-shirt. As he lay in bed and the days went by, the nurses merely scrubbed around the makeshift splint. It was not replaced with something better. This is the way most Third World medical facilities look and this isn't the worst I have seen. So be thankful for the amazing health care that we have in the US It may be expensive as hell, but at least it's clean.

We watched with disbelief as the trained Op-Smile volunteers turned these relics ORs into something that I would have almost been comfortable in as a patient. Almost. With the operating rooms now better equipped for the many surgeries to come and the screening room set up for the flood of families who would arrive seeking medical care for their children, we were ready to open the gates the next morning.

We arrived at the hospital in the morning to find a sea of children with facial deformities lining up to be screened. This was the first time that either John or I had been exposed to anything like this. I have never been the type of person who gawks at someone else's malformations but walking into this many children with deformities for the first time damn near took my breath away. The screening process started with a basic medical screening to first make sure that the children were healthy enough to undergo the surgery. If they make it past that, the doctors check the severity of the cleft palate and other facial imperfections. Cosmetic lip reconstructions can be performed at a very rapid rate; they only take from thirty to forty-five minutes. Cleft palates, however, can take much longer to correct because of the medical issue of the open cleft. A cleft palate can cover a range of deformities in the roof of the mouth, but it's essentially a syndrome in which the hard, bony palate of the roof of the mouth forms incompletely, leaving an open hole that leads from the mouth up into the sinus cavity. Some cannot be seen unless you look at the roof of the mouth because the child's face looks normal. Others can result in massive deformities, such as an open upper mandible. This is where you can see right into the sinus area through a gaping hole just below the child's nose. After the first day, though, the imperfections seemed to fade away and all I saw were the cutest children that I have ever laid my eyes or the lens of my camera on. Most volunteers will tell you that the imperfect smiles the children come in with are even more beautiful than the new smiles that they go away with after the surgery.

After two full days of filming the screenings, it was time for the staff to post the names of the accepted children. This is the most emotional part of the whole mission. Frantic parents swarm to read the list that is taped on the wall outside the screening room in hopes of finding their child's name. The accepted laugh with tears of joy, hugging their babies. The parents of those children not chosen walk back and forth reading every name over and over again hoping for a miracle, that somehow their child's name was accidentally misspelled or left off the list. Some parents just won't accept the decisions made and will camp outside for the next three days pleading to anyone walking past for the operation. This has worked in more than a few instances. After all the doctors are just human, They would correct all the children if time permitted.

CINDY'S ARRIVAL

Cindy McCain and Wendy were due to come in that evening as the surgeries were set to start the next morning. They would meet up with us at a formal dinner local government officials of Bao Loc were holding to honor the mission volunteers. Before the dinner, we all sat in a room next to the dining area and played the dreaded name game. This dreaded game is played on all of the Op-Smile missions. The volunteers sit in a large circle. Whoever starts the game tells the group their name and introduces the person to their right. That person then repeats the name of the first person, tells the group their own name and then introduces the person to their right. It continues around the circle until the names of all the volunteers are said. At this point most of the group is very confused and laughing. The purpose of the game is to not only get people talking, but to help them remember just who they are working with during the surgeries. Communication is of major importance. When you have doctors, nurses, anesthesiologists, and a host of other assistants who come from several continents and speak ten different languages all working under the stress of operating on children, it can get a bit daunting. John and I managed to escape the game because we were filming it – or, more honestly, we pretended to film the game to avoid playing. One of the volunteers was excited to meet Cindy and asked me what she was like. How she would be dressed when she showed up for the dinner? John and I explained how laid back she was and said that she would probably show up in a T-shirt and jeans, I don't think the volunteer believed me.

On cue, Cindy stepped through the door wearing a comfortable pair of torn jeans and a form-fitting T-shirt – elegant even in her comfortable attire. She and Wendy sat down with the group, introduced themselves and, like the goodwill ambassadors they are, charmed the room with answers to questions and a few impromptu stories about their experiences on past Operation Smile missions. Our hosts announced that dinner was ready, so we all moved into the next room where large round tables, seating about seven, were set up with very formal place settings that reflected the local vibe. Cindy and Wendy were seated with the local dignitaries at a table in the front of the room. John and I chose a table farther back and sat with a few of the volunteer nurses we befriended. The courses started to come out and, in typical fashion, I was handed everything to taste before many seated with us would try the local cuisine. This included a stew with some type of organ meat and an odd-looking fish that was fried, served whole and presented upright on a stick as if it were a piece of art. The fish almost looked appetizing until the server came at it with a pair of utility scissors and began snipping off pieces of crunchy brown fish and dropping them on our plates. They landed with a crinkled, thumping sound. My best trick of the evening was when I unknowingly drank the small bowl of hand wash that was put in front of me before the first course. I thought it was soup. As the table listened, I described the taste as weak, lemony and not really that good. Hearing my description, the server walked over, shaking his head, and shoved my hands in the liquid. He then helped me rub them together as if I were a three-year-old being taught something for the first time. With a look of accomplishment, he walked away, leaving me with my newfound knowledge and lemon fresh hands. I believe there is even a photo of me with a chicken head in my teeth sneering at the camera like a ravaged maniac. This was, of course, after quite a few glasses of the local, very strong, alcoholic drink of choice.

Halfway through the meal, a message came back to us: John and I were requested to join Cindy and the local governor of the town at the head table. After a couple of "Aren't you two special" glares from the people at our table, we got up and made our way to the front of the room. Remember, even though we acted like Cindy's big shot personal video guys, this was really only the second time we had actually met her in person. Dinner finished up with large amounts of wine and our conversation with Wendy and Cindy seemed to start up right where we'd left off in Cambodia almost six months earlier. This left us feeling extremely special indeed. And nicely buzzed.

As on most missions, morning came early after a good night out. Cindy was staying in a different hotel than we were, so, after our breakfast soup, we met her at the hospital. This was shortly after the team started the first surgeries. According to Cindy's instructions, John and I had already chosen a few children and filmed them through the screening process. This would allow us to follow them through the surgeries and get contrasting "before" and "after" shots of their faces. We walked around the hospital for a bit so Cindy could get a feel for how the mission was going and, when she was satisfied, it was time: Time to follow her into the operating rooms and view the surgeries that were in progress. I really had no idea how this would affect me, I was an emergency medical technician on an ambulance when I was twenty-one, but filming a facial surgery was something completely different and alien.

FILMING MY FIRST FACIAL SURGERY

We entered the OR, and the sounds of suction and scraping, and the beep of heart monitors started to echo through my headphones. The smell of sterile tools cleaned by peroxide, betadine solution and alcohol began to mix with the odor of flesh being cauterized. There was also the metallic, gamey smell of blood. Watching a child's face being opened to expose the bone that needs to be carved in order to create a stronger structure is not the easiest thing to view, but, after a short time, I noticed that the video camera acted as a shield between me and the operation. It was going on right in front of me, but I had to focus on the shot quality, the audio levels and framing out certain things in the monitor—all while not getting in anyone's way. It's very much the same as being a child and watching a scary movie with your hands over your eyes: You catch bits and pieces through your fingers. You know something is going on, but you are not looking directly at the movie. You're focused on it, but not totally watching it. That may sound weird but that's how I would best describe filming intense surgical procedures.

Cindy and I, in on our scrubs and our lime green sterile sandals, made our way through the hallways of squeaky swinging doors and spent hours filming in the operating rooms. The conditions reminded me of the TV show *MASH*. Sometimes there were up to three patients being operated on in one small room at the same time—much like in a mobile hospital unit during a war. The rule of thumb while filming in an operating room is to try not to back up. As long as you can see it, whatever it may be, you won't knock it over. Also, don't go into any blue or green sterile area where surgical tools are stationed for use. If you do, a friendly prep nurse will announce your unwanted placement and correct your positioning. I remember filming one amazing moment in which a small Vietnamese boy, about ten years old, was walked into the operating room, right through the tables where surgeries were currently going on. He could see the other children lying there, with tubes coming out of them and in a half-dead state induced by the anesthesia. He could hear the same sounds and smell the same smells as we could, but he bravely walked right through the room over to the empty table and, with the help of a friendly nurse, he undressed and laid down for his procedure without as much as a whimper or a tear. I was thirty-nine years old at the time and I don't think that I would have the strength or nerve to do what I saw that small boy do. As he inhaled the gas coming from the mask placed on him, covering his nose and mouth, the volunteers around him all started to sing *Twinkle, Twinkle Little Star* until he fell asleep. It was one of those moments that right out made me cry and I don't think there was a dry eye in the entire room. I was so fortunate to have captured that moment on video. Even though Op-Smile doesn't like to show children being put under anesthesia, this was one of those moments that truly shows the love and compassion of the volunteer doctors and nurses bring to these missions.

The filming continued as we moved out of the operating areas and made our way down to post-op. Here is where the real insanity happens. Because of scheduling, the children come out of surgery in waves, heading right into the arms of the pediatric nurses that stay with them as they wake from the anesthesia induced sleep. Let me tell you, they all don't wake up peacefully. Kicking, screaming and trying to pull everything off, or out, of their little bodies is what the nurses are usually greeted with. All while they are trying to check vitals, monitor IVs, stop bleeding and comfort the children. On more than one occasion we were either given an expressive look, or told outright, "Put the camera down and help me hold this child!" Of course, we always did. Filming these missions is amazing, but nothing compared to the feeling of being able to assist the team.

We continued filming continued throughout the rest of the day, until we thought we had enough footage to put some informative pieces together for the Operation Smile website and we had the shots Cindy wanted. As there were rumors that her husband, John McCain, was considering a second race for the US presidency, we filmed a couple of public service announcement style pieces where Cindy talked about what she would do if she were ever First Lady. Which was, of course, to keep doing the humanitarian work she loved. That's one reason why John and I respect her so much.

BACK TO HO CHI MINH CITY

The mission still had two days of surgeries and one cleanup day left, but John and I decided to take Cindy up on her offer and ride back to Ho Chi Minh in the private van she had rented, instead of staying the extra days with the volunteers and taking the bus back. Even though there was much more to experience on the mission, it only seemed right to us because we were here to film her. The other advantage of leaving early was that we could stay with her and Wendy in the Caravelle Hotel. The drive back to Ho Chi Minh City was great. Cindy and Wendy had the van stocked with beer, snacks and a large bag of candy that we kept passing around between the four of us, while the hired guide that came with the van kept Vietnam trivia flowing. This was the first time that we really totally relaxed, let our guard down and got to know Cindy. No work, just a few friends taking a scenic ride back to Ho Chi Minh City along one of Vietnam's most dangerous highways.

Oh, did forget to mention that part? National Road No.1 runs almost the entire length of Vietnam from north to south. It's a huge commercial roadway where buses and semi-trucks pass each other with only inches of clearance in between. These vehicles aren't the best maintained, nor are many sections of the highway. In more than one location, we saw where a bus or truck had veered off the highway and plummeted down the mountainous cliffs, never to be seen again. The highway is so isolated in areas that, at some accident sites, they just bury the bodies of the dead right there on the side of the road. We did see a couple fresh graves on our trips to and from Ho Chi Minh City along this highway, but as long as we paid more attention to the laughter and great conversations going on inside the vans, instead of all the near misses outside, the uneasy feeling of impending doom was manageable.

We reached the Caravelle Hotel and checked in. John and I went to explore our room, agreeing to meet Cindy and Wendy on the rooftop bar for dinner and drinks after we showered and rested up for a bit. This place was awesome; I couldn't believe that we were staying as guest of Cindy McCain in a five-star hotel in Ho Chi Minh City. Cindy has a travel rule when going on a mission to locations that can be less then hospitable: On the first night in and last night out, if the situation permits, treat yourself to a luxurious hotel. After sleeping in mosquito nets and taking cold showers in water that you can't let into your mouth for most of the journey, it's great to have a comfortable night's sleep before the long flight back home. After I took a much needed, long, hot shower, John and I found our way to the roof top restaurant. This was our first experience at the bar called Saigon Saigon, but it wouldn't be our last. The place, and the experience, was otherworldly; the open-air restaurant lounge sits atop the twenty-fourth floor of the hotel and from it you have an amazing view of the city.

On this particular evening there was a light rain falling and lightning created luminescent spiderweb patterns across the night sky. Sitting there, taking all of this in, I felt drugged. Part of that feeling might have been the drinks, and the fact that my body was drained of energy from the cliff hanging drive, but there's also this amazing sensation that you get after a mission. It's a sense of accomplishment—that you have just experienced something greater than yourself, sometimes even put yourself in harm's way to help someone that will never know you. Maybe it's the act of doing something truly unselfish that drugs you, I'm not sure; but it's there and it's real and it's a real addictive drug.

The morning came with more surreal events. Wendy called our room and told us Cindy had invited us to join them for breakfast on the club level. John McCain was having a debate stateside and, because of the time difference between Vietnam and the US, we were able to watch some of it with them. It was like watching a poker game. Cindy knew all the tells, who was bluffing, who was only running because his wife wanted him to do so and the dirt of each person in the game. I learned things watching that debate that I had to forget. Talk about feeling like you have been brought into the inner circle. After a breakfast fit for a monarch, we bid Cindy and Wendy goodbye as they had to head back to the states and went in search of some adventure. John and I had the room at the Caravelle for one more night before we met back up with the mission group at our original hotel, so we took full advantage of the amenities. If you ever get the chance to have a Balinese massage from a small Vietnamese woman in a five-star hotel spa in Ho Chi Minh City, I highly suggest you do it. I believe that John opted for the Swedish massage, but he seemed as satisfied as I was. So satisfied, in fact, that we both went back again later that evening for round two.

The next morning, feeling refreshed and spry from all the massages, John got the wild idea that, because we had the day with nothing to do, we should go and see the famous Chu Chu tunnels just outside the city. Here you can crawl through the tunnels the Viet Cong dug by as they fought off the invading American forces, and you can shoot a fully automatic AK-47. This highly excited John.

JOHN'S DEATH-DEFYING SCOOTER ADVENTURE

First, we needed to acquire tickets for the tour of the tunnels and the bus ride to the remote location, so John called the guide that Cindy had hired to take us from Bao Lac back to Ho Chi Minh City to see if he knew where to get the tickets. He got off the phone and told me that the guy was going to get us tickets and meet us later at the hotel. It couldn't have been more than nine minutes after John hung up the phone that the front desk called and said there was someone waiting for him in the lobby. We should have seen this as a precursor of events to come.

John hung up the phone, glanced at me with a slight shrug and proceeded to go down to get the tickets. This meeting in the hotel lobby actually turned out to be a ride to the location to buy our tickets and the mode of transportation was, of course, a scooter. John bravely straddled the two-wheeled death machine and held on tight for the "E" ticket ride. He is much larger than the average sized Vietnamese person, so he must have looked exceptionally funny riding on the back of a scooter, tightly gripping the small Vietnamese man in front, as they zipped through the traffic packed streets. To explain the scooter traffic in Ho Chi Minh City, the best visual aid that I can offer is to think of schools of fish, all swimming in tightly grouped packs, darting in and out of other schools of fish. One scooter moves to the right or left, and two hundred others scooters all follow the redirection. There is very little contact between them as long as they maintain their forward motion. If a person wants to cross the road on foot, all they need to do to is just walk into the traffic and *not* stop for the scooters. Like the schools of fish swimming around a rock, the packs of bikes just split around you and continue on their way without ever breaking or losing speed. The problem occurs when a person, usually a tourist, tries to stop in the middle of the road to avoid an oncoming two-wheel vehicle. This throws the school of scooters into a panic that results in lots of beeping and yelling, with many drivers shooting off onto the sidewalk through the food vendors.

It's organized chaos, but if you follow the rules, it works just fine. Now you can imagine what John must have looked like, sticking out like a large white tuna amid a million Vietnamese mackerels. All joking aside, it was very dangerous. He said that the guide just told him to hang on and to try to lean with him. When John returned, he looked a few shades whiter. He said that he Hung on for dear life and that, throughout the entire ride, he could feel the other scooters brush past his knees at full speed. There was nothing else he could do; he was already squeezing them in as tight up against the scooter as he could possibly get them. The guide had a hard time controlling the scooter with their combined weight and made no attempt to hide it; he would frequently yell, "Wow!" or, "Oh shit." But we now had our tickets and John had a firsthand new respect for transportation in the city. We decided to walk to the bus location.

The bus ride was very hot, not air-conditioned, uncomfortable and way too long for an excursion to a tourist trap. My discomfort was partially because the bus was full and the bolt holding the right side of my seat sheared off early in the drive, causing me to sit at an awkward angle for the two hours it took to get to the damn location. The tunnels, in their own historic right, were something to see though. I don't get claustrophobic and neither does John, but one of the tunnels was so cramped that our tunnel tour guide actually looked at John once and said, "You no go. You no fit." This was at the smallest and longest of the underground tunnels. These underground passageways were restricting and pitch black. They even gave *me* an uneasy feeling while I duck-walked through them, shoulders touching both sides, butt dragging at my feet and my head with my chin to my chest. My highpoint was watching John go to the refreshment counter and come back with cold drinks and dozen AK-47 rounds to shoot in the machine gun area. The guns are supposed to be fully automatic but most were so dirty that, after spitting out only three rounds at most, a round would stick and the machine gun tech/ concession stand register operator would have to forcefully unjam the stuck round and then cram another into the chamber. The barrel of John's rifle was also chained down, with a whopping six inches of play, which caused him to lean down to shoot the gun instead of raising it to his shoulder. This was probably done to stop some round eye from trying to restart the Vietnam war or accidentally shooting himself in the foot.

The remainder of the trip went relatively smoothly. After we checked out of the Caravelle, we met with the rest of the volunteers at the original hotel and swapped stories about our adventures with Cindy and their last couple of days of surgery. We showed them how we navigated the local streets by using a novelty cartoon street map on a paper placemat we'd taken from an Italian restaurant we'd visited. Although it was not to scale and looked like a child drew it, it was quite useful. We directed some of the group to places of interest we had found—like the Peace Museum and a huge street market with very fresh, although extremely visually unappealing, seafood for sale.

The night before we flew out, some of the younger local Vietnamese volunteers took John and me out to enjoy the night club scene and we Americanized them a bit with rounds of Tequila shots. The evening was a perfect end to our journey. You can't really get a good idea of a culture without befriending some locals and letting them show you the un-touristy side of their homeland. Operation Smile missions are very much like summer camp. You get ten or so days of bonding under extreme conditions; lifelong friendships are made, and there's stress, laughter and lots of heartfelt tears at the airport as the groups slowly get smaller and people depart to go back to their families and their regular lives.

KENYA, NOVEMBER 2007
WORLD JOURNEY OF SMILES

THE WORLD JOURNEY
OF SMILES

ABOUT A WEEK AFTER I RETURNED from the Vietnam trip, a stunt coordinator and great friend of mine, Cort Hessler, called me to work on a TV mini-series being filmed for the Spike TV. The show was called *The Kill Point* and it was being shot in Pittsburgh. I was hired to stunt double two different actors. One for a foot chase with a train and another for an incredible fight scene with John Leguizamo in which we destroyed an entire bank lobby. It was beyond great! The unbelievable story behind me getting this stunt job was that Cort had called me earlier about it and I turned him down. I had already made plans to go film Cindy in Vietnam. For a stunt guy, turning down a big job is a tough thing to do – usually. But for once, I had no trouble doing it. It was a soul changing epiphany for me to feel that there was something out there more important than the career I had spent so many years pursuing. The really cool part is that the universe was just fine with my decision and rewarded me with a surprise. I was at the airport in Orlando, returning from Vietnam, when I received a second phone call from Cort telling me that the stunt gig had been pushed back and, if I still wanted it, it was mine. How's that for good karma?

While I worked on the TV show, I kept in touch with the contacts I had made during the Vietnam trip with Operation Smile. My list of names was growing, and I had learned from the Freedom Fields trip to Cambodia just how important it was to follow up with my new connections and stay fresh in their minds. As with Cindy McCain, it seemed the people from Op-Smile had taken a liking to John and me.

A day after returning from the stunt gig in Pittsburgh I received a phone call from Katherine Taylor at the Operation Smile headquarters in Norfolk, Virginia. At that time, Katherine was the brand marketing director of Op-Smile and our names had been passed along to her from some of the coordinators on our last trip. She told me there was a thing coming up called *The World Journey of Smiles*. This was an event that Operation Smile was doing for their twenty-fifth anniversary. Their goal was to accomplish five thousand cleft lip and palate surgeries in over twenty countries around the world, all in a five-day surgery period. This was a mammoth undertaking, even for an NGO of their size. They were sending film crews to document ten of the mission sites around the world and wanted updated video segments for their website that showed the progress of these missions. Along with the updates, footage from the whole trip would to be used to put together a short documentary covering the entire *World Journey of Smiles* mission.

Katherine asked if we would be interested in joining in, and if there was any particular location in which John and I would like to film. It's not every day that someone asks you where in the world you would like to go for free, s. of course, we jumped at the opportunity. Some of the locations had been taken already so we quickly narrowed our choice down to Jordan and Nairobi, Kenya. After a little more deliberation, we told her that we would love to see what Africa was like. This turned out to be a good choice, because Katherine also wanted to go back to Kenya and agreed to join us on the mission as a kind of media coordinator. This way, with her help, we would know exactly what video footage would best suit the Operation Smile website and for us it would be yet another opportunity to make a future connection within the humanitarian world. Of course, she also became an amazing friend during this crazy adventure, and she still is to this day.

Katherine is much like John and me. She's passionate and has a wild streak for the dangerous places that the humanitarian world can take you. She has enough unbelievable stories to fill an entire book by herself and she has had a big influence on me. She's a big part of the reason I continue to venture off to the places that we travel to in search of stories and nonprofit groups to assist.

NAIROBI DURING ELECTION TIME VIOLENCE

What none of us could have known, was that we were heading to Kenya during a time of political uneasiness, one that would lead to a crisis that after the incumbent President of Kenya, Mwai Kibaki, was named the winner of the presidential election held on December 27, 2007. Raila Odinga of the Orange Democratic Movement claimed electoral ballots were manipulated, and international observers brought in by both parties confirmed this. The Operation Smile team, along with John, Katherine and I, were in Nairobi in November 2007, a mere month before the election that led to the start of the protests and tribal conflict. The slums of Nairobi saw some of the worst violence, violence which continued sporadically for several months in the Rift Valley and in Nakuru, the location where a second Op-Smile team had been sent to perform surgeries at the same time our team was in Nairobi. The three of us, John, Katherine and I, were walking into the headwaters of a possible African civil war and the evidence would soon show all around us.

Flying in from points around the globe, the Operation Smile team met up at the Jomo Kenyatta International Airport in Kenya. John and I ran into our old nemesis—landing in a foreign country at night. We loaded onto a bus—at least that's what it resembled from the outside. It had four wheels, a door and a very wild paint job that was half Jerry Garcia art, half colorful graffiti. The inside: now that's where the resemblance to a bus stopped. This thing was a rolling disco, complete with black lights and strobes that ran the length of the bus's roof line. The windows had so much tint and so many designs that, even during the daylight hours, it would have been impossible to see out of them. Paintings of modern recording stars plastered the walls and it had a sound system that could rival a WHO concert. Not the transportation you would have imagined for a group of the world's finest surgeons. Of course, these weren't your ordinary, run-of-the-mill world class doctors. They were more like super doctors, so this party on wheels suited our group just fine. We drove through the darkness to the hotel where we would be staying for the next eight nights. I had a hard time making out what the surroundings looked like through the bus's window art, but the roads looked much like the ones we had seen in other countries—with one major difference. There was much more walled security and barbed wire around the hotels and businesses. As we approached our gated hotel, I remember thinking, "Wow, this is going to be a real interesting trip."

The gate opened, we drove into the hotel property and then they immediately closed behind us. This would become our primary rule when we traveled after dark: We were not to walk anywhere. We would all pile in a bus or a few cabs, but only after the vehicles were safely inside our hotel's perimeter fence. There was to be no walking to the road to hail a cab. When we arrived at a restaurant, the bus or cab would pull into its safety-enclosed area, which was usually surrounded by barbed wire or razor wire, and we would walk as a group into the establishment. Street crime in Nairobi is supposedly among the worst in the world, and like in most places, criminals love nighttime. We all stuck out like sore thumbs. A bunch light skinned people in a non-touristy part of Nairobi, riding around in a disco bus does tend to draw attention.

The next morning started with a protein-filled breakfast buffet at the hotel, which included soggy bacon, dry eggs and baked beans. (Maybe it's the British influence, but every breakfast in Africa seemed to come with baked beans—not really what you want to start the day with at seven a.m.) Afterwards, we went with the Op-Smile volunteers to tour the Kenyatta National Hospital, where the surgical mission would take place. As we drove in the daylight, it became obvious that Kenya was not what I had been expecting it to be. I knew that South Africa was a very modern country, but I thought the rest of the countries in Africa would be open, with vast landscapes like I had seen in Cambodia. I expected open fires, huts, villagers and zebras. Yes, I was a bit naïve, but it was my first time in Africa. What do you expect? What I got instead of my imaginary vision was a modern city that rivaled Chicago. The place was huge and it just seemed to roll on forever. Every time we crested another hilltop, it was more city as far as I could see. It was a very humbling experience; my fantasy images were blown away by reality. And almost everyone in Nairobi speaks English. If you add that to the urban look and the skyscrapers, you really don't feel as if you're outside of the United States at all.

We were though: we were in Africa. We were in Nairobi during a presidential election, and even though I could easily be lulled into a false sense of security by the look of the city, this was a dangerous place, and even worse, it was a very dangerous time to be here.

THE RAZOR WIRE HOSPITAL

As with most of Kenya, Kenyatta National Hospital was also not what I had expected. With its five story gray concrete walls, guard gates and even more razor wire fence than the hotel, it looked more like a maximum-security prison then a hospital. If not for the beautiful trees and flower gardens that covered the hospital grounds it would have a ridiculously depressing location for health care. As we toured the facility, I could see that even though the overall appearance was of a more modern hospital, it still had a way to go to meet the standards that we see in the states. The operating rooms were much better equipped than the ones we filmed in Vietnam, but they still needed more attention to bring them up to the needs of the Operation Smile doctors. Pieces of the light fixtures over the operating tables were either missing or broken, the walls were in desperate need of paint, the gray terrazzo floor was stained from years of use and the operating rooms looked like they had been built in the 1960s. With exception of a couple newer pieces of medical equipment, nothing had ever been updated. There were two operation theaters that were attached in the middle by a large open hallway. The hallway also acted as a prep and cleanup location with access to the storage area where the Op-Smile equipment was to be kept. Operation Smile missions have a very high success rate, even though the doctors are sometimes performing up to a combined thirty surgeries per day. This is partly because, no matter where in the world the missions are being held, the equipment the doctors train on and use is the same. It's all shipped in from the states. Each doctor, no matter their nationality, can be sent to any mission site in the world and find the same life monitoring equipment and the same anesthesia machines. Right down to the portable lights, it's always identical equipment. This stops incidents from happening due to the lack of knowledge or faulty medical equipment that might exist at a foreign hospital. The mortality rate on Operation Smile missions is lower than then the average number of deaths during surgery in the United States. That says a lot for the organization and their practices. On this particular endeavor, *The World Journey of Smiles*, there were doctors from India working in Africa; doctors from Africa sent to work in China; German and French doctors in Vietnam; and loads of Canadian and American doctors in the Middle East and Russia. All these people worked side by side and they didn't always understand each other's language. But because they had all trained on the equipment that Op-Smile ships in, the success rate was almost one hundred percent. It's kind of like bringing your own game to a house party and knowing that you can win.

John and I took this first day tour as a time to orient ourselves with the layout of the hospital and, with Katherine's assistance, we worked out a game plan for which topics and volunteers to focus on. We wanted to film and upload as many short stories to the Operation Smile website as we could in the eight-day period. The next morning, after another wonderful protein and baked bean filled breakfast, Katherine asked if we would like to bail on the disco bus and walk to the hospital. Of course, we said yes; walking always adds that element of danger and adventure that we love.

The weather in Nairobi was not what I expected. Why would

it have been? Everything else in my fantasy image of Africa was off, why should the weather have been any different? In the mornings it was cold and wet—not a hard rain but more of a light, annoying drizzle that kept falling until the sun came out. Then it was beautiful and sunny, but not too hot. Luckily, I have learned from my mistakes to always bring a jacket of some type. I was thankful that I remembered this here. The hospital was about a two-mile walk from our hotel and although the streets were dangerous at night, they had a friendly vibe during the daylight hours. Street vendors would set up at the highway corners and sell drinks, candy and phone cards. People made their way back and forth along the sidewalks smiling and hooting at each other in a happy manner. The roads were much larger than the ones in Vietnam and for every scooter that we saw there, Nairobi had a bus to match it. They have a very large, although very confusing, mass transit system. The grab hold of anything and hang on system was much in use inside, outside and even on top of the buses the locals rode. As we walked past the traffic police, who wore long black trench coats and carried AK-47's, we watched them harshly shake down taxi drivers for hundreds dollar for crossing over a double yellow line at an intersection. These occurrences brought us back to reality and reminded us that this was still not one of the safest locations for a few white Americans to be.

Another unnerving experience was the random checkpoints along the highways where you were forced to stop your vehicle at a crude looking concrete and rebar spiked barricade. Armed men then approached your car with automatic rifles aimed at the side of your head and asked you to pop the trunk and to see your papers. They would then either take what they wanted or just let you go on your way. With a state police group, a state military group, a governmental military force and many private security entities, all wearing different uniforms, you never quite knew who you were dealing with. But they all had big machine guns and they seldom smiled at you. In fact, it would be creepier if they did smile because you never knew just what they are thinking. The other thing we noticed, as we walked along the streets to the hospital, was the ever intensifying political situation. Orange party posters were everywhere, and the current president must have purchased half the billboards in Nairobi to post huge photos of his face. It was the kind of photo in which the eyes follow you wherever you go. I don't know if it was meant to inspire confidence or intimidate, but on his face was a sneering smile that seemed to say, "Reelect me or I will eat your family."

Political rally busses would pass us from time to time. They overflowed with angry young men who wielded clubs and machetes, and yelled rallying messages over loudspeakers—both trying to drum up supporters and to intimidate those voting for the opponent. They were just looking for an excuse to instigate violence. We drew some strange looks from passersby as we made our way onto the hospital grounds carrying our Pelican cases and holding tight to our camera gear. Mostly, it was harmless curiosity, although one time, as John and I were walking toward the hospital entrance and passed a line of people, someone yelled out, "Hey white man!" in a slow, deep register. I can't say that it absolutely scared the shit out of me, but it did send a few chills down the length of my spine. John looked at me and said, "You did hear that, right?" to which I replied, "Yep... Just keep walking." Sometimes when trouble knocks, it's best to leave the door unanswered.

WHO GAVE YOU PERMISSION TO FILM HERE?

On day one, we made it to the hospital at about the same time as the rest of the volunteers. We decided to film the set-up of the operating room, recovery area, and like in Vietnam, all the work that goes into turning a Third World hospital into one that is clean, organized and safe enough medical area for the Op-Smile team to use. While I went off in search of some great shots, John went in search of an area to use as a production hub. We needed a quiet place with access to power outlets and enough room to set up a small editing system and charging station. This space was important because of our need to get continuous video segments uploaded to *The World Journey of Smiles* blog on the Operation Smile website. The room also had to be secure enough to trust leaving our gear alone without the risk of it walking off with some random hospital employee. After a bit of searching through spare rooms and storage spaces, John found a closet that had been converted into a makeshift office. It was perfect: It had a light, a locking door, a small window and enough power outlets to satisfy our needs. It was at the end of the hallway between the recovery room and the speech therapy area. It was also right in front of the patient check in station, an ideal placement. With the door open, the closet gave us the perfect vantage point to keep an eye out for good stories to follow while still editing our video footage to upload. It might have only been an eight-foot by eight-foot closet but it was our new fully working studio.

While John reconfigured the closet, I went to film the OR transformation. One of the video segments we wanted to put together was a piece on the equipment that is donated to Op-Smile from their many sponsors. I spent a few hours filming the volunteers unpacking the medical equipment from the large white shipping cases plastered with bright orange Operation Smile labels. They continued to morph the operating stations into usable spaces. The OR on the right had three surgical stations set up and the left OR had two stations, along with a table to the deal with local procedures where the patient would not be put to sleep under anesthesia. This was the second time that I had seen this transformation, the first time being in Vietnam. If I see it a million times, it will never stop amazing me. While modern medical equipment may be used, the rooms are assembled in a way that would make MacGyver proud. Orange extension cords ran back and forth across the room taped to the concrete terrazzo floor with ordinary grey duct tape or whatever was easily available. Some of these extension cords ran directly into the equipment while others met up with six-way power strips, the very kind that you buy from Wal-Mart around Christmas time to plug in all your tree and holiday lights. The type with the little red on/off switch at one end? Yeah, those. They are also taped to the floor, or maybe a wall, or to the leg of a table. Plugged into these power strips are the heart monitors, suction units and whatever else will conveniently reach. In some cases, the cords stretched across the room to their limits. When five surgeries were going on at the same time it was like a controlled, yet chaotic, dance of doctors, nurses and volunteers all trying not to kick a plug from its taped position or bump into the operation being performed at the next table.

After filming for quite a while I returned to our studio, the closet, to check on John and Katherine. John had the place all set up and ready to go and when I returned. He and Katherine were helping the other volunteers clear out space for more beds in a newly formed recovery area and they brought in boxes from the loading dock on the ground floor. John disappeared for a while to help someone track down more equipment, so Katherine and I decided it was a perfect time to explore the hospital grounds and get some exterior footage to edit into the rest I had filmed. We found an ideal angle from the road out front where we could get the whole hospital in frame. We filmed some gardeners working in a courtyard, and some beautiful mosaic artwork on the walls of a hallway, and then ran into a large man with a machine gun who wasn't too happy to see us wondering around his hospital with video cameras.

"Who gave you permission to film here?" he asked us. We told him we were with the Operation Smile group and we were filming for them.

"Who gave you permission to film outside the Operation Smile areas?" he asked. Katherine looked at him and politely replied, "My apologies, we thought there would be no issue filming around the grounds of the hospital." I piped in and tried to explain about establishing landscape shots, but that didn't work either. During this conversation with our new, expressionless African friend, a second guard came up behind him. I guess the second guard radioed for assistance because within a few minutes armed men were escorting Katherine and I to the security office. We entered a small, unmarked room and were asked to sit down and wait for the chief of security. Small is a gross understatement; the room was oddly longer than it was wide, like a shoe box, with a bar style desk along one wall where a receptionist type person sat. Along the other wall, opposite the reception desk, were four small, almost child-sized chairs. This is where we sat. The room was so narrow that our knees were inches from touching the desk in front of us even though the backs of the chairs were against the wall behind us. Along with that, the desk in front of us was so tall that we could barely see the gentleman seated at it even though he was just feet away from us. It gave me the sensation that I had just been sent to the principal's office in an elementary school in which the furnishings were made to fit a six-year-old. Katherine and I kept looking at each other, trying not to make things worse by giggling at our predicament. At the back of the long room was an office separated by panes of frosted glass mounted on top of a three-foot wooden wall covered with some kind of cheap paneling. It reminded me of a nineteen seventies bank. I half expected a shady loan officer in a polyester suit to walk out and offer me a great interest rate on a car loan. We could hear the guard that escorted us in speaking to someone, but I could not make out what this second man looked like due to the frosted glass. Every few minutes the conversation would stop, and the door would open just enough for the guard to stick his head out and look at us with a confused expression on his face. Then he closed the door and continued his conversation. We found the whole thing very funny. Each time he looked out, Katherine and I, seated in the kiddy chairs with our knees hitting the desk in front, would try to stop our giggling and then we would look back at him with as innocent a smile as we could muster. This went on and on like a well-executed *Saturday Night Live* comedy skit until the Chief of Security came to talk with us. By that time, we had been there for over an hour and I had taken the tape from the camera and pushed it down inside my shoe just in case they asked for the video footage. The Chief proudly introduced himself and, in a voice that sounded a bit like James Earl Jones' said, "We don't need any international situations to happen, if you know what I mean. Please stay within your group's allotted area and everything will be fine. Have a nice day" He then shook our hands, opened the door, saw us out, pointing us in the direction of the mission location, and closed the door behind us. We barely made it around the first corner before we broke out into tearing laughter and ran off like two kids to tell John about our adventure. Rule number one when confronted with a possible situation in a developing nation is to stay calm and use your brain. A friendly smile and the stupid tourist act usually work. Playing dumb can get you out of a mess of shit.

Later that evening John and I met up with Katherine in the hotel bar to look over the footage that I shot that day and to put our first segment together. As we sat in the corner of the bar, editing our footage, we couldn't help but notice how the upcoming elections were affecting the people that lived here. The TV was always turned to a news channel; most had pushed aside soccer games and were dedicated to round-the-clock coverage of the campaigns. The evenings would start out with a few people from each political tribe sitting in the bar having a drink or two, but as soon as one side outnumbered the other, someone from the more numerous tribe would find a TV channel supporting their candidate. The bar would then become much louder and more agitated. Comments and negative slurs were directed at the opposing tribe's candidate, causing the outnumbered to leave fearing possible violence. We would try to look busy and keep to ourselves because one smile or hello to the wrong person and it might look like the three white people in the bar supported a specific candidate. That could have turned out badly.

One night a news channel showed a segment on an election official who was merely delivering the paper voting ballots to a village outside of Nairobi. The ballots were in a box in the back seat of his car and, when he arrived to deliver them, it was discovered that some of the corners of the ballots had been damaged in transport. The crowd, seeing these damaged voting ballots, accused the election official of rigging them to create a fraudulent vote count. A violent mob formed and they chased the official's car down, broke out the windows and beat him within an inch of his life. Each day we saw the tension in Nairobi become worse. Violence escalated until one night some of our volunteers were almost caught up in it.

A couple of the doctors, along with a few other volunteer team members, decided to throw caution to the wind and walk to a restaurant that was only a couple hotels down from ours. Their mistake was that they went out at night. As the group walked back after eating, they were approached by a gang of uniformed young men, all wielding machetes, and bats. One of the doctors told me that he felt as if his heart was going to beat right out of his chest and that he knew he was going to die. Luckily, as the gang of men got closer one of the uniformed young men said, "You have nothing to be afraid of, we are not looking for you." Then the small mob disappeared into the darkness as quickly as it had appeared. We later found out that this was a political mob on its way to either convince people to change their votes or to make someone disappear permanently. As the week progressed, we would start to hear gunshots ringing through the streets near our hotel rooms. But we all still had a job to do; children were in need.

WE'RE NOT SURE WHAT SHE HAS, BUT IT'S NOT CHICKENPOX

The screening room for this mission was set up at the end of a long hallway. It was a large open room with concrete floors, some plastic chairs set up for a waiting area, a few tables for the doctors to examine the potential surgery candidates and an area where the children could play with a volunteer child life specialist. Echoing rooms and unhappy children made filming very difficult, as they always do. Even with wireless microphones on them, it was almost impossible to hear what the doctors were saying. John put together some last-minute finishes on the segments we edited the night before and I filmed families settling their children into the pre-op beds after they were accepted as patients for that day's facial operations. The morning flowed smoothly. We did not get the massive rush of people seeking surgery that we had expected, so almost everyone who came in was accepted—unless there was a preexisting medical condition that would make the operation unsafe. However, a smooth start to the morning can only be followed by something absolutely unexpected, something leading to a very interesting thing to write about. Like this for example:

About eleven-thirty in the morning, a doctor and a nurse headed in our direction with a thirteen-year-old girl. She and her father had walked, bussed and begged their way to the clinic site in Nairobi from the country of Somalia, which is located on the other side of Kenya. That's a hell of a trek. What made this weeklong journey even more amazing is that the young girl was covered from head to toe with some type of unknown pockmarks. The father was questioned about this and he replied that his daughter came down with this visible ailment days before they left for our mission location. She was hurried out of the screening area by a couple nurses for a better inspection, in hopes that they might identify the cause of the pockmarks and to keep the girl from possibly infecting any of the other children seated in the screening room. The room they chose for this inspection was our editing closet, where John was busy working on one of the video segments. The nurses barged in the closet, along with a few curious volunteers who were also anxious to figure out just what the girl had brought into our semi-clean environment. One of the nurses asked John if he had had the chickenpox as a child and if he had a problem with them doing an exam with him in the room. In reality, the questions were a moot. John would have had to climb over the desk and a few boxes, then squeeze past the infected girl just to get out of the room. There was also the fact that the nurses had already closed the door, stripped the girl down and begun their examination of the pockmarks. John was stuck. After about five minutes the door opened and the girl, followed by the nurses, walked out of the room. I peered into the closet to see John still sitting behind the desk in the same position that he was in when the door was shut. He had a horrified look on his face—the same look you would find on someone's face who accidentally walked in on their grandmother while she was showering. Yes, I laughed. As the nurses walked past me, I very confidently said, "chickenpox," like I knew what the hell I was talking about.

A nurse replied, "No, good news; it's not chickenpox."

"That's good, what is it then?" I asked.

With a slight grin she looked back to me and said, "Umm..., we have no idea what it is." She shrugged her shoulders and sniggered, "At least it's not chickenpox."

Still in the closet, still sitting behind the desk in the same position, with a blank stare on his face, I could see John listening attentively to our conversation. He glanced at us and then at a letter that was posted on the wall describing the symptoms of an incurable disease called Rift Valley Fever. Thank God it wasn't that either, because one of the symptoms of Rift was all of your blood leaking through your pores. To this day we still have no idea what the girl was covered with. She was, however, accepted for the cleft lip operation. Upon seeing his daughter after the deformity was repaired, her father's eyes filled with tears. Thanking us all, he said that maybe now his daughter could finally find a husband and bear children for the village. Up to this point she was had not even accepted as a woman, Now he could be proud of her.

It might seem like a harsh statement but this is the way

these children and adults are regarded. They are monsters, a curse on the parents that brings shame to the entire village. There are just as many cleft lip cases in the United States, but most of them are repaired when the children are very young so the deformity is almost unheard of and rarely seen in public. In developing countries, though, where healthcare is almost impossible to find, children can grow into young adults, or even into full adulthood, without ever being able to get their deformed features corrected. They lead very hard lives filled with rejection and shame.

THE GIFT OF AFRICAN INTERNET ACCESS

After having all the armed guard fun right before lunch, we felt the urge to leave the hospital grounds for some fresh air and to see if we could find a place to upload our first two video segments. There was no Internet access at the hospital and the service back at our hotel was so slow that we would have been waiting for days. It was also pay by the minute. Lucky for us, that one of the women working with Operation Smile Kenya had a contact for us. It was a local internet provider that was a short cab ride from the hospital. Through this woman they had given us permission to patch into their server and upload our videos. This was wonderful news. The other film crews that were covering *The World Journey of Smiles* in other locations around the world were running into the same problem, and this would give us a leg up on the competition. Okay, there was no real competition and no prize waiting for the film crew with the greatest number of uploads. But, come on! The bragging rights alone were worth it. As Katherine put it so eloquently, "There was no competition, but we still won."

The Internet provider was in a downtown district, located on the upper floors of a very modern skyscraper. The three of us were welcomed like celebrities and given full access to whatever we needed. We were even assigned an employee from the company who was happy to help us out. We took full advantage of this golden opportunity and used it daily to get our videos out and to communicate with friends back home. It sure beat waiting in line to use the antiquated computers at the hotel at three in the morning. After we finished with our first video upload, Katherine suggested that we treat ourselves to a tasty, non-hospital cafeteria meal. She had been to Nairobi in the past and remembered a great hotel with a restaurant right around the corner from the building that we were in. A cold beer was sounded mighty good.

THEY'RE GUARDING WHAT?

The Friendliest Checkpoint In Kenya. That's what the sign posted at the beginning of the road we turned onto said. Walking down this road would have been no different than any other we had conquered on foot, but driving down it was a another story. There was a maze of strategically placed concrete cylinders, painted with black and white rings, running across the width of the street. This was truly an improvement over the homemade, rusty rebar barricades we had seen in so many other locations around town. The gun carrying guards also seemed a bit more organized and less in your face at this checkpoint. Just beyond the barricades and set back off the right side of the street, was the gated entrance to a beautiful colonial style hotel. This was the location of the restaurant Katherine had chosen. As we entered the gate, I could not help but notice the walled complex across the street from the hotel. I couldn't make out what it was. There were no signs posted and, further-more, a massive, unpainted concrete wall topped with razor wire blocked most of the view of the facility. The only access to whatever was behind this wall was through a heavily guarded iron gate. I don't use the words heavily guarded lightly. There must have been two dozen military looking troops, machine guns in hand, posted along the wall. Unlike other locations where we had seen armed guards, here they were more regimented. The wore black berets and long black trench coats covered their modern camouflage uniforms.

For some reason that even eludes me, I love trying to get photos of myself posing with armed military and militia units around the world. Do I have a death wish? No. Maybe it's the element of danger; maybe it's just to show people that it can be like the wild west in other places around the world. I don't know. I just tend to gravitate in their direction, and you can probably see where this is going. I turned to Katherine and said, "I wonder what that's all about. Think I should try to go get a picture?"

Katherine, being an adventurous type said, "Why not? What's the worst that could happen?"

John had heard our exchange of words. He looked at me like I had grown a toe from the center of my forehead and tilted his head like your dog does when you say, "Want a cookie?" Under his breath he growled, "Kevin NO!"

I smiled at him and started in the direction of the street, then stopped and looked back at him over my shoulder.

"What? Are you insane?" he asked. His voice became quieter and more whisper- like the farther away I got, until I could only see him mouthing pleas not to continue. Me being the people person I am, I figured why not try? Maybe they would jump at the opportunity to make a white man's day by posing for a photo op. Yeah, right. So I crossed the street and walked right into the pack of them.

Some came forward to greet me and others stayed at their

post along the wall. As one guard approached me, I did my best to give a stupid tourist smile and, with a Do you speak English? tone in my voice, I asked, "Would you mind if I took a picture with you guys?"

Thankfully the guard cracked a smile as he looked at me, like he wanted to say, "You're a crazy little white man." Then politely he said, "No, you can't."

With a tone of disappointment, I pushed back a bit, "Come on, please?"

"I am sorry, but no," the guard replied. I could see that the guards in the back were amused by my brazenness, or stupidity, so I said, "Okay, well can I just take one of you all from the road?"

The smiling guard replied, "You can take a picture of the hotel you were entering from the road, but please do not aim your camera in this direction." Even I know when to not push my luck. I graciously stepped back while maintaining eye contact and, with a polite nod and a smile, I scurried back to the hotel side where Katherine and John were standing.

Katherine gave me props and said, "Hey at least you tried," and John gave me the same look that Oliver Hardy would give to Stan Laurel after dropping a piano onto him. We headed in for a great lunch but I was still inquisitive about the guarded estate on the other side of the road.

When we left the restaurant, nightfall wasn't too far away, so, to be safe, we decided to call for a cab ride back across town to our hotel. As we waited out front for the cab, I watched the guards meander around in front of the walled compound and I would catch one of them occasionally glancing over at us. I still had no idea what they were guarding, but I did have a strong feeling that if someone were to run toward them, they would shoot first and not even care why you were running. Our cab pulled up and we piled in. As we drove away, I asked the driver what was behind the walls and why were there so many guards out front. He too looked at me like I had a toe growing from the center of my forehead and said, "That is the Israeli Embassy, my friend."

John's look was priceless and Katherine just broke out in laughter. The poor cab driver, not knowing what I had done, must have thought we were escapees from an asylum. It seems that I had walked up to one of the most heavily guarded embassies in Nairobi, during a time when pre-election violence was rising daily and asked for a photo with the guards. No one ever said I was boring.

SURGERY DAYS BRING NEW KNOWLEDGE

The next three days were surgery days. When John, Katherine and I arrived at the hospital, things were already running at full speed. There were children in the operating room undergoing procedures, children waiting with the child life specialist for the next table to open up, children in recovery and families reunited with their children in the post-op area. It was running like a well-oiled machine. John and I took turns filming in the OR and assisting the nurses in the post-op room. Although we were there to document the mission, John and I are humanitarians first and it is inspiring to get a chance to put down the cameras and give some hands-on help. Bringing children from recovery to their parents in the post-op rooms has to be my favorite thing on these missions. To see the look on a parent's face when you hand them their child after surgery has been performed is worth all the money in the world. Sometimes the parents don't even recognize their own children because the facial changes are so drastic. After a long stare, they hold them tight, and then tears start streaming down the faces of both the parents and the volunteers. It's very emotionally uplifting.

I left John bouncing back and forth between helping the nurses, editing in the closet and filming around the post-op room, while I ventured into the operating theaters to see if there were any good stories to follow. Africa was somewhat different from Vietnam, and since this was still only my second time filming in this type of environment, I eased myself back into the surgeries slowly. Because of the smaller than expected turnout at our mission location, the Op-Smile doctors were able to take on more than just cleft lip and palate surgeries. Burns on children are an ever-present problem in Africa because so much of the cooking is done over open fires. We saw many children with horrific scars on their faces from the boiling liquids they had pulled off onto themselves from the easy- to-reach fire pits. Two problems arise from this. First, the scar tissue that replaces the preexisting skin does not have the same elasticity as healthy skin does, so while the child grows, the skin doesn't. This causes a limited range of motion, especially when it affects the arms, shoulder-to-neck area and the legs. In these instances, the doctors shave off the skin with what looks like a giant potato peeler. The afflicted area will then heal, allowing for more scar tissue to build up. With more scar tissue, more mobility is gained. The other medical problem associated with burns and skin injuries in Africa is a scaring issue called Keloids. With Keloids, there is an excess growth of scar tissue at the site of a healed skin injury. Although race is not a factor, people with darker skin pigmentation seem to be afflicted more often. Even small burn scars can be affected with Keloids, and they can grow to extremely large sizes if not removed. Often when the Keloid has been removed, a new one will form over the scar and, over time, the procedure must be repeated—sometimes throughout the lifetime of the person afflicted.

On this trip, we were very lucky to have a surgeon from Canada, who, along with facial procedures, did quite a few hand reconstructions. On more than one occasion we have seen the Op-Smile teams run across children with a disease called Apert Syndrome. It is a congenital disorder characterized by malformations of the skull, face, hands and feet. Most of the parents who bring in children in with this syndrome have no idea that their child has it, as, due to the lack of access to modern medicine, it was never diagnosed. Cleft palates, however, are a common visible trait related to Aperts Syndrome and parents know that the Operation Smile doctors fix this problem, so they bring their child in for that reason.

The most noticeable and identifying trait of Aperts Syndrome is that a child's fingers will fuse together, forming one large, flat, paddle shaped-finger with a single, solid fingernail growing across it. On this mission there was one child that I specifically remember who had this problem. His eyes were set far apart, his cranium was oversized and his forehead elongated, but he was still so damn cute. He was about four years old and even though his manual dexterity was impaired due to his inability to fully grasp objects, he was always smiling, very rambunctious, super smart and just a quick little thing. I followed up on his charts to see when it was his turn for surgery and, when his time came to go in, I filmed his mother handing him to the nurses as he barely shed a tear. I donned my scrubs and entered the operating area to film some of his surgery and to have the Canadian surgeon talk me through the procedure as he went along. First some fresh skin was removed from the boy's thigh to be grafted onto the sides of his new fingers, after they were created. The x-rays showed that the bone structure to support individual fingers was all in place, so the plan was to separate the two finger bones on the outside of the hand, creating three fingers—one large one in the center and two normal ones on the sides. Later, in a second operation, the child could have the middle two separated, giving him four functioning fingers. The skin removed from the thigh would be sewn to the inside areas where the separation cut had been made. The hardest part, I was told, was to restructure the veins, tendons and muscle tissue so that the fingers would work as they should.

I documented this for a while and then stepped away to see what else was going on in the OR. I filmed the work at a few other tables and then, from the other side of the room, I thought I heard the doctor working on the hand ask for the bone nippers. Bone nippers? That got my attention. So, I turned and started to walk back to the hand surgery table. I must have only been about ten feet away when I heard a loud, crunchy snap, and something small shot from the table. It was followed by the comment, "Anyone see that finger on the floor?"

I raised the camera to the doctor's face and he looked at me with a smirk and said, "Better three working fingers then a single big one that he can't use.

I could see him grinning behind his surgical mask as he then said, "Who really needs a pinky, anyway?" I just looked at him and laughed. Even though it seemed a bit extreme, he was right. Kids are so resilient, and the finger bone he cut off was too malformed to support a functioning digit. Only hours after the surgery, I saw that small boy on the floor of the recovery room area. Both his hands were wrapped in bandages and he was playing with a toy truck, still smiling like nothing had ever happened. Like I said before, I can't stop singing the praises of the volunteer doctors who go on these medical missions. Even in less than perfect conditions, the skill and caring they bring to these procedures is equal to the care you will find in any modern medical facility on the globe. *The World Journey of Smiles* was a huge success, almost hitting its goal of five thousand surgeries in the ten-day mission schedule. Since only three or four of those days were actually surgery days, it was an amazing accomplishment.

THE CRADLE OF LIFE TOURIST TRAP

With the last of the children out of surgery and the Op-Smile medical equipment packed back up for shipping, the team was ready for a day of recreation and relaxation before the long flight home. We set up a trip on the disco bus to visit the Rift Valley. The Great Rift Valley is basically a 6,000-mile crack in the crust of the earth. This fissure runs from an area near Lebanon to the country of Mozambique in East Africa. The Rift actually cuts Kenya into two segments. It is thought of as the cradle of civilization as the skeletal remains of hominid ancestors of modern humans have been unearthed here— some dating back over 3 million years. The valley is bookended by some of the highest mountains in Africa and is home to Lake Tanganyika, one of the world's deepest lakes. The depth of the lake has been recorded at an astonishing 4,700 feet.

From our roadside viewing point, the valley seemed to go on forever. Also, at our roadside viewing point, as in most places that people flock to visit, was a tourist trap loaded with useless trinkets to buy. It carried the same crap as the markets in Nairobi did, only with a slightly higher prices due to this being a natural wonder location. John and I both found out on our first trip to Cambodia, where he bought a strange looking violin at the temples, that he is a target for people selling their knickknacks. While I must have a no nonsense look about me, John has sucker written all over him:

the harder they push, the quicker he relieves himself of cash in the hope that the pestering people will just leave him alone. I am happy to say that it only took about five trips for him to harden his shell to pleading merchants, but at the Rift Valley stop, John didn't even make it ten steps away from the bus before he had doled out almost seventy-five dollars for a bunch of hand carved soapstone effigies of local animals. This time it was my turn to look at him and say, "You did it again, didn't you?"

Furious with himself he just stood there, looking down at his arm full of buys and, in self-disgust, glanced up at me and said, "What the hell am I going to do with this shit? I hate this. Why can't I just say no, or ignore them like you do? How do you do it? I just wasted seventy-five bucks."

I laughed real hard, shook my head and walked away to see if I could find some cold beers. Our day continued with a tour of a local wildlife park, where for five dollars the workers opened up a gate and allowed us to enter a pen and pet a wild cheetah. This made for a great photo op and helped John forget about his earlier financial losses. After a long, sleepy bus ride back, complete with a beautiful sunset over the African plains and a herd of wild Zebras running along the side of the highway, the evening festivities continued with a dinner party in honor of the volunteers. As the stress from the last week of surgeries melted away, we drank and danced on our last cold, rainy night in Africa. I found it dreamlike and surreal that the DJ played *Rains Over Africa* by Toto, which happens to be one of my favorite songs. In an almost perfect Hollywood movie ending to our trip, I walked outside into the cold, drizzling rain and listened to the words of the song: "Hurry boy, it's waiting there for you." I knew something special was happening to me and that experiencing all the world had to offer was my destiny.

Katherine, John and I made it out safely and were back in the states before the serious political violence started. The airports were shut down and areas of town burned to the ground only two weeks after we left Nairobi, but happily none of our new friends in Kenya were displaced or killed.

A BUDDHISTS TEACHER'S PHILOSOPHY OF LIFE

This is a teaching that I heard from an old Buddhist practitioner. For some reason it seems like a good time to tell it.

Life. As Buddhists, we like to base life on one hundred years. Whether we live past that age or die before, one hundred is a good number. For the first twenty years of your life, you are under someone else's care because you do not know enough yet to be on your own. If you live one hundred years, you will spend the last twenty years of your life under someone else's care because you are too old to be alone. This leaves you with sixty years to truly live—which it not too bad. Now, consider that we sleep for half of our lives. This cuts our sixty good years in half to thirty years. So, if, per chance, you do live to be one hundred years old, you really only have thirty years to make conscious decisions on your own. Why, therefore, would you want to do anything but live with kindness and gratitude in your heart?

After I heard this, I meditated on it for quite a while and realized just how true it is. But the statement was said a long time ago. If you inserted the formula into our modern, busy lives, you would also have to figure out how long we spend in our cars, waiting in lines, doing yard work or focusing on our jobs. If you put all those variables into the equation, we barely have any time of our own to actually live. Come to think of it, how do we live?

KOSOVO, MARCH 2008
THE HALO TRUST

OUR INTRO TO KOSOVO

BACK AT FEAR FACTOR LIVE, John and I were becoming the two to talk about. People were amazed that we kept getting the chance to travel around the world, most of it paid for by someone else. Already offers to carry our equipment around were coming from our friends, but we were too focused on finding our own future to worry about anyone else's at that time. Along with the humanitarian filming, I was having a good year with stunt jobs. Sometime in February, I had received a phone call from one of my Miami stunt contacts about a movie called *Sex Drive*. It sounded more like a porno movie to me than the teenage coming-of-age picture it was purported to be, but it's hard to turn down a good stunt gig. They needed me to double an actor in a scene in which a pissed off redneck in a jacked up four-wheel drive pickup truck speeds into a parking lot and slams into the side of the hero's parked car. My good friend Chris, the same one I worked with on *Miami Vice*, was driving the four-by-four and my job was to sit in the driver's seat of the car as he drove the truck into my driver side door. Special air bags were placed under my side of the car and, when fired off, they would give the car just enough lift to allow the four-by-four to launch my car—and me—up onto its passenger side, without, we hoped, flipping me all the way onto the roof. As it was, John and I were already heading down to the Florida Keys to meet up with Nigel, our friend from Cambodia who trained new deminers for The HALO trust. He had a new, part-time job with another group and they were having an event that he wanted us to be a part of. So we managed to get another free trip with all expenses paid—this time to a private resort in Key Largo. And the timing worked out great. After my last night of work on *Sex Drive*, I drove down to meet up with John for a fun few days in our free, private two-bedroom condo.

Our stay in the Keys was also informative. The organization putting on the event had been developed by a bunch of former British military officers, and it used strict military efficiency, combined with fun and games, to help the top brass of huge corporations learn to work together better. We were invited there because of our stunt backgrounds. The organization's future plans included rope challenge courses and even mock battles, and they wanted to pick our brains about potential safety issues.

I was the way back from a run to the mainland to pick up a sign for one of the group's leadership building activities when my phone rang. It was Wendy, Cindy McCain's assistant. We had the usual catch-up conversation, and I told her where we were and about the trouble we were getting into playing with the Brits in the Keys. We both laughed and then she asked, "Are you and John free in March?"

"Of course we are," I replied immediately. Hell! Like I had any idea what I was going to be doing in March. But my years of stunt work had taught me to always say yes first, and worry about how to accomplish the trip later. She told me that Cindy was going to visit The HALO Trust guys in the newly formed country of Kosovo. She would tour the landmine fields and areas where cluster bombs were still live in the ground. I had almost no idea where Kosovo was or just what a cluster bomb did, so of course I said, "Count us in! I love that place." Wendy and I bonded from the start, and by this time she knew that we would follow her and Cindy into a full-on gunfight in Rwanda if asked. The fact that we were now almost experienced enough to actually make it to a location anywhere in the world, without a babysitter telling us where and how to find the correct connecting flights in obscure foreign airports, was also a huge plus on our side. She scheduled us to join a conference call later that day to go over the logistics of the trip and what we needed to film, bring and expect to see in Kosovo. I was so excited that I had to pull off the two-lane road onto the shoulder to call John and fill him in on our next great adventure. John was just as giddy as I was and I hurried back as fast as I could. Why? I don't really know. The trip was over a month away, but talking about it, in person, to John solidified it in my mind.

As I waited for the agreed upon time of the conference call, John and I decided to kill the Heineken mini keg that was chilling in our fridge, and then go down to the convention room to see what strange activities the Brits had the businessmen attempting. We found a large group of business professionals, dressed in suits, in the parking lot of the convention area playing a game of playground tag. This, it turned out, was part of the course's regimen: Fill their minds, tire them out, reenergize them, then hit them with new motivational facts and challenges—all day, nonstop. The funny thing is that it works. The businesspeople taking this team-building course worked for a liquor distribution company, and the owner of that company was smack dab in the middle of the games, learning with his employees. This CEO just happened to be Rocky Wirtz, owner of the Chicago Blackhawks. Somehow, once again, John and I had accidentally stumbled across an amazing opportunity. By assisting this group we not only got a free, if short, vacation in the Keys, we were also able to acquire the same knowledge that others were paying thousands of dollars to learn. Pretty cool.

I was so enthralled by what I was witnessing that I almost forgot about the conference call with Cindy McCain. My instructions were to dial a certain number, punch in a secret code, then state my name and enter the call. With some butterflies in my gut, I dialed, and when the recorded message told me to do so, I stated my name. Unfortunately, due to my nervous, dry mouth, it came out sounding more like Vevin than Kevin. But I punched in the code anyway and waited.

The call was in progress when I joined in and Wendy was already laughing at my attempt to introduce myself. I was there mostly to listen and answer any questions that came up about the filming, but there was one other item on the agenda. Wendy, as I'd learned during our earlier call, was stepping down as Cindy's travel assistant and passing the job over to another of Cindy's dear friends, Megan Latcovich and she wanted to introduce Megan to me. Right off it was clear that Megan had been very well informed about the antics of the two humanitarian stuntmen and she made it clear that, as a Navy helicopter pilot, she was just as crazy as we were.

This was going to be a very fast paced but amazingly fun trip, and they weren't kidding about the fast paced part. John and I were to meet Cindy and Megan at the Mandarin Oriental Hotel Hyde Park, in London, where we would stay the night before our flight into Pristina, the capital of Kosovo. In Kosovo, we would go to The HALO Trust headquarters for a briefing on local issues, tour some minefields and cluster bomb impact locations, and meet the principal of a primary school that had been taken over by Serbian forces during the war. The trip would also include an opportunity film Cindy meeting the president of Kosovo and end with a visit to the recently established US Embassy in Pristina. Then we would all head back to London for a relaxing night before we flew back home. As I listened to the schedule of events and tried not to pace around with excitement, John just stood there staring at me like his head was going to explode. Hell, I was jumping up and down inside and just as anxious to tell him what I was hearing as he was eager to know what was being said, but I had to maintain some sense of maturity during my big boy conference call with Cindy.

LONDON CALLING

We arrived at Gatwick Airport in London and, for a change, it was during daylight hours. I was just glad that we weren't landing in Heathrow, which is just way too busy and confusing, Gatwick is also a large international airport but it's less affected by tourism. We exited the plane and headed toward immigration to get our passports stamped.

Bags now in hand, we navigated our way to the Victoria/ London Express train which took us to Victoria station and, from there, we caught a cab to the Mandarin Oriental in Hyde Park. As we were advised to do, we caught a trusty brown cab—they are sanctioned by London— and were at the steps of the hotel within fifteen minutes. Did I mention that it was cold? Really cold, ice forming from your breath cold, freezing cold. I had packed for colder weather, mind you, but not for permafrost. Two men dressed in proper red and black British bellmen's uniforms grabbed our bags from the cab and put them on the curb beside a grate from which visible steam arose, condensing from the cold air. Our bags would be carried up to our rooms after we checked in with the front desk. This was a very proper and somewhat exclusive hotel, so I am sure they were looking at John and I as if we should be checking in to the Stop and Sleep Motel around the block. However, our names were in their book, and the young woman behind the desk smiled and checked us in. Had I noticed just how she had checked us in, I might have had time to correct another embarrassment for John before it happened. But I didn't. Maybe there was a global conspiracy or maybe the guys from airport immigration called the hotel as a joke. I had referred to John my partner, and sure as shit reservations had been placed for Mr. and Mrs. Kevin Ball. Now, that would mean that someone thought that I was the man in the relationship and that Dear John was my betrothed spouse. Oh, it gets better. The room itself proved this theory to be true as the female desk clerk who showed us the accommodations made no attempt to apologize for the two beds that had been pushed together to form one king-size bed, or the his and hers bathrobes with matching slippers that were laid out on either side of the large bed. Large slippers had been placed on Mr. Ball's side, while Mrs. Ball, and that would be John, received petite woman's footwear. There was a lengthy pause as the woman smiled and told us to call down to the front if there were anything else we needed. Then, before we could collect ourselves to correct the situation, she backed out of the room and shut the door, leaving John and I to at each other in complete silence.

"London thinks we're gay," John said. This humorous realization, along with the travel fatigue, caused us to laugh for nearly an hour, and we almost had the room reengineered to accommodate two straight guys when John looked out the window and noticed that it was snowing, really hard. I had heard that hardly ever snows in London, and it was an amazing site to behold, but this snowy trend would follow us throughout our adventure in the Balkans and the warmest pants I had with me were a pair of denim jeans.

Cindy and Megan were due to arrive at the hotel later that evening. This gave John and me time to search for an authentic British pub, for some real British food and a properly poured pint of ale. We walked and it was so cold that, after a couple of miles, I could no longer feel my feet. My thin socks and dress shoes with a quarter inch sole offered no insulation between my feet and the frozen London sidewalk. The wind was howling through the streets, blowing small snow flurries around, but still we walked, in search of the perfect pour. Bag O' Nails Quality Ales was that perfect place. Perfect mostly because it was so miserably cold and this was the first place that we ran across, but it turned out to be the type of pub that John and I would have chosen anyway. A few pints down and some warm meat pie in our stomachs, we braved the weather again to find the palace, which luckily was just a block away. It looked nothing like what I'd thought it would. I believe we walked past it a couple times before we realized that it was indeed the one and only Buckingham Palace. There is a great photo of John standing in front of the gate shrugging his shoulders with a look on his face that plainly says, "This is it, I'm freezing. Let's go back to the pub." We probably would have gone back, but we knew that Cindy was due in soon and we'd made plans to go to dinner with her and Megan and discuss the trip to Kosovo. The London part of this story wouldn't be complete without mentioning the dinner.

We met Cindy and Megan in the lobby later that evening. It was our first time meeting Megan in person and we hadn't seen Cindy since Vietnam. A car was waiting curbside in front of the hotel to take us to this wonderful Italian restaurant that Cindy had found on one of her earlier trips to London. We entered and were seated at a table for four. The hostess obviously thought that

Megan and I, the youngest looking, were a couple. This led her to the assumption that John and Cindy were a couple as well. What happened next will go into my mental archives as one of the funniest things I have ever witnessed. John, as the oldest looking male at the table, received most of the waiter's attention, starting off with the wine menu. Let me state that while John is quite the connoisseur of worldly beers, he knew little to nothing about fine wines. Nor could he pronounce anything on the menu. He humbly studied the wine menu for a few moments until Cindy, who does happen to be an expert on wines, asked sweetly, "Would you like me to pick one John?" He graciously handed the power of choosing our libations over to the wine guru sitting across from him. Cindy chose a very nice Sauvignon Blanc, pointed the name out to John and handed the wine menu back to him just before the waiter walked up to our table.

"Have you decided on a wine sir?" John pointed to the one that Cindy favored.

"Very good choice, sir, thank you," the waiter said, and then he disappeared into the back room only to return a few moments later with the bottle of wine. When you buy a bottle of wine in a fine dining establishment, it is presented to you first so that you may inspect the label. The waiter did this and, with a fancy swish of the wrist, offered the bottle for inspection. John looked up with a polite nod as if to say, "That's fine."

Next came step two of the process, the tasting. As he should, the waiter opened the bottle at the table, poured a small amount into a wine glass and handed it to John to taste, smell and ultimately approve. This is why we all love John; he managed to keep a straight face while he pulled off this next trick. He took the glass, held it up and swirled it around, looked at the waiter, then at the glass, then at the waiter again and, with one quick slurp, emptied the glass. Still without cracking a smile, he flawlessly reenacted a Listerine commercial, swishing the wine into his right bulging cheek, then his left and topping it off with a full-on, head tilted back gargle of the pricey wine. As the waiter stared in confused amazement, John swallowed loudly, looked up and said, "Ah yes. That will do nicely."

After a delicious meal of Italian wonders and slaphappy conversation, we ended up back at the hotel bar for a couple of thirty-dollar martinis. I ordered them shaken not stirred, in my best James Bond voice, before I realized that the exchange rate at this time was 2.2 pounds to 1 US dollar. That meant that, converted to dollars, everything on the menu, or in the United Kingdom for that matter, was double the price shown plus twenty cents on the dollar. Oh, the lessons we learn while traveling: among the most important is check the exchange rate before you shop. The exchange rate was almost as shocking as finding out that we were mocking James Bond and his beloved MI-6 in what turned out to be a gay bar.

SERBIA REFUSES OUR FLIGHT PLAN

This is one of my favorite stories to tell because Kosovo was unlike any place I had ever been. The next morning, we woke early, made some coffee—the only thing that I like better than beer, grabbed our bags and met Cindy and Megan in the lobby. Two cars idled out in front of the hotel waiting to take us to Luton, a small private airfield located somewhere just outside London. Upon arrival, we were taken into a guest lounge where our passports were taken, our luggage was checked and put through a portable x-ray scanner, and we were pampered a bit.

After all, we were traveling with a senator's wife. While all this was taking place, I noticed Cindy at the far end of the room discussing something with our pilot and Guy Willoughby, the founder of The HALO Trust. He would be accompanying us on the flight, along with a reporter by the name of Jill Zuckman from the *Chicago Tribune*. Guy can best be described as someone who stepped right out of an antiquated adventures club—a quiet man of few words, but strong in stature. You only have to be in his presence for a moment and you can visualize him sitting in a library, surrounded by oversized mahogany bookcases and walls adorned with maps and the trophy heads of animal he'd hunted around the globe. After many years of military service to Queen and crown, Guy founded The HALO Trust to rid the world of the abandoned weapons of war. I continued to watch Cindy and could tell from reading her body language that something serious was going on. What that turned out to be was something I never thought I would encounter. I could make out a few words of the conversation and walked closer to determine if what I thought I heard was correct.

Cindy made no attempt to hide the conversation from us. "Tell the Serbian government that we are on a humanitarian mission," I heard her say to the pilot.

He responded with, "They still say no; diplomatic passages only."

"Then tell them this is a diplomatic mission. I am a US Senator's wife, aren't I?"

"They still say no."

"This is ridiculous. I can't believe they are trying to pull this," she said. Since the topic now seemed open for discussion now, I asked what was going on.

"Serbia's government won't give us permission to fly through Serbian air space on our way to Kosovo," Cindy replied. She, the pilot and Guy then disappeared to work out a resolution for our little predicament. I turned my questions to Megan who remained in the lounge with us.

"What does this mean exactly?" I asked. She replied that we would probably be considered a hostile enemy if our plane ventured into Serbian airspace.

"Hostile?" I choked out through a bite of my complementary blueberry muffin. "That doesn't sound good. Does Serbia have an air force? Will they come after us?"

I still don't know if it was Megan's dry sense of humor or if she was dead serious when she responded with, "No, they don't, and I seriously doubt they have any surface to air devices that could reach our plane at the altitude we'll be flying." She smirked, raised one eyebrow and walked away to check on Cindy and the pilot. This left John and me standing in the room alone, looking at each other, motionless, silent and inwardly trying to grapple with the idea of having our airplane blown from the friendly skies. I think John broke the silence with, "Beer would be good right now."

A couple of minutes later, a now happy Cindy appeared from the other room and said, "You two ready?" she said as she and Guy passed us on the way to the door that led to the tarmac. The pilot had rerouted our flight path to one that was a bit less direct but wouldn't create any international news by pissing of the government of Serbia. The new path would take us out of the U.K. and over central Europe, where we would hang a right and follow the Adriatic Sea, hop over Greece and come up through friendly Macedonia into Pristina, the capital of Kosovo. This would be comparable to flying from Colorado to Atlanta by way of Cuba, but at least no one was going to be calling this little plane load of Americans *hostiles*.

Megan, who had falling into the role of big sister, was right on Cindy's heals, followed by Jill. As she passed us she barked out, "Come on Sally and Nancy let's go." Would you believe that, out of all the nicknames I have had in my life, this is the one that stuck? From that moment, up to present, John and I have been known as Sally and Nancy.

Allow me to present a brief history lesson to let you know why Serbia was pissed at the announcement that a bunch of happy-go-lucky Americans, including a Senator's wife, wanted to fly over their beloved country. Serbia has been a hot spot for at least the last 1,500 years. Kosovo was, at one time, a very important part of Serbia and contains many religious and historical sites. After many changes and multiple wars, Kosovo was finally given the designation Socialist Autonomous Province within Serbia—meaning that Kosovo had the right to rule itself. In the late eighties, Slobodan Milosevic thrust himself into power in Belgrade, Servia's capital, by taking advantage of Serbian patriotism and questioning Kosovo, which was primarily occupied by Albanians. From Belgrade, he ordered that all Albanians be fired from state jobs and that Serbians replace them. Kosovo protested peacefully, but these protests eventually lead to the formation of the KLA, or Kosovo Liberation Army. With a title like that, I'm sure you can see where this is going. Milosevic let loose a brutal military campaign against the KLA. This included widespread atrocities against innocent civilians in an attempt to ethnically cleanse over 800,000 Albanians. NATO forces stepped in to help regain peace. Following this action, the United States, under the Clinton administration, sent forces to help NATO prevent a full-on genocide of the Albanian people. As John and I would find out later, the people of Kosovo are in love with Americans and feel that it's only because of God and the United States that Kosovo and its people exist today. There is even a Bill Clinton Highway and the label on their locally brewed beer has the Kosovo flag next to the American flag, with a heart in the middle joining the two. If you ask me, getting on a country's beer label is one of the highest honors you can achieve. Kosovo had only received international recognition as an independent state about ten days before our trip, and, because of this, there was a lot of anger and anti-American sentiment at the Serbian border. It was probably good judgment to fly around and leave them be.

Strolling onto the tarmac, John and I followed the group around the terminal to the location of our parked aircraft. As my eyes met the blue and white jet, I felt joy, excitement and wonder all slam together and knot up in that area of your body that makes you speechless and weak-kneed. One glance over at him and I could tell that John's emotions were playing the same game of tug-a-war with his body as mine were. I really don't know what I was expecting our transportation to Kosovo to—maybe one of those twin turboprop planes, like the ones that take tourists to the Bahamas from Miami. With all the Serbia no-fly zone talk, the question hadn't really hadn't crossed my mind. What stood in front of us, and beckoned us to come aboard, was a full-sized private jet. Not a prop plane or even a small Lear jet; I think this was a Challenger 604. This craft comfortably sat up to twelve people and was big enough to allow you to stand up and walk around. You could even take a nap in the bedroom at the rear. With only six of us on board, it was the most pleasurable flight I have ever taken and it ruined me for coach flights for all eternity. I think Cindy was pleased by our surprise and excitement. She just kept smiling at us as we slowly took the stairs, one at a time, up to the door, trying to savor the feeling for as long as we could. That ended when a laughing voice hollered, "Sally! Nancy! Get on the plane."

The inside was even more grand—all leather tan seats that moved in more directions than I could contort my body, gold-colored fixtures and real wood everywhere. It was like a flying law office. John and I just sat there with the biggest shit eating grins on our faces for the whole flight. I purposely had to contain myself from giggling continuously. I kept thinking, "How did I get myself and John into this one?" Then I remembered how life works if you just move forward the way you are supposed to, and I felt right at home.

During the flight Jill interviewed Guy about forming The HALO Trust and coining the phrase, "humanitarian demining." She also asked why there were so many factors contributing to landmine removal problems in Kosovo. Guy told us all that he would speak about that topic in greater detail at the HALO compound, where there were maps and documents to help us understand why the United Nations had all funds pulled back from demining efforts in Kosovo. It turned out that this would our primary objective on this trip—to document Cindy and Guy's meetings with local government officials to get the removal of abandoned landmines and cluster bombs brought to the top of the list of Kosovo's critical needs. As I listened to Guy and filmed some of the interview, I knew this was going to be a memorable and eye-opening trip. I couldn't wait to hear more of what Guy had to say throughout our journey.

I could see through the plane's windows that the sky was growing darker as we neared the end of our flight into Pristina. For some reason the word "Balkans" has always brought to my mind images of snowy mountains and crumbling stone buildings damaged by years of civil unrest. I know, I watch too many movies, but this time my imagination was very accurate. As we closed in on the runway, through the gray sky, I could see that the ground was covered with snow, and I could feel the cold crosswinds that pressed on the plane's cabin walls and pushed us around on the runway as we taxied in. When our friendly flight attendant opened the plane door and that first frigid gust of snowy air blew in, it became very obvious to me that I had underestimated the weather in Kosovo and stupidly under-packed my cold winter gear. Yep, this was extremely bone-chilling cold. As I descended the stairs onto the tarmac, the wind blew right through my jeans as if I wasn't wearing pants at all, and my feet could already feel the frozen concrete through the thin soles of my cheap dress shoes. Fortunately, I had brought a couple heavier weight Mountain Headwear jackets, so from the waist up I was able to maintain comfortable warmth. My lower body, however, was going to suffer something awful in this climate.

Bob and Tony, our private security team, waited for us at the bottom of the stairs. I am still not sure if those were their real names, but what I do know is that these two were ex British Secret Air Service (SAS)—real hardcore commando shit. They were there to be our escorts on the tour around Kosovo and to make sure we all made it out safe. When you're married to a US Senator and an heiress to a company worth a small fortune, you can never be too careful. Cindy always had some little security trick up her sleeve, which always made me feel sufficiently protected. We followed Bob and Tony to a small immigration room where our passports were checked, but not stamped. I really wanted a stamp from Kosovo but because it's a place to which the US frowns on citizens traveling, there would be no cool Kosovo stamp for Kevin's collection. With Bob in the lead and Tony bringing up the rear, we made our way out of the terminal and headed to the parking lot. There we found our old friends, The HALO Trust's British Land Rovers— the same ones that we had grown to love in Cambodia. They were waiting to take us to the HALO headquarters for a quick briefing before we headed to our hotel. John and I grabbed our bags and loaded up. We somehow managed to get stuck in the Rover that had been converted into a medical transport—an ambulance of sorts. The main difference was that instead of back seats, this one had a couple bench seats along the sides and we had to enter through the door at the rear. No real problem, other than the low ceiling and the fact that the rear of the vehicle was not insulated, which made a long drive through the snowy conditions just a bit uncomfortable. Of course, we made another nighttime entry into a country, so we had absolutely no idea what the landscape looked like. With my line of sight stopped by the snow banked up on either side of the highway, I could only envision what I had seen from news footage taken during the war. Images of bombed out buildings and scorched earth ran through my mind as I peered into the dark, bitter cold, remoteness. This and the fact that the driver was once a rebel soldier kept me a bit on edge. My body was getting stiff and achy from the cold and it felt like my hip bones were pushing through the thin seat cushions into the sheet metal frame of the truck, so the right hand turn we made into The HALO Trust headquarters couldn't have come at a better time. The line of Rovers pulled in and parked, and, with a symphony of moans, grunts and crunchy sounds, John and I unfolded and got out of our frosty box on wheels. Even though we were tired from our travels, Guy wanted to waste no time in giving Cindy the lowdown on what was going on in Kosovo and what we would be seeing in the days to come.

Thank God there was some hot coffee waiting for us. We all needed a bit of an internal warming up. After a leg stretch, bathroom break and, for me, even more coffee, we all went into a small room for our *Intro to Kosovo 101* lecture. We also met some of the local HALO staff who would be accompanying us as we toured the minefields and locations affected by cluster bombs. Matthew was introduced to us as the acting area manager for HALO in Kosovo. His job was to oversee the efforts of the local deminers and act as a general supervisor for this location. Like Guy, Matthew was a man of few words unless he was speaking on the issues at hand, and in no time we were deep into a lecture on Kosovo and how the United Nations had been using independently paid demining companies to aid in the removal of all the leftover war debris still buried in the ground. A company making a profit from removing mines and cluster bombs would consider getting most of them out of the ground quite the success. To HALO, leaving only one landmine in the ground would be a complete failure. Their goal is one hundred percent clear and usable land and they have the reputation to back up that promise. The UN essentially set a date and said, "Okay, it's clear. There are no more mines in the ground." They then pulled all funding for landmine and UXO (unexploded ordinance) removal from the books, listing Kosovo as clear and forcing HALO to stop work. This left many local HALO employees without jobs and, worse, Kosovo simply wasn't clear. We heard this in the briefing and we would see first-hand examples of it in the days to come. Guy was going to take us to locations where the ground was loaded with mines and cluster bombs, show us land that could not be cultivated or built on, and even allow us to speak with the locals whose lives were disrupted by the unknown locations of these buried weapons.

While he spoke on the topic, Matthew passed around inert versions of different types of landmines to hold. Visual aids, and actually holding a landmine, bring you closer to the issue. You become part of the circle, especially when you realize that this thing you are holding in your hand once rested in the earth with millions of others and they were all placed there for one purpose—to kill or maim human beings.

Most of the types of mines that Matthew passed around I had seen before in Cambodia, and in displays set up at the different HALO facilities we had visited. One device, however, was completely new to me. It was called a BLU-97/B Combined Effects Cluster Bomb. This specific cluster bomb is a combined shape charge, fragmentation and incendiary device, used against personnel, tanks and armor. It was Kosovo's biggest problem. Even though there were quite a few landmine fields that needed to be cleared, they had been designed as a protective boundaries. Most mine fields were located in border areas or near places that were used as fortified military facilities during the war. Cluster bombs, though, were still being found in schoolyards, on mountains, along highways and even in backyards throughout Pristina and other village towns. What exactly is a cluster bomb, you might ask, and how does if differ from a landmine?

WHAT I LEARNED ABOUT CLUSTER BOMBS

A cluster bomb is a type of cluster munition. they can either be dropped from the air or launched from the ground. Each bomb dropped is an explosive weapon that, upon detonation at a preset altitude, ejects smaller explosive charges. Each bomb can contain hundreds of these individual bomblets, and they each then make their way to the ground, some aided by small drone parachutes for more stability. Each bomblet explodes upon reaching a set distance from the ground and, ideally, over the enemy target. The altitude of the original drop, the time of the original bomb's detonation, and the arming timers, chutes and altitude all play a part in determining whether the bomblets explode in the air at their intended elevations, or if they malfunction and plummet to the ground without properly arming. This gives cluster bombs up to a thirty percent failure rate. The math is very simple, really. Hundreds of bombing runs by NATO and US aircraft, each dropping hundreds of cluster bombs containing hundreds of individual bomblets with a thirty percent failure rate, equals thousands of live cluster bomblets, possibly armed but all extremely unstable, buried in the ground. This is what they were finding in Kosovo.

Unlike a landmine, which is designed to maim a person, cluster bombs are intended to achieve maximum amounts of destruction. The intended use of cluster munitions covers a broad spectrum. Some of the bombs are designed for use against personnel, while others are created for use against tanks, destroying runways, distributing landmines or even delivering chemical weapons. The bomblets, no matter their original purpose, do not discriminate and if stumbled upon or hit with a shovel, each will explode, leaving very little trace of the innocent man, woman or child who was ill-fated enough to discover it.

Another major problem in dealing with children and the bomblets is the color, size and shape of each. Bomblets range in size but, on average, most are about the dimensions of a coffee canister or softball and they are usually painted bright yellow and orange. What else is painted bright with bright colors and about the size of a coffee can? UN aid and food packets. These are also dropped from planes, often over in the same vicinity that the cluster bombs are dropped. Really? What genius came up that plan? By nature's design, we know to stay away from most berries that are either red or black. How about we use those colors?

Why do military forces use these monstrous devices? Because they are extremely effective! Imagine you are a soldier, pinned down by enemy forces and there are hundreds of opposition troops between you and your destination. Now imagine that one bombing run can clear a path of everything—from men to tanks to fortified bunkers -thus saving your entire platoon. Trust me, you will now think this monstrous weapon is an angel of mercy.

That's why groups like The HALO Trust and individuals like Guy and Cindy spend so much time clearing the ground and slowing the rate of *civilian* casualties.

A BIT SLEEP DEPRIVED

The briefing went on for some time, until it was obvious that we all needed to get some rest. I, for one, was becoming tormented. My mind was absolutely captivated by what I was hearing from Guy and Matthew, but my body was refusing to allow the muscles in my neck to hold my head anywhere near a twelve o'clock position. I believe poor Megan was drooling on her sweatshirt. John was fast asleep for most of the ride to the hotel and I nodded in and out while still trying to get a good look at the cityscape. One thing that the stopover and introductions at the HALO compound did achieve was that it gave us a chance to feel a bit more comfortable around the local HALO crew and our drivers. After all most of them were ex KLA soldiers, the rebels, and many of them had actively fought in battles against the Serbian forces. Like many other people we met throughout our travels, they were amazing and I was humbled by their stories. They motivated me to continue to pass their words along.

It was only a short drive to the hotel, but by the time we arrive, Bob and Tony had already scoped out the place. Although it was a perfectly safe environment, it was nice to feel checked up on. These two had a totally different approach than the American security groups we had been around. Instead of muscling up and letting everyone know that they were security, both Bob and Tony dressed down, as if they were just average locals and they were very quiet, never making a scene. Bob usually sat in a chair, reading a paper with his back to the wall and most of the time I never knew where Tony was. At dinners they each took a specific seat that allowed the best view of the doors. Tony always went in first, before we ever entered a room, and Bob walked in with us as if he were one of the gang. I learned much from observing them both.

John and I jumped into the bar in the lobby to see what the brew of choice was in Kosovo—no big surprise there— then made it up to our room just in time to witness a unique spectacle from our hotel window.

Evening prayer time started up a few minutes after we made it to our room. The haunting sound of the call to worship could be heard echoing through the streets, sung from distant mosques. As I sat on the foot of the bed checking out what the local TV had to offer, I heard the strangest sound outside the window. It was like a billowing wind caused by something otherworldly. An unnatural sound, it came past the slightly ajar window so fast that I could feel the air pressure in the room change. There was a humming sound that accompanied the wind, but not one large hum; more like many small hums all joining together forming this unearthly resonance It was chilling. We listened for a few moments while blankly staring at each other in puzzlement, our expressions saying, "I'm not going over to look out the window, you go." Slowly, we both made our way to the glass. Through the dimly lit streets we could see that there was a black cloud moving around in the air at a high rate of speed. It changed directions as quickly as a school of fish, darting around at about the third-floor level, sometimes coming so close to the hotel that it almost hit the building before vanishing out of sight. The sound always came first, followed by the black cloud. Cautiously we opened the window during one of the moments of quiet stillness, stood there for a second waiting, then, like a jack-in-the-box, we both leapt back as the swarm shot past us. Swarm really is the appropriate word here.

Birds, all black and tightly packed. Even though we now knew what the cloud was, it was still hard to grasp what was going on here. The wailing of the prayer calls from the many mosques and over the loudspeakers nightly brought tens of thousands of birds into an enormous, crazed frenzy. Like a surreal dream, the flock darted around—backed by the haunting prayer from the mosques. I managed to grab the camera and film the event that continued on for about a half hour, I should really send that footage to National Geographic. After the avian commotion died down, we both crashed hard and slept like babies till the morning wakeup call roused us from our restful slumber. For some God forsaken reason every morning with a mission group starts at first light—way too early. This was no exception.

RUN AND GUN FILMING STYLE

After enough time for a quick breakfast, we all climbed into our trusty transportation and hit the road. Morning light cast transformed the image I thought I had seen the night before, Pristina was beautiful. Blue skies with high, white cirrus clouds gave me the feeling of being is a snow globe, and the freezing air helped with that feeling. What I thought was dark and ominous the night before turned out to be soft, rolling hills leading up to snowcapped mountains. The mountains surrounded us on all sides, creating the rim of a mountainous bowl, with Pristina being the cereal left in the bottom. Kosovo looked more like a scene from the 1937 movie *Heidi*, staring Shirley Temple, than a country recently out of a war. I was told that during spring and early summer the rolling hills turn into lush green hills, blanketed with vibrant wildflowers that flow to the base of the mountains. Kosovo could be a tourist destination for summer downhill mountain biking and a new Mecca for extreme winter sports enthusiasts. Unfortunately, the extreme angle would take on new meaning if you tried to giant slalom down through one of the numerous, unmarked landmine fields that still lay hidden mountains. Looking at all this beauty, it was hard to imagine a war had ever taken place here, and that there were still thousands of unexploded, possibly armed, munitions lying hidden just below the surface of the ground. On the way to visit the primary school, Matthew had the rovers pull off the road at some specific locations so that he and the local HALO staff could fill us in on some demining activities. We were shown where the removal process had been halted because of the UN funding issues. We visited areas that had been cleared, suspicious locations and even some spots in which a cluster bomb was known to be just below the surface of the soil. These bomblets were found, reported, then left alone by the persons who exposed them, hoping to have them removed when HALO had the go ahead to actively restart the removal and destruction process again. This is why it is so critical, in urban environments like Kosovo, to keep the removal process going until no mine or cluster bomb is left unexposed.

In Cambodia all the mines had been buried in the ground by the hand of man. Even though the locations of some mines are unknown, once a field is located the mines usually follow some pattern. This is because humans are creatures of habit and will follow a repetitive pattern even if not instructed to do so. Chance, however, has no logic or need to create patterns, so bombs and mines that are dropped from an aircraft could be hiding anywhere. Locals have found them along sides of highways, in parking lots and in school yards. We even looked at a hole in the center of a major roadway where a single cluster bomblet had punched through the asphalt leaving a perfect cookie cutter circle behind. The live bomblet was still living under the road at whatever depth its forward motion stopped. Without HALO nothing would be done, it would remain below that very active highway, with any luck undisturbed.

After seeing a few more locations like the road, we continued on to the school. Let's not forget that it was still freezing outside and that John and I were stuck in the back of the medical Rover, cold and uncomfortable. You would have said we resembled two of the Three Stooges if you had watched us, 1) try to escape from the back door of our Rover with video cameras and microphones at the ready, and 2) rush to the front vehicle, from which Cindy was emerging, in time to capture some useful conversations on tape. I got good at my escapes by using my right foot to pop open the inside door latch while simultaneously sliding down the bench seat, camera in my left hand, and using my right hand to support myself during the getaway. As my feet hit the ground I would rush toward the conversation, often getting there just in time to get a sarcastic "What took you two so long?" look from Megan—which always came with an "I'm kidding" smirk and a flick of the hand motioning us to run and get back in our vehicle. At a couple of stops, by the time I made it to Cindy's group, they were already loading back in and driving away, giving me nothing more than a comical run around the convoy of Land Rovers—which just perpetuated our circle of tardiness. I didn't even always make it to her; sometimes I made it just far enough to see that they weren't even planning to get out into the cold. I would see a couple of hands pointing out the window at something in the distance and they would start to drive away while I was ten steps from my Land Rovers open rear hatch. I would then run back quickly, catching John before he managed to lumber out of the back. He is a full size larger than I am, and we both slow down in the cold from old stunt injuries.

There was much laughing amidst the cursing on that day of many stops. The laughing both from us and from the children who always managed to show up just in time to watch and point at our meticulous motor vehicle exit and entrance strategies. Everywhere in the world we go, we always seem to somehow get in this predicament while filming Cindy, but it always makes for great stories later, over drinks. Everyone loves to laugh at the class clowns.

EXPLODING SCHOOLYARDS

Children were walking around the front courtyard as we pulled in for the first school visit of the day. The war hadn't caused much surface damage to the building itself but, as we would soon find out, the surrounding area—including the school grounds—was notorious for holding unknown numbers of cluster bombs. Run ins with unexploded munitions by the local villagers were usually the first and most reliable notification that led the HALO team to areas that needed attention. We saw this in Cambodia, with farmers working around the landmine fields. but here, in the more urban areas of Kosovo, the locals were informing the authorities about cluster bombs. This information helped lead HALO to these remote locations while also allowing them to map and keep a running database of the sightings pertaining to the abandoned cluster bomblets.

In this particular instance, the principal of the primary school had been trying to plant a small tree in the front courtyard area. He grabbed a shovel and randomly chose a location to dig a one-foot by one-foot hole in which to plant the small tree. After only a few shovels of earth, he exposed the bright yellow outside wall of a live bomblet. Fortunately for the principal and any children that might have been around him, he only unearthed the device instead of striking it with enough force to cause detonation. The first attempt to dig one small hole and a cluster bomb is found. That ratio suggested that the schoolyard might have been laden with unstable bomblets. Yet life went on, and children continued to walk over the grounds as they went to and from school every day. Without reinstatement of the funding, this horrific situation would remain as it was and the chances of a child being destroyed were very real. Matthew put it best when he said, "Children will be children, but they should at least be able to find safe passage to school."

How real was this danger? Two weeks after we left the country, a literal stone's throw from the school we visited, two people were injured and five people killed, blown up along with their cow, when the grazing animal nudged a live bomblet that was half buried on a hillside trail, This was the same trail that we walked up to get a good view of the school, I assure you, the danger is extremely real.

Even though our visit was timed during local Easter break, when children were out of school, word of our coming spread throughout the surrounding townships, enticing children and parents to come meet Cindy and to hear how HALO was trying to restart the removal process of the cluster bombs. Almost none of the staff and students attending that day knew who Cindy, Guy or Matthew were, or even that funding had been pulled back from the mine and bomb removal activities. What they did see was an

American woman and a couple of British men acting as goodwill ambassadors, acknowledging that there was an enormous issue that needed to be addressed in this post war environment. This simple visit helped reassure and raise the confidence levels of these local townspeople, letting them know that others were trying to help them regain a foothold on a safer and more productive way of life. As we approached the front of the school's main building, two young girls that led a mob of smiling children were the first to greet Cindy and present their bouquets of flowers. They were followed by the principal and what seemed like half the town. The friendly flock of onlookers funneled into the school building after us, proceeded down the hall and into a classroom where the other half of the town was already waiting for us. The small classroom quickly became tightly packed. Most of the kids were probably just bored and wanted to see their first real live Americans outside of a conflict situation, but the well-mannered group contentedly listened as their principal spoke with Guy and Cindy, through use of an interpreter, about the topics affecting their friends and families. After a selection of random questions from the kids and their parents, we continued our tour of the school. Down the halls we went, still followed by what seemed to be the entire town. John and I did our best to keep up with the Cindy and our group while squeezing through the sea of three-foot tall kids, who, like us, were all trying to get to the head of the pack where the trendy American lady was. Anticipating just such a situation, I'd had the nifty idea of hooking a wireless lavaliere microphone on Cindy before we arrived. This allowed me to keep up with and record any conversations going on, even if the herd of youngsters had me pinned down in another room. As I listened to the conversation through my headset, I heard Cindy ask,

"Why are there so many mines and cluster bombs around the local schools?"

"Glad you asked that," Guy said, always happy to share his wealth of facts. The same question had been running through my mind all day. Was it because of the children, or to terrorize families? Why? The answer turned out to be much more strategic then vicious. It is because of these buildings' structural design—the layout—and the fact that schools and hospitals are better fortified against an attack than other structures. No matter what country you visit, and no matter how poor the people are, education is the means to escape from a dismal life. Children want to go to school to learn and a location is needed to teach them. To give their children a place to learn, people gather to build schoolhouses in their communities, villages, and towns—sometimes with help from the government and international charitable funding. Like hospitals, school buildings need to be well designed to contain people. They also need to be durable, to keep out as much outside noise and distraction as possible, and provide protection against the rain, dust, wind and heat from the sun. Sometimes schools and hospitals are the first places to get running water, sanitary bathrooms and even electricity. It makes perfect sense that an invading force would seek out these locations first and use these organized facilities. With their many hallways and connecting rooms, they make a perfect place to house troops and set up command centers.

In the instance of this particular school, after the invading Serbian forces captured it and set it up as a base, they needed to protect it. They lay down a defensive perimeter of landmine fields just outside the school yard. This would make it more difficult for the KLA to take back the seized establishment from the Serbian army. Of course, where you find one landmine field set up to defend a location, you will usually find a second mine field set up to contain the first field. In this case, the design plan was to suppress the movements of the Serbian soldiers as they traveled to and from their new base. It was very reminiscent of a chess game with each side trying to counter the moves of the opposing armed forces, defend, attack, contain and advance. While this tug of war for supremacy was going on, the call went out to big brother NATO.

TIME TO GET A BIT TECHNICAL

For those that don't know, NATO stands for North Atlantic Treaty Organization. It was based on the North Atlantic Treaty, which was signed on April 4, 1949 and acts as an intergovernmental military alliance, in which the affiliate states agree to joint defense in response to an attack by outside parties. Here's where the big guns come into the situation. NATO forces, for the most part, try to create peace through superior firepower. In this case they wanted to help level the playing field, and to stop the eradication of the people of Kosovo. Air strikes over the invaded locations began, and the cluster bombs began to rain down onto strategic targets in overlapping patterns from organized bombing runs. Each of these airdrops, over their target, was about the length of two football fields. These supportive attacks on the forces that were holed up in the schools and in other strongholds ultimately left behind thousands of bomblets that remained in the ground long after the conflict ended. That, my friends, is why schools and hospitals are highly valued military targets and why so many pieces of unexploded ordnance are found in and around them years later. It creates a *shitty* state of affairs for the people who happen to live in the area.

Finishing our visit to this first location, we loaded back up and drove out of the gates, off the school's property. A horde of waving children followed us. As I watched them run down the street after us, playing as children do, I couldn't fight off the morbid thought that one of the young faces I just filmed might be that of a future innocent victim.

MINES IN THE MOUNTAINS

Our next stop was somewhere up in the beautiful Dinarides Mountains range that encircles Pristina. With the town and the foothills in the rear-view mirror we headed off to a place that made our Land Rovers feel very much at home, even though they had seen many miles of torment in their days. Their suspensions flawlessly navigated the uneven, rocky trails. I could only imagine how comfortable the ride up the forty-degree incline might have been if my ass had actually been in a seat, and maybe facing forward. As it was, John and I had a great view of where we had been, and, thanks to the steep, awkward angle, my feet were now securely planted on the rear door of our converted medical Rover. It was almost like standing up in a freezer.

Following nature's grand design, the higher up we went the colder it got, and, due to the lack of any green foliage to act as a wind block, the chill factor intensified to a very uncomfortable level by the time we reached the summit. But the view made it all worth-while. From where we stood, I could see more snow-capped mountains on one side and all the way to Pristina when I turned around 180 degrees. The vista was astounding. Then Matthew, with his dry British wit, had to spoil my beautiful daydream by scaring the crap out of me and reminding us that we were standing in the middle of a very large and unmarked active landmine field.

In Cambodia all the places we toured were well marked. It might be only with red wooden stakes, but it still gave you a good idea of where you didn't want to go. Here in the mountains of Kosovo there was nothing. Not a sign or a red stick; a just the small trail that we used to get from the vehicles (parked on the other side of the mountain slope) to our present location. Well... , a small trail and Matthew, standing in front of us at the side of our trail with his arms out making a human T shape.

As I paused in my tracks to look at him, he addressed our nervous line of sightseers and said, "Please do not venture off this trail," Still with his arms out acting as a visual barricade, he continued, "From where I stand and behind me there are landmines! Behind you, about the same distance on the of the trail there are also mines."

This trail that we were on, all carefully placing one foot directly in front of other in a heel-to-toe pattern was only the width of your foot—not your feet, your right foot, or your left—pick one. The point is that it was really tight. Sure, there was a bit of room on either side of the foot path before you would hit some low brush, maybe three feet, but dammed if I was going to place my feet on any spot that wasn't obviously etched into the ground by a year or so of uninterrupted foot traffic. To add to the fun, Matthew had that type of British accent where you couldn't tell if he was excited Everything he said rolled of his tongue without a sense of urgency. Each word was well pronounced and calmly spoken. This is probably great trait to have when one is a remover of highly explosive landmines, but I couldn't tell if he was serious or joking most of the time. Therefore, I adopted the same attitude as Short Round did when he followed Indiana Jones, "I step where you step, I go where you go, I no touch nothing!"

All joking aside. it was very intimidating to know that we were surrounded by a mountainside that had been mined by the airdrop method. These landmines had not been placed by human hands; they had been scattered from the air. This meant that there was no pattern to the mayhem and even though the trail that we walked on was well worn in, no one knew with any certainty the proximity of the nearest mine. At the end of the trail was a small, cleared spot of ground that afforded us the ability to spread out just a bit, and allowed John and I to get in front of the conversation for some better shots. Over the years I have become very efficient at walking backwards and filming at the same time because most people don't stop and talk, they walk and talk. Here, however, stumbling over a loose rock and awkwardly tumbling rearward into the nearby scrub brush seemed like an experience I could do without.

Matthew and Guy talked about the lives of the local villages, how their livelihood from wood cutting was impeded by the presence of the landmines and how an occasional cow would wander off a path in search of the perfect morsel of grass just to be taken out by an explosion. To put it in better perspective, one cow costs almost half a year's salary, so it is a huge loss to a farmer. Almost on cue, I glanced up to see four cows on an adjacent hillside slowly lumbering along. It was an evil thought but I couldn't help but laugh inside at the mental image of one of the cows spontaneously going poof, leaving three bovines to look at each other like, "Where's Ralph?"

The other thing that I noticed were the children. They weren't walking through the hills like the cows; they were right next to us. Children have no fear and even though they all learned landmine safety in school, they were kids. Kids walk places kids shouldn't. Sometimes they follow the adults down a small trail between two known landmine fields. Where they came from and how they made it this far up into the mountains was a mystery but they sure as hell followed us everywhere, probably because Security Bob and Tony kept giving them candy. One thing was becoming very clear, though. Kosovo was loaded with unexploded munitions and children, both sharing the same extremely inappropriate locations.

The trip down the mountain mirrored the trip up with the exception that our heads were now at the bottom end of the forty-degree bouncy ride. At least the rear door stayed shut at this angle. After turning off onto an alternate, but equally rocky, road we made our way to a bombed-out building, left in ruins by the war. We were told that this location was still much safer to walk around, even though it looked more intimidating, and it would give us a good vantage point to see another mountain range that was inundated with mines—without actually walking through the damn things this time. The mountainside we were now shown had proven itself to have mine activity during a recent forest fire. It seemed the local UN chief also ran the fire brigade and was sending his men in to fight the blaze, all the while telling them that there were no landmines in the area. To quote Matthew, one local firefighter said, "We aren't going in there! Because, bang, bang, bang." There were mines popping off all around them.

Again, the location was so picturesque that were it not for the crumbling building and the large crater next to it that had been formed by a mortar shell, it would have been hard to imagine that atrocities happened here. The group's conversation slowly turned from war to tourism and how Kosovo wanted to place itself on the map for winter and summer outdoor sports, which could give a huge boost to the local economy. Until the land was cleared; however, this would remain a pipedream. As our breakfasts were wearing off, and with the sun located straight overhead, pointing to lunch on the sky clock, we decided to eat. I, for one, was ready. It's true that when you are cold your body uses up much more energy. Trying to maintain my macho, nothing phases me attitude, while constantly thinking about being blown up added to my fatigue and hunger. We all needed a breather and a beer.

Over lunch, we tossed around the idea of restructuring our tour by next heading back to the HALO compound for a detailed visit of the facilities. There, Cindy could also address the locals HALO employees before our group headed back out to yet another school. This school was located on the other side of Pristina and would show us just how vast the cluster bomb issue was.

Daylight always puts a whole new spin on what you think you saw at night. A good example of this would be my reaction to what Kosovo itself looked like with the lights on. The compound in daylight would prove to be no different. I have to say that I love visiting HALO compounds around the world. They are all so military and so raw at the same time. I feel like the world should turn to black and white imagery each time I drive up to one of them. To me, personally, they're really just that captivating. HALO uses the recycle, modify and recreate approach. All the equipment they use was originally designed for some other purpose. The front-end loaders and bulldozers reinforced with extra steel plates for blast protection, and retrofitted with heavy rollers and devices to sift landmines from the sand are some of my favorites of their many creations. Of course, everything is painted white and then labeled with the blue oval HALO design.

Even the compounds themselves are usually old warehouses or office buildings converted to suit the needs of the many men and women who live and work there. They come complete with communications rooms, map rooms, medical training facilities and space to hold all the landmine removal devices. Think of it like this: Imaging if Hannibal and B.A. from *The -Team* helped the Rebel Alliance from *Star Wars* to fabricate a bunch of devices to go up against the evil empire. This is the stuff they'd come up with.

The main headquarters for the entire HALO global operation is located in a converted horse barn in Scotland. Need I say more?

The base in Kosovo lived up to my expectations. It was a bit smaller than the one we saw in Cambodia but the layout made better use of space. We pulled off the road, passed through the gate, parked alongside the fleet of other rovers and made our way inside to film the inner secrets of the compound. Not that it's really secret; there's just a lot of neat stuff laying around inside. The tour went on for a little over an hour and Cindy impressed the crap out of us with her vast knowledge of the entire HALO operation. How it runs, equipment uses, map and country statistics—she knew it all. This only added more evidence to support the assertion that she is an amazing human being.

Nigel, our HALO guide from Cambodia, loves to tell a story about the time Cindy walked up to an African warlord and asked for a flight out of Angola on his private plane. Her aircraft had been appropriated by another UN team and she needed transportation. To Nigel's surprise, the warlord agreed immediately. Nigel tells the story with a laugh and adds that he thought that there was no way he was going to live to tell the story. Cindy's retort is simply, "Come on, where's your adventurous side?"

Before we headed out to visit the second school and make final stop for the day, Cindy stepped into the goodwill ambassador role and spoke a few words to a large assemblage of local HALO deminers, who had come to the compound to meet her. She eloquently introduced herself and spoke of the bonds between the people of Kosovo and the United States, and she promised to do everything she could to help obtain the speedy return of the funding that had been pulled away from the removal effort. After her short speech, John went to work setting up a group shot with Cindy, Guy and Matthew in the middle of very large group of

HALO staff—who all seemed confident after hearing Cindy say that people were really trying to get the mine removal effort in Kosovo back up and running. Upon completion of the photo-op, we set off again. John and I were both overjoyed to learn that there had been a vehicle swap out and that we were now assigned to a different Land Rover—one with a backseat. Now we could finally face forward, and if you think a country is beautiful while you're looking at it through the back window in a chilly rear compartment, let me tell you that graduating up and gaining the ability to look out the front window to see where you're going, with the heat on, is a euphoric sensation. My defrosting body was finally feeling human.

Guy had the vehicles pull off the highway right before the entrance to the school to show us the pattern of some bomb strikes. From where we stood, on the shoulder of the road, he showed where the NATO planes took aim and let loose the deluge of cluster bombs. They chose a path that led across a field, over the traffic lanes and on top of the primary school-grounds before it tapered off in the neighborhoods beyond. Closing my eyes, I could see it happening as he spoke.

This particular school was totally void of activity, again because of the Easter Holidays, so we parked at the edge of a cement basketball court near the backside of the school building. John and I exited out of an actual vehicle side door, instead of the rear hatch, and wandered over to see what Guy and Matthew were telling Cindy and Jill. To create the appropriate visual for this particular story, I really should change this to *I* went over to hear what Guy and Matthew were saying. The wandering part is what John was doing along the far end of the schoolyard, near some ground that had recently been turned up for future construction of a second football pitch. John was just looking for a good spot from which to take photos. I listened to the statistics that rolled off Matthews tongue as he explained to us how the school had been planning on putting in a second soccer field until the construction equipment ran into serious snag. One of the tractors leveling the ground for this future field unearthed a bright yellow cluster bomblet.

Guy piped in, pointed at the chewed-up ground and said, "Right over there, where John is walking, we expected to find at least twelve, if not more, cluster bomblets in the soil."

As if John had supersonic ears, he somehow heard what Guy said and, with a movement that mimicked the famous monochromatic film clip of the Bigfoot sighting, he slowly turned his head and looked directly into my camera. It looked as if his brain wanted to tell his body to stop, to cease, to not to take another step, but his legs were confused and uncertain where a safe spot was to place his feet might be, so he kept moving forward—even though he didn't want to. From what Guy was saying, he was in no real danger unless he were to start probing the ground with a broom handle, but he clearly didn't hear that part and, yes, this made me laugh inside, real hard. Through the view finder on my video camera, I had a perfect frame-up of Matthew, Cindy and Guy in the foreground discussing the problems the school faced. In the background, however, was a Woody Allen skit, featuring one John Evanko trying to side step invisible bomblets by gingerly dancing on his tiptoes, his eyes focused on the ground. He looked like he was navigating through a maze of dog shit, and his speed increased exponentially until he finally reached a place close enough to the rest of us to feel safe. Approaching us, a little pale but deliberately casual, he said, "So, there's bombs in the ground where I was just walking?"

Matthew, imperturbable as ever, replied, "Yes. There are quite a few in this yard."

John's expression was a mixture, "Thanks' for the heads up," and "I want to kick you in the balls."

Realizing what was going on, Cindy deflected a bit. "So you're telling us that there are cluster bomblets in the field through which I just saw a small boy ride his bike?"

"Yes," Guy said. "But sources other than ours are saying that this whole area, and others like it, are clear."

That was why all the funding had been pulled back for mine removal in Kosovo. UN staff members had manipulated the numbers.. This last stop really fueled Cindy's determination to get demining in Kosovo back on track before more innocent people died, and it readied her for the next day's agenda—which was full of presidents, political visits and an uninvited stop at the US embassy.

OUR NEW MUSLIM FRIEND

With a full day of new experiences behind us, and a much more comfortable vehicle under us, it was time to go back to Pristina for a good night's sleep before our next day of political shenanigans. This was a great drive because, for the first time on the trip, John and I had the opportunity to talk to our HALO driver, David. I think we were all equally excited to learn about the differences in our cultures. He was an ex-soldier from the Kosovo Liberation Army who was now working for HALO and helping to fix the damage caused by the war. For the first half of our road trip, he bombarded us with questions about where we lived. What it was like in the states? He also wanted us to know how appreciative he and the people of Kosovo were of the American involvement in their fight for freedom.

After some time, though, he paused and asked, "Do you have any questions for me?" John fired back with a great one, one that we had been asking ourselves about but hadn't had the time to ask anyone else. The ensuing conversation was one of those life-changing moments, and John and I have been telling people about it since the day. John even wrote an email about it, a month later. In response to one that was sent to him about all the evil Muslims in the world. I believe his words can do more justice to this situation than mine could. Here is what John wrote:

> On the ride from the school to Pristina I asked our driver, David, "What's with all the Mosques in the country and all the calls to worship?"
>
> He looked at me with a smile and, with the deepest respect for my question, simply said, "We're Muslim."
>
> Well, I compounded my stupidity by saying, "No way. You're Muslim? You drink beer at dinner, you don't have a beard, I haven't seen you pray once..."
>
> "When was the last time you went to church?" he asked.
>
> Sadly, I had to answer, "A funeral."
>
> David said he couldn't remember the last time he went to Mosque. He said the work he does ridding his country of unexploded ordnance should more than make up for missing a prayer or two, and that he thinks that God/Allah will forgive him for the beers.
>
> "Yeah, but as a Muslim, don't you have all those rules?"
>
> "As a Christian, don't you?"
>
> "Yeah, I guess I want to be a good Christian, but it's not really that important to me." "Yeah, me either," David said.

I also feel people should know that they, the Muslims
of Kosovo, as a people, love us. English is a required
language in their schools and there is a popular movement
to rename the country Little America. I kid you not. Just
ask any Kosovar when you're walking down Bill Clinton
Boulevard. I'm not kidding about that either. It's the name
of a major central street in Pristina. These are the Muslims
that I know. I like these people. These Muslims.

- John Evanko

If someone started a sentence with, "A Catholic, a Muslim
and a Pantheist were riding in a car," you would think there
was a punch line coming up in a few minutes. But that was us.
We were hanging out with a Muslim who loved to go out to
bars and drink beer with the guys, one that wasn't running off
every time a prayer call went out. This wasn't the evil enemy
that our media wanted us to believe in. This was someone that
I would welcome into my home. And John wasn't the right-
wing, evangelistic Christian, preaching and telling people they
were going to hell for practicing Islam, that David's world had
led him to expect. Me, well, I really confused David when I
described myself as a spiritual person who was half Taoist, half
Shamanistic and totally followed what the universe wanted me
to do. Surprisingly, he loved my off-kilter directions and said,
"We are all the same person."

There were no enemies here. We were becoming friends, and
what transcended everything was our desire to help others and
our love for humanity. I have taken the lesson I learned, and this
story, with me to all corners of the globe and whether it's Islam,
Hindu, Christian, Buddhist or any of the other practices that I

have come across, the people have always treated me with respect and understanding. Even though our sacred principles may be different, we all want to live in peace and freedom and have a prosperous life. For the rest of the trip, the three of us laughed and opened up about our thoughts on the ways of the world. Our new Muslim friend even went so far as to say that if the United States were ever invaded, he and his friends would come over, fight and gladly die protecting the American way of life. This is how well loved we are in Kosovo, a country that is ninety percent Muslim.

MAYBE YOU SHOULD SHAVE

Just when you think an adventure is going to slow down, a higher power decides to hit the accelerator. Because of all the traveling around the day before, we were very happy when Cindy suggested that we all sleep in the next morning and meet in the hotel restaurant for a late breakfast before our day began. This hotel was a bit nicer than the one we stayed in on our first night, so John and I took our dear, sweet time getting up. We caught up on some TV watching and enjoyed some good, non-rushed bathroom time. Not sure of just what to expect for the day, I casually strolled down to brunch in my jeans, comfortable and unshaven—the condition my faces stay in throughout many of my international missions—only to run into a table of very well-dressed individuals who had almost finished eating. "Good morning" and "How did you sleep?" talk started from Cindy and Megan. Then Security Bob, who was sitting at the table in a suit, looked over at us, finished a sip of his coffee and said, "So, are you two ready to go?"

My ass had barely touched the chair, so I thought he was joking, until, in a more serious tone, he added, "You should hurry up, return to your room, shave and get into your suits." My blank stare and momentary pause were enough to persuade him that we really didn't know what was planned for the day.

"Boys," he said, "you are going to meet the president of a country today. You should respect him by dressing for the occasion."

Bob's words hit me like my dad's had, years before, when I did something to embarrass him in front of the neighbors. He was dead serious and when a British secret military soldier, ex or not, looks at you like that and suggests you go shave, you step quickly. I believe John and I both managed to spit out something that vaguely sounded like, "Yes sir," as we hovered over our seats inhaling what we could of our food in as few bites as possible. We then grabbed our coffees and hightailed it to the stairs. Megan, of course, found this scene quite amusing, and sneered up at us like the big sister who never did anything wrong.

Luckily, traveling with Cindy had taught us both to be fashion Boy Scouts. "Be prepared" was our motto—for snow, desert, jungle and semi formal occasions, sometimes all on the same trip. In this situation I had packed a formal dress shirt and tie, and I believe that John had packed an actual suit jacket.

We had found this amazing packing system created by Eagle Creek that flattens everything down into an easily manageable size, even a full three-piece suit. It helps keep clothes better organized and less wrinkled, and it's definitely on my must-have-when-traveling list.

Again, the Abbott and Costello routine started up in the room, with both of us trying to get presentable enough to meet a president. I guess I never really thought that meeting another country's president was that big of a deal. I'm ashamed to say it, but I had rarely even voted for the US president. But, as I sheared the six or so days' worth of coarse growth from my face with a very dull razor and no shaving cream, it hit me how high of an honor this actually was. We were going to go into the inner sanctum, the Kosovo version of the oval office and, behind closed doors, we were going to film and chat with the highest elected official in a newly formed sovereign country. A nervous excitement flowed through me. What should have taken thirty minutes, we managed to condense down to only ten, which pleasantly surprised Bob as he waited for us at the bottom of the stairs. With a nonchalant gaze to see how good we had cleaned up, he smiled and with a pat on the back said, "Very good boys."

The rovers were waiting out front, and even our drivers, who weren't coming inside the presidential office with us, were dressed in their Friday go to mosque best. Yeah, this was a big, big, very huge, big deal.

ON THE OTHER SIDE OF THE VELVET ROPE

Cindy, as usual, was a pillar of confidence. If she's ever been nervous around us, I've yet to witness it. She and Megan were both wrinkle free pictures of business elegance. Guy, Matthew, Jill, Bob and Tony were all suited up for the day of dignitary meetings as well. John and I looked like two guys who took ten minutes to shower, shit, shave, unfold something and choke on ties—which was still much better than the vagabond look that we were planning on going with for the day.

Let me start this next bit off in the right context. Our group was greeted by a woman at the front doors, or maybe rear doors, to a large building. We entered, were greeted and then hurried to the right, through another door, then down a long hallway which led to a bunch of stairs. Maybe everyone else knew what was about to happen next, but no one bothered to inform John or yours truly, Captain Fucking Clueless. Sometimes I think Megan purposely held back information just to get a laugh out of seeing how we reacted to interesting predicaments, but I think this one might have even caught her off guard.

I had the camera rolling the whole time, and, as usual, half the shots were of the floor, the stairs or my shoes, but, as I got closer to the top of the flight of steps, I raised it and focused in on Cindy, who was a few steps ahead of us. I could hear something going on, some commotion off to the left, but couldn't see around the edge of the stairwell's top wall, and I was trying to keep everything framed up nicely in the viewfinder. As Cindy's feet left the last step, a man, who turned out to be the president of Kosovo, approached her and offered his hand. With his right hand locked in a firm handshake he placed his other on Cindy's shoulder and slowly turned her to the left, the direction where the commotion I heard from the stairwell was still actively going on. As they turned, I followed their motion and rotated to see an entire media circus. All of Kosovo and a lot of the adjoining countries sent their press corps to cover the breaking news story of Cindy McCain's meeting with the president. As God is my witness, there must have been close to a hundred reporters and photographers standing on the other side of a red velvet rope connected by stanchions. I felt like I was on the red carpet on Academy Awards night. I tried to keep my focus on what I was doing, but with the cacophony of thousands of rapid-fire clicks rattling off from the camera, along with the stroboscope of blinding flashes, I was a bit overwhelmed. Let's not forget to reiterate that John and I were on the other side of the red velvet ropes—the side with Cindy and the president. If you search online, you can find a news clip shot from the press side of the ropes. It captures our surprised expressions nicely.

After the president's staff thought ample time had been given for the photo-op, we were escorted into his office where the discussion of the issues at hand would take place. John and I followed the group from the rear and, as we got close to the door, John and I were halted and given a look by one of the president's staff that clearly said, "And just where do you two think you're going? How dare you cross the press line." Cindy glanced back and motioned to the gentleman that we were with her, so he let us pass a bit reluctantly. I looked back with a cocky grin as if to say, "Do you know who we are? Get the hell out of my face." and then slipped past before someone changed their mind. The door shut and we were in, filming our first full-fledged diplomatic meeting. This was one of those moments where, on the outside I was as cool as a cucumber but the little kid inside me had a huge, power tripping boner.

You could tell by the layout of the room that this was where all the important diplomatic meetings went on in Kosovo. Two high backed chairs took front and center and were angled slightly so that whoever sat in them could speak to each other but still include those sitting in twin couches that flanked the conversation area. All of this was centered around a small coffee table and on the wall behind the big chairs were two pictures—one of Gandhi and one of Mother Theresa. Cindy sat in the chair on the right and the president sat on the left. To mirror this, his staff and interpreter were seated on the couch to his left side and our group took the right side. It looked as if two debate *teams, headed by their coaches, were getting ready to face off. Coffee was offered in* small teacups and everyone was introduced. John stayed standing so that he could meander around the room and get shots from different angles, while I chose a spot and sat on the ground at the foot of the coffee table. This gave me a direct view of the conversation and allowed me to reach my coffee. No reason I couldn't enjoy my first cup of presidential coffee while I worked. Bob and Tony took their usual posts at opposite locations in the room and Megan found a chair with its back to the wall at the left side of the office entrance door, as if she were ready for a quick escape. Everyone was settling in for a good, down-to-earth chat, when, just as I got comfortable, the door flew open and all hell broke loose. The entire press corps invaded the room in a mad frenzy, each person looking to get the perfect shot of Cindy and their good old president, Fatmir Sejdiu. It seemed that each one of them decided that where I was sitting was the perfect spot.

I am not, nor have I ever been, with the press. I don't know their ways or their etiquette, but I guess they were given about three minutes to come in and get their shots before they were hustled back out of the room by the staff. My boss, Cindy McCain, was the only person I was worried about filming, so when these media maniacs pressed up against me, jockeying for position, I fought back. I am used to one-on-one interviews and filming run-and-gun style, but not this. There were elbows and assholes hitting me from all sides, people crawling up my back and camera lenses bouncing off my head. Of course, all my idle threats were wasted because not a damn one of them understood English. The stuntman side was building up in me. I am not a violent person but the shock, and their rudeness, had my blood pressure elevating to the point that I could hear my heartbeat in my skull. Then, as quickly and chaotically as they swarmed in, they all left—so fast it almost created a vacuum when they shot back out the door. I took a breath and a moment to regaining my presence, and, just as I was back in my zone, I felt a hand upon my shoulder pushing me and saying something in a language that I couldn't understand. I ignored him, so he pushed a bit harder. Without looking away from the viewfinder, I shrugged my right shoulder to let whoever this was know that I wasn't moving. Persistently, this person then poked me in the shoulder again, this time hard enough to make me shift the camera shot. This pissed me off a bit, so, using my right hand, I shoved him toward the couch and continued filming. With obvious amusement, Cindy looked over and said, "They're with me. Would it be okay if they stayed in the room to film?" The president nodded his approval and from then on nobody bothered us as we continued to document the incredible event unfolding in front of us. Most of the discussion was about the funding being pulled back from the mine removal efforts, but, occasionally, the president would say something about the US and how close our two countries were. The one comment he made that still lingers in my memory was, "God and America saved Kosovo." That was a very powerful statement and a true testament to their love of Americans.

Throughout the hour-long session, Megan sat in her chair drinking her coffee from a tiny cup and trying to be as invisible as she could. This is only funny because each time I pulled back to get a wide shot of Cindy and the President engrossed in their dialogue, you could see Megan, just off to the right, sipping gingerly from her teacup and checking out the room. This was when we coined the nickname that still sticks with her today – Teacup. She will be known as Teacup for the rest of this book.

The talks ended with a room full of handshakes and wishes for goodwill between our two allied nations. Cindy and the president exited his office to a more friendly press setting in the hallway just out front—the typical podium backed by blue curtain setting that all countries seem to use when filming elected officials for the local evening news. They both spoke, a few questions were asked, everyone clapped and then we made our way back down the flights of stairs, through the long hallway and back out into the parking lot where this whole fiasco started. Gathering in a semi-circle everyone congratulated each other on a job well done. I figured this would be a good time for a candid conversation so I raised the camera to Cindy and said, "That seemed to go well. What, to you, were the most memorable part of the conversation?" Without missing a beat she looked at me and said, "It had to be when I looked up to see you trying to push the vice president of Kosovo over the couch." Then she laughed and said that's why she loved to have John and me around. We keep it interesting.

I stood there while she walked away, blankly staring into the distance, focused on nothing, but contemplating her words while replaying the event over in my head. Who knew? Teacup walked past, patted me on the back and shook her head., "Way to go Nancy," she said. Then John appeared next to me, with the same blank expression, and we just stood there in awkward silence, watching our group walk across the parking lot to our next meeting location. Then we spontaneously burst into crying laughter.

"That will make a great story someday," he said.

We caught up with the group as they were heading into the office of the prime minister of Kosovo, Mr. Hashim Thaci. As a side note, in 2010, I believe, Mr. Thaci was accused of involvement with an organ trafficking ring and having ties to the local Mafia, but at the time of our visit these accusations had yet to become public.

This gathering was less formal and lacked all the pomp and circumstance of the presidential meeting, but, just the same, John and I were looked upon as pests by his staff. At one time the prime minister himself looked over and said, "Do you mind?" with a perturbed sound in his broken English. Again, Cindy graciously asked if we could stay. He allowed it, but you could see in his eyes that he didn't like the fact that we were filming him. Where the President had a soft grandfatherly kindness to his persona, the prime minister's eyes were colder. His was a more ominous, militant presence.

This meeting also ended with handshakes and well wishes. We saw ourselves out and hit the road for the next stop on the day's agenda, which was a visit to the local representative of the European Union (EU). This guy was so reclusive that John and I were asked to stay in the car while Cindy and Guy went in for a fast chat. We figured that two out of three dignitaries on camera was a good percentage and maybe we would have better luck at the US embassy, our last location of the day.

At the time of our trip, Kosovo had only been acknowledged as a sovereign country for about ten days, and the US Embassy was far from fully staffed, but Guy figured that we should make a stop just the same. It was the first sign of Americanism that we experienced. The gate, guarded by US soldiers in recognizable camouflage fatigues, armed with standard issue AR-15 assault rifles, showed that we had a presence here. The guards allowed us to enter the embassy compound and we were met by a rather excitable fellow who seemed to be enthralled by our arrival. Even John and I were met with exuberant handshakes and, since our greeter had no problem with the presence of our cameras, we filmed everything while he was leading us up to the more formal offices on the second floor.

In a typical US government, lack of communication scenario, I think that our happy new friend forgot to inform his superiors, or anyone else for that matter, that we were in bound for a visit. Halfway up the flight of stairs someone below us started yelling, "Hey, you can't film in here," and started up the stairs in pursuit.

"Go, go," I said, pushing John from behind and laughing out loud as we rushed to catch up with Cindy, who had already exited the stairwell at the conference room level. Our pursuer caught up with our group, but seeing we were with the assemblage of important people, he stopped yelling and did a hasty retreat back to where he came from. Pulling my attention back to Cindy and Guy, I could see that a new face had emerged from a door on one side of the hallway and was addressing our group. It was a very frazzled woman who looked as if someone had just woken her from a deep sleep by yelling in her ear, "Holy shit, the Senator of Arizona's wife is here." Seriously, no one had told this poor US delegate anything about our visit. She was still buttoning her shirt and trying to fix her matted bedhead as she led us to a private conference room. In short, we raided the US Embassy in Kosovo. Check that off the bucket list.

To make things worse, Guy totally overwhelmed her with statistics about the unexploded ordinance issues in Kosovo and how the funding had been pulled back from HALO.

At this point, she looked at him and asked, "Just what does HALO do?" Guy raised his eyebrows and glanced at Cindy as if to say, "We aren't getting anywhere here." Trying to be diplomatic as one could be when confronted by a group of people speaking on a topic that you know nothing about, she then said something like, "I'm sure our people in DC are on top of this issue and someone will be in contact as soon as I get all the facts." At that comment, and seeing where this was going, Guy decided to bow out and not give this poor woman a total brain screw. As we walked back to the Rovers, I heard Matthew say to Cindy, "I believe we can write that one off for now."

The US embassy would wrap up our political trekking for the trip and Matthew, Guy *and Cindy were extremely happy with what they'd accomplished. They had rattled an* enormous number of doors for a single day and caused quite a bit of commotion in the press.

So much, that shortly after our visit, the powers-that-be decided that Guy and HALO weren't just talking shit and the funding for landmine removal was reestablished.

HAVE YOU TWO EVER BEEN TO SCOTLAND?

Upon returning to the hotel that evening, Teacup asked John and I if we had ever seen The HALO Trust headquarters in Scotland,

"No," I said.

"Oh good," she replied,

"If you and John don't mind, Cindy would like to have you take some pictures and video of the annual board of directors meeting tomorrow."

"Don't mind?" I said, feeling a little giddy. Keeping our cool, John and I looked at each other, then at her and replied, almost in unison, "No, that's cool. Whatever Cindy needs." Teacup walked away to inform Cindy that the boys were cool with extending the trip for a couple day—in Scotland! I am sure she realized how inwardly excited we were to have our adventure continue in yet another country we had never visited.

Morning came with ample excitement during the short drive to the airport, and a couple of last-minute photo ops with local Kosovo HALO employees before we boarded our luxurious limo in the sky and took wing to Scotland. Even Guy was enjoying the flights because HALO keeps an amazingly low overhead. He was used to flying coach for the cheapest available airfare. Total travel time to Scotland from Kosovo was about the same as it took to get to Kosovo from London and John and I took advantage of our time in the jet, realizing that we might never see this extreme style of lavish travel again. Guy Willoughby, when not running the HALO trust, liked to wind down by racing horses. Not just any, simple race though. Guy competed in some form of Scottish style steeple chase run. This is where the horse and its jockey must race around the track leaping obstacles that most people would need a tall ladder and a shot of liquid courage to clear. Not Guy though; he did it on a horse. It was his way of relaxing.

Meeting us at the airport in Scotland were his wife and daughter, with a carload of his jockeying equipment and attire. It seemed that John and I were in for another first. We had just enough time to make it from the airport to the track to watch him compete in one of his last races. His wife and daughter had convinced him to retire before he broke his neck.

Never having been in Scotland before and finally have landed somewhere during the day, I thoroughly enjoyed the ride through the Scottish countryside. Arriving at the track, unshowered and still wearing our unwashed travel clothes, we were invited to a Scottish lunch buffet before the race. This is where I fell in love with Haggis, a wonderful mix of organ meat, blood and grains that was originally cooked in a sheep's stomach. Gross as it may sound, the stuff is absolutely wonderful and, if you ever get the chance, I highly recommend trying it. It's like meat oatmeal.

Guy was off somewhere getting ready to ride. His wife and daughter, along with Matthew, who had flown back with us to attend the annual HALO board of directors meeting, joined John, Cindy, Teacup and I for the Scottish feast. We were also met by another woman, a donor who sat with Cindy on the board of directors for HALO. Her name was Marilyn Burke, the founder of the Julia Burke Foundation. She named the foundation after the passing of her daughter, Julia. Marilyn reminded me of Kathy Bates' character in the movie *Titanic*—the Unsinkable Molly Brown. She had a huge heart but wouldn't take crap from anyone. Over lunch, and in between my many trips to the all-you-can-eat

Haggis bar, we struck up a great dialogue that spanned many humanitarian topics and, of course, ended up with me volunteering our services if the need ever arose for video production work.

While Marilyn and I were talking, Matthew had been quietly listening to the conversation. When Marilyn excused herself from the table, Matthew leaned over to John and me, and in his calmest Matthew voice yet, said, "I owe the two of you a grand apology." John and I looked at each other a bit perplexed, and Matthew continued, "I shouldn't have, but I assumed that the two of you were just some guys that Cindy paid to come film. I had no idea that you volunteered with NGOs the way you do. Listening to your exchange with Marilyn, I can see that I had completely misjudged you two and I am truly sorry." Caught a bit off guard, John and I stepped over each other's words while trying to let him know that it was no big deal to us. We was just doing what we do, but to make him feel Okay, we accepted his apology. Now, years later, he is usually the first to greet us with kind words whenever we are in contact. I took two lessons away from this: never assume without asking first, and always be adult enough to express regret if I read someone wrong.

Dinning completed, we all made our way out trackside to watch Guy tear up the competition. I know absolutely nothing about betting on the horses, but Guy's thirteen-year-old obviously did because, upon hearing that we placed a bet on Guy to win, she looked up at us like we were completely clueless. (We were.)

"You just bet on my dad to win the horse race?"

"Have a little faith in your dad," I said.

She then stunned me with, "You should have bet it on him leaving in the back of an ambulance."

"Wow, such harsh words from a young woman," I jokingly exclaimed,

"Just watch," she said.

As the race started, Guy seemed to be doing well and was way out in front of the rest. It was a quick, one lap race so it didn't take long for him to lead the pack out of turn three and into the home stretch. I glanced at his daughter and raised one eyebrow as if say, "See? weren't you wrong!" She wasn't impressed and looked back at me with a "Just wait. It's not over yet." expression on her face. Down the last bit of front straight he came, clearing each jump and water hazard with ease. He approached the last hedge to hurtle and it was a massive. He disappeared out of view for a fraction of a second and then we saw him and his horse, both in the air, both moving forward, but not quite occupying the same place in the space-time continuum. At this point his daughter's eyes went from watching the race, to a fixed gaze up at me. After what seemed a very long pause, and with the most perfect timing you could ever imagine a child having, she mouthed the words, "I told you," just as Guy's body slowly rolled off the hindquarters of his horse, bouncing a few times before it came to a stop on the freshly chewed-up dirt. As daddy's little girl had predicted, an ambulance drove out from the infield area and two obliging gentlemen got out and helped Guy up off the ground and into the back, to be driven off to the medical station. We caught up with him as he was entering the jockey village area to find out if he was all right. I personally couldn't imagine falling from a horse while it was leaping for its life to clear a hedge at full gallop, but I guess that comes with the game. Guy just looked over said, "I'll be a bit stiff in the morning but the only thing that's really bruised is my pride." I guess that getting pitched from his ride in front of board members was not at the top of his list of expectations for the day's events.

From here the plan was to drive to the inn where we would all be staying for the night and to have a nice, relaxing evening before an early start in the morning. I use the word inn, and not hotel, because that's exactly what this place was—a good, old-fashion story book inn, complete with an elderly husband-and-wife caretaker couple and, other than the fact that I am sure my room in the basement was haunted, it was great.

I may have an over-active imagination, but as soon as I walked down the tight stone staircase and passed across the threshold of the basement door, I could feel an eerie presence. I had the sensation that someone was constantly watching me. So much so that I slept with the television and all the lights in the room on.

After a less than perfect night's sleep, I walked up to the breakfast to find the view outside the windows was just what I thought Scotland was supposed to look and feel like—gray and cold with a constant light rain blown almost horizontal by the wind. It was a picture-perfect location to eat the first meal of the day. I opted for the blood pudding and eggs. This was the closest thing that I could find to my newly beloved Haggis. Leaving nothing on my plate that even resembled food, I went down to my haunted room, showered off and grabbed my bags. Traveling the way we do, it's sometimes hard to commit to unpacking because we have the habit of never coming back to the same place twice. This was one of those situations. Hell, this entire trip was one of those situations. I got so used to Teacup asking, "Where's your stuff, Nancy?" that I just started showing up packed to go whenever it was time to load up into the Land Rovers.

The board meeting at the HALO headquarters began around noon, which gave John and I plenty of time to explore and film this kick-ass horse stable that had been converted into The HALO Trust HQ. It was kick-ass because it was once the stables of a very old Scottish castle. The stone building made a perfect residence for the inner workings of The HALO Trust and it seemed to make the NGO even cooler because it was like they had their very own Hall of Justice, right out of the *Super Friends* cartoon series. Also cool was that we were allowed to roam freely among the superheroes as they worked to rid the world of evil, abandoned weapons of war. Cubicle by cubicle, we filmed staff members focused on different global locations that contained landmines, cluster bombs, rockets and artillery, all preparing their annual reports to give to the board of directors at the meeting. It was an amazing thing to witness.

John was called to the boardroom to take a group photo of all the members at the session and then we were cut loose for a while to explore the local countryside. This meant a visit to a nearby medieval castle and many, many miles of sheep wandering through rolling green pastures. The cold, misty weather only served to make the Scottish Highlands even more intriguing and this was turning out to be one of the most magical trips we had taken. Later that afternoon, a strange twist of events created yet another wonderful surprise. When John and I returned from exploring, we found Teacup on the phone with the travel agent. It seemed that the new terminal, recently opened at Heathrow Airport, was having some issues and they couldn't guarantee that we and our baggage would make it to our destination. So, we were stuck in Scotland unless she could find us a way out. "Next time, try the train," a quote from a movie I once watched, is exactly what Cindy suggested. For the next hour Teacup battled, over her cell phone, with a local agent until she found the only way out. Sir Richard Branson was our ace in the hole. Well, not him personally, but his beautiful Virgin Atlantic Railways was. With Cindy's go ahead,

Teacup booked four first class tickets from Glasgow, Scotland to London, England on board the beautiful red and white Virgin Train. Time wasn't really on our side and we had just enough of it to say our goodbyes, hop in a rental bus and speed across the countryside to Glasgow to catch the train at the station. I think we beat the train by less than twenty minutes and it nearly took that long to navigate the station and find the right track. If you have never taken the train, it's not like an airplane that sits at the terminal for an hour while people call your name over the intercom. If you're running late, you only have a short window of time to load onto the train before it shoots back out of the station and heads to the next stop. First class or not, no one is looking for you to board.

This was one of my all-time favorite journeys with Cindy and Teacup. It was just the four of us relaxing in first class on a train There was an air of romance and it felt as if we were escaping from something. We were still in seats, mind you, not a James Bond private suite on the Orient Express, but it was still quite elegant. At one point the steward came past with a cart full of libations—beer, wine, mixers, etc.—and asked if we would like something.

After a few minutes of deliberating Cindy said, "It's first class, just leave it all. I am sure the boys will drink it, and come back and check on us in a bit, if you don't mind, please." And once again Cindy became my hero. I don't know how many times the universe allows a person to become your hero but Cindy has managed to do so at least a dozen times, if not more. Half were probably related to buying us ice cold beer in some exotic, Third World environment. I will always sing her praises loudly.

Our foursome parted ways at the Victoria station in London. Cindy and Teacup headed to Heathrow; John and I were off to Gatwick. Waving goodbye from a platform in the famous Victoria train station, as we walked away in opposite directions, seemed a very fitting end to our UK adventure.

INTERNATIONAL HEALTH EMISSARIES

Back home from Kosovo, John and I got busy with the footage that we had just shot. Logging, downloading and editing became our new habit. John McCain was getting deeper into his presidential campaign and the frequency of getting small segments ready for the McCain website was growing. We could tell that we were going to have a busy year dealing with Cindy's projects, and, if that wasn't time consuming enough for the two of us, I had also come across another NGO that needed our assistance. The new nonprofit we were getting involved with went by the name International Health Emissaries, and it was founded by the father of one of the women of the Freedom Fields NGO, the group with which John and I traveled to Cambodia. (IHE) International Health Emissaries (IHE), is also based out of the Carmel/Monterey Bay area. It actually has two founders, Jack Faia and Mark Bayless Both are amazing friends of ours now, more like actual family. This NGO, as their mission statement reads, accomplishes two things:

The first goal of International Health Emissaries is to provide medical and dental care, at no cost, to indigent people throughout the world who otherwise would have no access to such health services. The second goal of IHE is to provide an opportunity for American volunteers to positively and effectively represent the United States of America and give the volunteers the opportunity to make lasting relationships with people throughout the world.

Both Mark and Jack got their start working with a group called Los Médicos Voladores—The Flying Doctors—and, as Jack put it, "After one too many close calls while trying to land a friend's little Cessna aircraft on a small, almost nonexistent, runway in the jungles of South America, I found the need to do something else." The two knew each other from the Monterey dental circles and decided to team up and do things their way. So they formed IHE and they haven't looked back since.

Mark and I had been emailing and talking for almost a year and we came up with a game plan. John and I would go on two separate missions with IHE, document their work and put together a marketing video that combined the two trips. The first location would be Lima, Peru in June of 2008; the second would be Guatemala in November of the same year. Add to this the Asia tour that we ended up going on with Cindy, also in June, remember that we had just returned from Kosovo and you can get an idea of just how much globe hopping we did in 2008.

Mark and I chose Peru and Guatemala because of the stark contrast between these locations. Peru is dusty, dry and cold, while Guatemala is tropical and lush. Both would provide ample footage of poor, indigenous people in need of dental care but the different types of poverty would be obvious to anyone who viewed the videos. I came close to overloading our capability because we both still had regular jobs at *Fear Factor* and film season was picking up, which meant more stunt work. If we didn't work, we couldn't afford to continue to donate our time and skills to the humanitarian world.

Like always, the universe has a sneaky way of stepping in and putting everything just where it wants. John received a call from a friend of ours who was coordinating a movie in New Orleans. It stars the wrestler John Cena and was called *Twelve Rounds*. There were a couple of action-packed stunt sequences and our friend needed some stunt bodies to throw into the mayhem, so John booked a flight and headed out to Louisiana while I stayed and worked on the Kosovo video footage. If you watch the movie *Twelve Rounds,* look for the scene in which a fire truck, driven by Cena's stunt double, comes barreling down a city street, careens off of parked cars, mangling them, and sets off a chain reaction that causes a cable car to lose control and run right through a street fair. Left and right, stunt people dive out of the way of the oncoming trolley until it finally reaches some concrete barricades at the end of the road where John and another stunt guy friend of ours, Bill, are located.

There is one rule to follow when running away from an object in a stunt sequence: Don't look back to see what's going on behind you; just keep running to a safe zone as fast as humanly possible. The phone call that I received from John late one night started off with, "You know how you're not supposed to look back to see the crash? I looked back."

"What happened John?" I asked. He then informed me that as he was leaping over the concrete barricade and still in the air, he looked back—not at the ground where his feet were landing. One leg turning the wrong way on impact, causing a snapping sound so loud that Bill turned to John to ask, "Did you hear that loud pop?" and found John on the ground, holding his knee and writhing in pain. That loud pop was the anterior cruciate ligament in John's knee ripping nearly in half, a mere two months before we were to travel to Peru with IHE. Oh, what fun we have in our chosen line of work.

The injury shut John down from working at *Fear Factor* as the multilevel stage layout on the job required climbing up and down lots of ladders and stairs He tried but, after his first day of shows, he realized that there was no way he could continue. So he was sent home and remained away from *Fear Factor* until his leg was repaired and healthy, almost six months later. The doctor told John that surgery was needed to fix the ACL, but the trauma from the initial injury needed to be dealt with before he could be scheduled for the operation. It would take about a month to strengthen the muscles around the knee and for the swelling to subside. That set his surgery date to sometime in mid-July.

Realizing that everything truly happens for a reason, John used this downtime to completely throw himself into editing the footage that we shot in Kosovo. He put together some amazing segments that were all used in Cindy's section of the John McCain for President website. Along with this, he completely reconfigured and organized our ever-expanding video footage library and continued to school himself in video compression techniques. Instead of getting depressed and lazy, John took one of the lessons that we preach to others and applied it to his own life: *Things happen for a reason and you mustn't stress over situations in which you have absolutely no control. You must accept, adapt and overcome"*

WE SHALL SEE

There was once an old man who had one son and one horse, both of whom he valued very highly. One day the horse ran away and his neighbors came over to console him. "Oh what great misfortune," they said, "your horse is gone! How will you ever afford to get another one?"

The old man sat and smoked his pipe and only said, "We shall see."

Then, a few days later, the horse came back, accompanied by several wild horses, tripling his herd. Again, the neighbors visited, this time to congratulate the old man on his great luck. Again, he merely sat and smoked and said, "We shall see."

A short time later, his son was thrown from one of the wild horses and broke his leg in several places. The neighbors all arrived, calling out, "Ah great misfortune, your son will never walk again!" But again, the old man merely sat quietly in front of his house and, between puffs of his pipe, said, "We shall see."

Sometime after that, the army came through the village, rounding up all the young men to press them into service and send them to the battlefront far away in the frozen north. But with his crippled leg the old man's son was left behind. Though crippled, he managed to care for his old father until his death many years later.

- Lieh Tzu

I love this story because it so perfectly illustrates the idea that everything happens for a reason. The reason may not be clear at that particular time or place, and the universe's decisions may not even affect your life at all, but everything and every person on the planet is deeply interconnected to everything else. This is the way that life works, It's all cause and effect. You can accept this and try not to dwell on just why something happened, or you can rack your brain trying to find an answer that you will never be able to locate.

My girlfriend and I were recently at Disney World during the Christmas holidays, enjoying the Festival of Lights at EPCOT with her mother and sister. She had been bugging me to get tickets to Mickey's Christmas Party at the Magic Kingdom, where we could look at more lights and drink free cocoa as we walked around. The tickets were fifty dollars each, and that close to the Christmas extra money was running short. We left EPCOT a bit early and started to head home. As disappointed as she was, she still totally understood my reasoning on the money issue.

As we approached the monorail transportation hub to head back to the parking area, a woman, whom neither of us knew, yelled to us. "Hey, are you two by yourselves tonight?"

"Yes," we responded,

"Would you like two tickets to Mickey's Christmas Party?" she said. Stunned, we approached her and she told us that she and her husband were on the last day of their vacation. They had both come down with colds and were due to fly out early in the morning to head back home. She didn't want any money for the tickets; she just didn't want to see them go to waste. Within minutes we were on a different monorail, heading not to our car, but to the Christmas Party that Ashley, my girlfriend, had been longing about going to see. She was dumbstruck by this and kept saying, "How did this happen? Why us? What if we had made the decision not to leave EPCOT a bit early?" The bombardment kept coming

"How can you be so calm?" she asked.

"Dear, this is the way that the Universe works," I told her. "You can spend the rest of your life trying to piece together all the facts, times and what ifs into an equation and you will still never come up with an answer that explains why we are now going, for free, to enjoy something that you wanted to see so badly."

At times like this, smile and let life unfold as the universe wills it to. Examples like this happen in everyone's life every day. There's no magic involved; nor are they miracles, as some people call them. There is simply the flowing nature of existence.

NEXT STOP LIMA

June came and John's leg was healed enough that he felt confident about traveling to Peru with the International Health Emissaries group. Mark and I had been emailing and talking for a while now, getting all the dates and logistics set. Jack, even though he had not talked to me directly, felt comfortable about letting John and I tag along. Usually, he saw the need to personally meet everyone who accompanied the IHE group, but because of our reputations, the fact that we knew his daughter and that I had bonded with Mark, it was cool. The plan was for John and me to meet up with the rest of the group at the airport in Lima. They were flying in from San Francisco; we would head out from Orlando and change planes in Miami. Once in Lima, John and I were also to look for two nuns who had shuttle buses coordinated to take us to a hotel that was just outside one of the largest and poorest barrios in Lima.

I did my best to find flights that would arrive as close as possible to the group's arrival time, but to keep our costs as low as I could, I went with a small airline that shuttled between Miami and Peru. This would put us in Lima a few hours before the IHE dental team—enough time for some food and, of course, a local cerveza. In our typical fashion, I arrived at John's house to find him scurrying around stuffing last minute items into his carry-on and wondering just how many things we would forget to bring on this trip. As tradition commanded, we had our lucky shot of Tequila before at the airport before we left. We toasted our new adventure, boarded the plane and then we were wheels up for South America. If it had been a movie, this is the point where the theme from *Raiders of The Lost Ark* would start to play softly over my words, building to a crescendo, and the scene would fade to a model airplane flying over a hokey map of South America. The camera would slowly zoom in and push through the plane window to reveal John and I in deep conversation or trying to drink enough beer to help induce sleep on this extremely small, uncomfortable aircraft.

PERU, JUNE 2008
INTERNATIONAL HEALTH EMISSARIES

OUR FIRST DENTAL MISSION

OUR AIRLINE TICKETS CHEAPER for us than those of our traveling companions flying in from the West Coast, so I was hoping that their internal aircraft amenities were a bit grander than ours. John and I seem to go from one extreme to the other on these trips; it's enough to bewilder the brain. On the flight to Kosovo, only two months before, we had our own private jet, complete with a staff that catered to our every request. Now, we were lower equatorial bound and we damn near had to barter for water. The beer was super expensive, and I believe the airline's idea of cutting frivolous expenses was to remove the padding from the seat cushions. There wasn't even a headphone jack for some kind of audio. Sometimes it's good to spend the extra cash on an airline that provides a higher standard in comfort, and, if you can bypass immigration at Ft Lauderdale International Airport, for all that's holy, do it. Flying out is not too bad, but passing through immigration to get back into the US makes you feel like a cow being to the slaughter. A maze of small, confusing hallways funnels you through cramped doors that eventually lead to a tram that only goes one way. When the tram reaches its destination, travelers, packed like sardines in a can, squeeze out and walk ten feet to a downward moving escalator which much too small to handle to the perpetual load of tourists and the locals trying to get home. And all of this is what you can expect before you reach the immigration officers. Ft. Lauderdale's international area is much smaller than Miami's, so you can expect a very long wait in lines that move at a snail's pace.

Landing at Jorge Chávez International Airport in Lima was pretty painless, until we got past immigration and ran into a sea of locals who clamorously gladly offered to carry our bags to their vehicle and transport us to our local destination—whether we wanted them to or not "Transportation, señor," was all we kept hearing from the guys who were trying to walk off with our bags. Finally, after one too many hand slap competitions for dominance of my luggage handle, between myself and the latest señor bag carrier, John and I found a place to sit just out of the view of most of the indigenous porters. By this time, we were so proud of ourselves for being such superb world travelers that it took us until then to realize that we had no idea what the nuns we were meeting looked like. Nor did we know what a single member of the IHE group looked like—including Jack, who was our contact. To add to our dilemma, neither John or I had bothered to bring anyone's phone numbers, or even a printout with the number or address of the hotel in which we were registered.

"Holy shit," I said as we laughed; very vocally, I might add. We had come all the way to Lima and had absolutely no idea who we were looking for. Truthfully, this put us in our place for a few minutes, and a mild shot of panic came over me. John just kept looking at me, without a hint of facial expression, and shaking his head until he had a stroke of genius.

"How hard can it be to find a dental group coming out of the customs area?" he asked.

"Yeah, let's just look around. They're bound to be here somewhere," I agreed, feeling a bit of relief start to ease back into my body. Calmly we started to look around for signs of dentists. They were everywhere! There must have been five different dental and medical groups running around outside the customs area. Young dental groups, old dental groups, and student volunteers were gathered at the concession area, emerging from customs or digging through their bags. We were surrounded and outnumbered by dentists. As I stood in one spot, spinning in circles looking for some sign of an IHE volunteer, T-shirt, of banner, I began to wonder. "What's wrong with the locals? Does anyone who lives here actually have teeth left? What's the need for so many dentists? Either that or, because of the number of humanitarian dentists at the airport, the locals must have amazing smiles and no dental bills." The thought of being lost in Lima snapped into my mind again as John and I reunited to come up with plan number two. We stared at each other for a dramatically long silent moment.

"Nuns!" I said. "We should look for nuns!"

"Yeah, they should be easy to pick out of this crowd," John happily exclaimed. Penguins, is what we both expected to see, right out of the Vatican City in Rome. They would be dressed in long, formal habits and flow through the crowd, blessing those that humbled before them. Yeah, that's what they must look like. How could we miss that? Wrong! Just where I get my fucking delusional imagination from, I don't know. It wasn't from either of my parents, that's for sure. I must have some strong powers of delusion though, because John was now also trying to track down the nuns I'd envisioned and he's Catholic. Hell, surely that should help. We worked our way up one side of the crowd and down the other, over and over, until, probably because of John, we got a Catholic inspired miracle. I noticed a woman standing in the crowd and wearing jeans and a red blouse. Pinned to her shirt was a small, handmade yellow nametag in the shape of a tooth and written on it was, "Sister Joan." Pay dirt! Could this be our nun? Like two curious sharks we circled the woman, trying not to look too obvious, until I gained the nerve to face her and utter the letters, "I H E." That's all I had to say and the quiet women came alive with smiles and hellos. This was our nun.

"You two must be Kevin and John, the filming guys" she said, "How was your flight?" I don't think we ever let on to Sister Joan, or anyone, that we started this trip running totally blind and without bringing a scrap of contact information to a country that was completely alien to us. We stood there with our nun, contently awaiting the rest of the group to come join our happy family.

A very short time later, Jack Faia and the rest of the IHE volunteers wandered out from customs, dragging big red bags behind them that were loaded with equipment, toys and clothes that would be passed out to the locals after they had a procedure done. Had we remembered about these big red bags a short time earlier, we wouldn't have stressed so much. Now we know. The sisters and Jack spotted each other instantly, and the rest of the group followed him over to where we were. All was well in the universe. We introduced ourselves to the group and John and I played everything so cool that no one suspected a thing. They would never know that we were almost abandoned in Peru by our own stupidity and lack of planning. When we had everyone together, we headed out front to our awaiting rides.

PRIMITIVE ACCOMMODATIONS IN LIMA

Driving through the streets of Lima, Peru reminded me, in many ways of an apocalyptic war movie. This was a town that gave you a very insecure feeling. Like many places we had visited, it was a very well used town and it provided some of the most extremes examples of urban poverty that I have experienced in any location I have visited on the globe. Even the heart of downtown Lima, where all the fancy hotels and government buildings are located, is in a sad state. The vibe was kind of early French Colonial meets *Pirates of the Caribbean*, with countless street merchants selling everything from shoes to fruit to homemade goods from makeshift stalls and reinvented tables.

Remember what I said about our trips sometimes being polar opposites from one other? Well, the hotel into which we were now booked, The Hotel International, could, only in its wildest dreams, aspire to the standards of ancient Days Inn, somewhere in the Midwest, that had been long abandoned and was now being run by an assemblage of carnies. Am I being over dramatic? Perhaps? But not by much! The people running the establishment were very cordial, however, and extremely happy to have us there, but my windowless ten-foot by ten-foot room looked more like a place to be imprisoned than a place to sleep for the night. Actuality, I loved it. This is the type of place that makes you feel like you are truly immersed in the local flavor and it makes you appreciate what you have back home so much more than staying at the Ritz would. A/C would have been a plus, though; not to cool the room down, but to dry it out enough to keep the condensation from building to the point that my concrete walls sweated all night long. Watching the droplets run down the walls each morning reminded me of tent camping during Florida's hot summers. This depiction of our lodging for the week wouldn't be complete, though, if I left out the part about the 1980s style, slim line touch tone phone that hung in the stairwell just between my room and Jack's. The ring tone was, and I'm not lying, *It's a Small World*, and it went off at least thirty times a night to notify the hookers who hung out in the building that their pimp had found a client for them! Two nights in, Jack and I opened our room doors simultaneously as the phone went off, breaking the silence with the sickening Disney melody. Directing a mischievous grin at him, I walked over and casually ripped the phone from its perch on the wall. Wires and all came twanging out of the poorly drilled hole in the concrete. I poked the wires back into the hole, placed the phone back onto its roost and we contently returned to our rooms to sleep for the remainder of another damp, but now quiet, night.

In the mornings we all met in the dining room on the first floor, which opened out to the polluted highway that sat a crumbling sidewalk's width away, and ate a meager-yet-filling scrambled egg and bread breakfast. This was pretty much all you could get, and I think the fact that there were more than ten of us had overwhelmed the kitchen in a big way. I feel this way because, first thing in the morning, all the plates and cups kind of matched and the egg platters all bore a resemblance to each other. As more of us came down to eat, however, the plates started to look like the proprietors were walking next door and borrowing. This would go on until, when the last of our members arrived, they were lucky to get half an egg on a plate which looked as it had been used as a Frisbee by the local children, then given back after being washed off in a roadside puddle. All this I found absolutely acceptable as long as I could get a cup of coffee—not even great coffee, just strong, black coffee. Coffee is the yin to my beer yang, and I find that they are both critical on humanitarian travels to developing countries. One reason is that no matter where you are on the globe and no matter how bad the conditions, both are very safe to drink and even have healthful benefits. Coffee, along with helping you get going in the morning, is also helpful to, well, get you going in the morning. Let's face it, your system is on a different time schedule and you're eating stuff that makes your bowels sometimes say, "Nope!" A few cups of strong, black, burnt coffee will make the toughest bloke do the poopie dance all the way back to his room. Holding a hot cup of coffee helps trigger a memory response from home—a comforting sensation—and, no matter how bad it tastes, most coffee comes out boiled, which kills damn near everything. Beer, whether it's cold or warm. gives my mind the same lighthearted memory recall. It's a bonding beverage when shared among friends after a hard day's work and it has nourishment because of the yeast. Think of it as liquid bread. But most of all, it's safe. There is no need to refrigerate it and its shelf life is a long time. Really. When is the last time you had a beer that had gone bad to the point of spoiling? In locations where water will damn near kill you, a brewed, canned beer is a super safe and a fun substitute to local H2O.

*Just remember Kevin's ABCs of travel and you will be just fine: Acclimate through **B**eer and **C**offee.*

Now, the coffee in our windowless hotel was like none that I had ever come across before and I've seen a lot of bad coffee. The process was very simple. First they would take massive amounts of freeze-dried coffee—not Sanka, but some cheap local off-brand—and they would mix in just enough hot water to create a tar like instant coffee sludge. This would come out in an array of small vessels that were probably used for salad dressing at dinnertime. A teapot of boiling water was placed at the table alongside the java muck and with a precise combination of the two, we could create an appalling, but caffeinated, liquid that would tide us over until we arrived at the clinic where the nuns had a slightly better tasting coffee substitute for us to drink.

THE BLUE CLINIC IN THE BARRIO

In the United States, the word "barrio" refers to lower-class neighborhoods with largely Spanish-speaking populations. It's the Latino equivalent of "ghetto." The word implies that the poverty level is high in the neighborhood. To say the clinic in Lima was located in a poverty level area would be to give it a huge compliment. Many parts were so far over the poverty level that dirt, cardboard and copper speaker wire could be listed as the building supplies for its meager homesteads. Driving from the hotel to the clinic, some fifteen or so blocks away, I noticed the same pattern I had seen in many of the developing cities in which we had filmed. As in Cambodia and Vietnam, the farther away from the main road we traveled, the higher the poverty level became. Concrete, multilevel buildings on paved roads led to the same buildings but on dirt roads. This led to smaller storefronts and houses, which ultimately continued on until we were driving on powdery, dust-covered roads lined with handmade, red clay brick structures. Some were lucky enough to come with windows and roofs; many were not. But all of them were occupied by families. One thing that I found interesting in this location was that the center of the barrio was a community soccer field and this field was constantly active. It was the hub of the community and even the children with nothing would run around in tattered shoes, kicking not a soccer ball, but plastic bags stuffed into more plastic bags—enough to fill out a rudimentary sphere for them to kick around. There was one other structure that stood out among the background of red, dust covered buildings. It was the clinic that had been newly constructed by our two nuns and the Sisters of Mercy organization. If their goal was to make the clinic easy to locate, they had succeeded with flying colors. This place stood out like a brilliant blue sapphire in a sea of light sepia tones. The outside walls of the entire building were covered with a glossy blue tile and it sat across the street from the head of the soccer field. If you couldn't find it, you weren't looking very hard.

Our bouncy ride continued until we the corner onto yet another dusty, pothole infested road and pulled up to the front of the clinic. We were greeted by a line of smiling, applauding people. These volunteer dentists were received like they were international pop stars as they passed the locals and entered the clinic to set up the rooms. The configuration of IHE clinics varied from location to location. At some sites, small makeshift clinics had already been created, complete with surplus and donated dental chairs and properly functioning compressors, while at some (like in Cambodia), rural schoolhouses that offered nothing but an open room for work were used. At these blank canvas locations, everything the volunteer dentists used was either brought from the states or modified at the facility. Children's desks were pushed together, duct tape and towels used to make headrests to add some comfort to the hard surfaces and compressors were shipped in. Then air hoses were MacGyvered to run from the outside to a network of valves and hoses that gave each table the ability to be used for cleanings, extractions or other procedures. It was amazing to see the transformations that happen on the first set up day. At our location in Lima, the building we were in was very new and modern, considering what surrounded us outside the clinic walls. If you didn't look out the windows, you would swear that you were working in a location in the states. It even came complete with a small dental office on the second floor where a full-time local dentist aided the township on certain days. This building was the nuns' pride and joy. Our spot to set up on the first floor was just a big, open, but very clean, room, and knowing this in advance, Jack brought in portable equipment, lights, portable suction units and even folding patient tables that resembled something that you would take a nap on at a tailgate party. Usually, the most difficult part of the endeavor was clearing customs in the chosen country with a ton of medical gear and drugs. Sometimes the words, "volunteer organization" get lost in translation and proving that you're not a bunch of quacks coming in to charge for work takes a while.

By the end of the set-up day there was a fully functioning dental clinic ready to be used, complete with four procedure tables, a checkup station, injections table and a post-op area for those patients undergoing a more invasive procedure. As we all sat back and marveled at the transformation we had pulled off, you could tell that the crew was really excited to get their hands on some rotten Peruvian teeth. And that would come soon enough. Knowing that this was a once-a-year event, people would start lining up as early as four in the morning. If we hung out much longer, we were going to be bombarded with locals looking for a pre-clinic-day tooth pull, so we decided it a good idea to head out. We loaded onto our bus, which had now morphed back into public transportation and made our way back to the hotel for a pre-diner drink before we ventured out to a special location that Jack knew for a well-deserved meal. I believe the cuisine of choice that night was Asian, and we all needed food in a bad way, so Jack ordered these huge family-style portions of damn near everything they had on the menu. There was so much food and beer that I was sure our table would collapse. The flimsy thing somehow withstood the load, however, and our ravenous gorging ensued.

Jack would always choose restaurants for lunch or dinner that were notorious for the portion size of the food platters. He would then inadvertently order up a glutton's wet dream. Peruvians must love their meats because there is a chain restaurant—one there that Jack took us to—that goes by the name of Norkys Authentic Style Peruvian Rotisserie Chicken. If you think the name is a mouthful, try eating everything on your plate. The menu is very simple. You can get a half chicken order with fries, a whole chicken order with fries and something that was just called The Meat Platter. That's it. When I say half chicken order, I mean an entire rotisserie chicken cleaved in two. The whole order just leaves out the cleaver. I saw some tables of four people with four whole chickens on them, each accompanied by an order of fries that must have weighed two pounds.

The granddaddy in the Norkys food arsenal was The Meat Platter, and it was as ominous as it sounds in context. As we passed the pounds of poultry being served up, John split off to find the bathroom and told me to just order him some fries.

"Copy that," I hollered back to him as our group was led to a table large enough to seat us all. Jack's Spanish is good, especially when it comes to dental conversations. Here however, I think something went wrong because Jack rattled off something in the local tongue that caused the waitress eyes to light up before she disappeared.

To use the word "underestimated" to describe the amount of food that Jack accidentally ordered, is an injustice to the modern dictionary. He had misjudged the size of The Meat Platter and ordered one per person. This was not a slight error. Each platter was a six-pound smorgasbord of meats—pork chops, three cuts of steak, half a chicken, sausage, grilled pig intestines and a hodge-podge of other unidentifiable meaty slabs John made it back to the table just in time to bear witness to the parade of silver serving dishes, complete with dual Sterno can heating elements, being set in front of each of us. They just kept coming.

"All I wanted was an order of fries" John said scolding me and causing me to point the blame at Jack—who sat there bewildered, trying to see over his own mammoth pile of meat. All he could do was laugh at what his Spanish had ordered for the table.

Then the fries came out—not just John's, but one two-pound order per each meat platter. There must have been a minimum of twenty-five pounds of meat and eight pounds of fries sitting atop our three, small pushed-together tables. If I am exaggerating, it's not by much. Oh, it was so good!

The next day came with the same bland breakfast, the same sludgy coffee and the same bumpy, dusty ride to the clinic. The weather this morning seemed different, though. I hadn't paid much attention to the weather earlier—probably because of the initial rush of getting here and the fact that the previous day had been more pleasant than normal, but Lima has some of the oddest weather that I have ever encountered. It's classified as a desert zone and has relatively no rain throughout the year. This makes it super dry and dusty. However, its proximity to the ocean gives it a very high humidity level. It stays cool through most of the early morning, gets hot during the day and cold again into the evening. This creates a cold, constantly damp environment that leaves you confused about just how to dress, Ultimately you realize that, no matter what type of attire you put on, you are going to feel completely soggy. The damp also allows the ever-present dust to adhere to you in a very short period while you are outside, making everyone filthy. Just a helpful travel hint if you ever travel to the outskirts of Lima: synthetic materials are a necessity! Jeans and other cotton garments will soak up so much moisture that, by lunch, they will be stretched out to twice their original weight and falling off your body.

The line of people waiting at the clinic when we arrived was as predicted. It wrapped around the building and extended down the street. And again, as our bus pulled up to the front entrance of the clinic, the waiting line of people applauded and cheered. Each volunteer who exited the buss received the same heartfelt greeting. The team took a few last minutes to organize the dental equipment and then, with a quick prayer and a dousing of holy water from a rose by Sister Joan, the chaos of volunteer dentistry began. One by one the patients came in, pointing at a tooth or group of teeth and wanting relief from the constant agony of their toothache. The pattern was that they registered with a local volunteer at a desk placed near the front door and were then led to a holding area where they were educated on the importance of tooth care and given proper instructions on just how they should use a toothbrush to achieve the best cleaning results. Gentle up and down motions! It's the opposite technique of one that most of use, which is to scrub away, as if trying to remove grout stains from tile, until our gums bleed. I know, I used to do it too.

When their name was called, each person would move from the waiting area to the examination, or triage, chair for a shortened dental exam to locate the problematic tooth (or teeth as it usually was). Injections were given—to many an individual's surprise, a tag was placed on the patient to avoid removal of the wrong tooth and they were seated in the hall to give the Novocain enough time to take effect. Upon achieving total numbness, each person was sent to the appropriate chair for their procedure, be it a filling, an extraction, or an occasional crown, if time allowed. When the procedure was complete, the now numb and drooling individual was led to the free store, or as Jack called it, the Macy's of the barrio, where they could choose a couple items that the group brought from the states. Shoes, hats, clothing, toys for the kids and whatever else the IHE group could stuff in their luggage would supply the makeshift store. At most clinic locations, the children's shoes always went first—probably because of the rough conditions in these developing areas and the fact that children are constantly growing out of their shoes. By the end of each mission the store is picked clean. In these impoverished places, it wouldn't surprise me at all if most of the people came in and put themselves through the dental torture just to gain access to the free loot. This is really how poor some of these people are. Some, however, have very serious dental problems, including debilitating pain that keeps them from eating and dangerous amounts of infection that, if not taken care of, can even lead to death.

This was the first dental trip that John and I had ever been on and it thoroughly changed my opinion of their importance. I always looked at dentists as being second to doctors. Dentists save teeth, but doctors save lives. Well, that's a big misunderstanding. Dentists do save lives, and in many ways. Their treatments are instant. Within a few minutes the patient has no pain, where moments earlier it was incapacitating. If you can't eat because of a toothache, you become malnourished and weak. Dangerous amounts of infection can form in a relatively short time, which can cause fevers and lower an already frail immune system. In extreme situations this can even lead to death. While both volunteer doctor and dental missions are very important, dentistry can be relatively

inexpensive and it can be performed in the most unsuitable locations with an almost one hundred percent success rate. An entire
village or township can be treated in a matter of a few days, leaving
a crapload of happy, pain free locals now capable of eating again.
There are also the often-overlooked psychological issues that come
with teeth. People tend to not interact with others because they
feel self-conscious due to missing or rotten teeth. Beautiful young
women won't smile and get overlooked by the boys, and vice versa.
Even in these Third World conditions, a bright smile is a status
symbol and a smile can stand out in a crowd. I can't count the
number of men and women waiting in the long lines outside the
clinic who would keep their hand in front of their mouth when
they spoke to one another. This is a form of shame, but it quickly
changes to pride when they leave with a healthy new smile. I have
personally seen and filmed this beautiful transformation on many
occasions now.

By noon of day two the line was already reaching the end
of the building, turning around the corner and extending halfway
down the next road. With this many people already, Jack came
out front to examine people in the line to help speed up the triage
process, and to see where they would have to stop for the day. On
average the team of four dentist would see about eighty patients
per day but, because of the large turnout, Jack was pushing it up to
over one hundred. Even then it was hard for him to pick a cutoff
point in the line and to tell the rest that they would have to come
back in the morning. No one ever became upset, though. The
people that were not taken in that day would simply thank us for
what we were doing and come back in the middle of the night to
form a new line for the next day's dental activities. Sure enough,

A young Kevin Ball performing a motorcycle crash for the TV series
Unsolved Mysteries. *We were filming this episode in Orlando*
Florida, I flew over twenty feet and nearly over shot my safety pads.

This was another episode of Unsolved Mysteries. *We shut down an entire section of the interstate in Connecticut to create this reenactment where a man rescues a baby from a fiery car crash.*

Here I was working with a local deminer in the K-5 mine-belt near the borders between Cambodia and Thailand in 2007. This was the first trip that John Evanko and I made with the nonprofit group Freedom Fields USA and the trip that started our journey into the world of humanity.

Part of our first trip in 2007. A HALO Trust supervisor carefully dusts off the last bit of soil hiding yet another Russian made PMN landmine due to be destroyed. Mines like these are littered by the millions across the Cambodian countryside.

Part of our 2008 campaign tour of Southeast Asia with Cindy McCain took us to a massive landfill in the capital city of Phnom Pen, Cambodia. Thousands of children live and work in this festering refuge site.

While in Scotland visiting the headquarters of The HALO Trust in 2008, John and I found a presentation room containing a museum of weapons of war. This combat boot, missing the front half, was at one point on a soldier's left foot when he or she accidentally stepped on a buried landmine.

*On a river tributary, deep in the jungles of Guatemala, in 2008
John and I went in a long boat with a group of K'iche' Indians
on their way to a dental mission being held by the "International
Health Emissaries" organization. Most of these people couldn't swim.*

Father and daughter waiting to see if they have been accepted for a facial cleft surgery during Operation Smile's inaugural mission to Guwahati India in 2009.

*We were always greeted by the smiling faces of the children in
Lima Peru during the weeklong June 2008 dental mission, held
by International Health Emissaries and sponsored by the Sisters of
Mercy Catholic humanitarian support group.*

An image of the urban poverty in the barrios of Lima, Peru. This same view went on mile after mile and was some of the worst that John and I had ever been exposed to.

2012 Operation Smile mission to Bogota, Columbia. Sharing some smiles with a young girl on her way into the operating theater for a life-changing cleft lip surgery.

Engaging with an inquisitive Bolivian boy while on a facial surgery mission in 2014 with the international NGO Operation Smile.

there they were, standing in front of the clinic the next morning as our bus pulled up, clapping and cheering again.

Day three started up pretty much just like day two had—patients and volunteer dentists all doing their thing and the process flowing like clockwork. By noon there was a huge line out front, a large collection of broken teeth in a hazardous waste bag and one very ill John. For some reason, South America and John's digestive system seem to hate each other. He ate the same stuff that everyone else did but something hit him hard and shut him down for the day. I found a Peruvian version of Pedialyte to help keep his electrolyte count up and a quiet place in the nun's office on the second floor for him to lie down and recuperate, then I accompanied Sister Joan and a couple other IHE volunteers on a tour of the poorest section of the barrio. I was amazed at just what I saw.

THE WORST URBAN POVERTY I'VE SEEN

I have had many opportunities, over the past five or six years, to get up close and personal with poverty and see its many faces. In locations like rural Cambodia, poverty was harder to judge because the needs were so few. If you lived closer to a water well than your neighbors did, you were wealthier than they were. If you had a plastic tarp to keep the rain out of your hut, then you were better off than others and if you had access to food and some form of transportation, your status was elevated even more. As I always preach to people, poverty is location specific. In the dumps of Vietnam that we visited, poverty was obvious because people made their homes in the garbage, living for free in the landfill. As destitute as that may seem, I believe the barrios of Lima were, in some way, even worse. Urban poverty, like we found in Lima, may be the most difficult type of poverty for human beings to deal with because of the proximity to those in the lower and middle classes that live near nearby. To say that there is no way for people to escape this penniless existence is merely to state the cold, hard facts of reality. The people that we met in the cardboard houses we toured in Lima that day, are still there today. All but a very lucky few will remain there until they die. These people had nothing but a collection of cardboard and mismatched pieces of wood for their roof and walls, and the few items that they had been given or found.

This is not a dumpsite where you can scavenge for items, nor is it a jungle setting in a warm climate where you can hunt and farm. This is an active community in what is sometimes called a shantytown, and these people have bills to pay. The land they live on is not homesteaded like in rural Cambodia. It must be rented or bought. There is no running water, so it must be bought daily from the water trucks. The land cannot be farmed, so food must be acquired at local markets. In many ways, these people live in a way that we in the US can easily understand; their lifestyle is a dark mirror of ours. Families have taxes, fees and payments—all with no employment except for hand making very inexpensive items to sell, or reselling stuff for a few cents more than they paid for it. On this trip we were honored to be allowed to film inside some of the houses in which these families lived. What I saw, I will never forget.

To put it into understandable numbers:

From what I have researched, most people who live in extreme poverty in rural areas, and this can be up three out of every four people, survive on less than $1.00 per day. It's probably actually closer to 70 cents a day. About twenty-thousand children die quietly each day in some of the poorest *villages on earth, far removed from news coverage and the conscience of the world. These children die an invisible death. Because of this absence of money, most of the children are suffering and dying from malnutrition. In cities, urban slum growth is outpacing urban growth by a very large margin.*

Less than a single dollar a day, to buy food and water, and to take care of a family. These numbers come close to representing the income at this location in Peru, and because of a lack of sexual education and proper protection, the families in these settings are usually large. Some women had as many as nine children and one was actually using her own breast milk to feed all of them. If you think about it, education costs money and so does a condom, but sex is a free source of enjoyment. So the poorest of the poor, living in these urban slums, continue to procreate because they can.

ON THE MOUNTAIN OF THE POOREST, SHIT REALLY DOES RUN DOWN HILL

We had two opportunities to tour and film the hillside barrio with our nuns, The Sisters of Mercy. I should say, I had two opportunities; John missed the first one because of his Peruvian parasite conundrum, but, although a bit weak, he made the second trip up the mountain. To avoid my own confusion, I will just combine both treks into one from here on out.

I use the word "mountain" because it towered over the entire barrio. Actually, it was an enormous hill with a very large water tank perched atop its summit. The water tank, constructed of concrete, was about twenty feet tall and took up about the same area as a professional football field. It was built many years before, but never completed or filled with water. So there it sat like a useless monument mocking the poor that lived in its shadows. The very same poor who had to journey down into the township each day to buy water and then lug the heavy, sloshing load back to their dwellings. At the crest of this mountain, you could stand in one spot, rotate, and get a three-hundred-and-sixty-degree view of the entire barrio. On a clear day, at an elevation of five hundred feet, you should see for almost ten miles. We were somewhat higher than this, but the haze impeded our vision a bit, so ten miles is a good rough estimate. For ten miles, in a three hundred sixty-degree circle, all I could see was the barrio. Square it off and throw in some fancy math, and I figure it was well over a forty-mile area of people living well below the poverty line of one US dollar per day. This was both an amazing and stomach-turning sight to behold. From the sea to our rear, to the mountains to our left and the larger city to our front and right side, all you could see were the dusty reddish brick, dusty cardboard and dusty scrap wood structures that created the landscape. Added to this image, which gave the scene a surreal modern art feel, were an occasional red or blue painted wall and an assortment of colorful Peruvian fabrics and clothes hanging to dry on outside clotheslines. Beautiful images sometimes create themselves in the most unimaginable locations.

Of the three dwellings that we visited, one stood out more than the rest. It belonged to the woman with nine children who was using breast milk to help feed them all—even the older ones. Her husband had been injured on a construction site and could no longer work, so he would go off in search of scraps to sell as a means to support the family. As we stepped across the threshold to the dwelling, I could see how bad this was going to be. The long, dirt floor hallway that connected the makeshift door to the living space was less than six feet high, causing me to duck down as I walked, and it was so narrow that John almost had to turn sideways to keep his shoulders from touching the sides. One wall of the entrance hallway was constructed of mismatched pieces of wood, once painted but now so distressed and rotted by the constant cold humidity that it had faded to an off-white hue. Along the other wall was a selection of small sleeping rooms with entrance openings covered by colorful tattered fabric to give the illusion of privacy. The entire place reminded me more of the kind of fort or a clubhouse I would have built when I was in elementary school than a place to raise a family. The smell of stale mildew became stronger the farther down the hallway we walked, and just like in a cave, the deeper in we went, the darker and danker it became. Pushing through more damp hanging cloth, we entered the common room, which housed the cooking area and a small table to eat upon. There stood the house's matriarch holding a small child balanced upon her hip. She was probably in her early forties, but the environment and stress of such a hard existence had aged her face so that she appeared to be in her sixties. The first thing that I noticed, after my eyes adjusted to the dimly lit room, was that it was a partial cave. The rear wall was earth and had been dug out by hand. The room was actually half mountainside. The roof was made of cardboard boxes, opened up flat, fitted together and laid over wooden posts that were jammed into the earthen wall. Water from random rain showers and the tainted runoff from the shanties above had carved small channels into the brown clay wall, keeping it constantly wet and the dirt floor always muddy. The cooking space at the far end spanned the distance between the hillside and a structural wall that had also been created from found wood and other random building materials. The entire shack had been created from scrap. When Sister Joan asked the woman if there was anything that the family needed, she humbly replied that, with the onset of winter just a month away, she could really use some more cardboard to fix the holes in the roof and to give added insulation for the cold nights. I remember asking myself, "Did I really just hear what I think I did?" as the poor woman spoke. This is the reality, the truth of the way people exist in places like this around the world. This is why groups like IHE come to these locations and set up these free dental missions.

Can they solve all the problems of these impoverished people? The honest answer is no, but they can help to take the pain away and allow them to live with a bit more dignity. They can acknowledge that this existence is real and offer these people a small glimmer of hope, which is sometimes enough to keep them going.

Slightly scarred from what we had seen, we trekked around the mountain to visit a couple more families. One lived a bit higher up the mountain, in a better fortified home; the other was closer to the base. Sister Joan explained the hierarchy of the elevation and described, in her sisterly way, that shit really does run downhill. When you live in a location with no running water and no proper form of sewer drainage, everything at the top of the mountain runs accumulatively runs downward, all the way to the bottom of the hillside and, eventually, into the streets below. The benefits of having your home at the top of the mounting are obvious if you don't like pungent odor and the sight of your neighbor's shit making its way through your living room. File that away in the recesses of your mind for later.

The rest of the dental clinic went extremely smoothly and, with the demise of the hooker phone at our hotel, I slept much better. Even John was back to his perky self. Life was good. Our small, helpful dental group was pretty much all that these people would ever know of Americans. We represented our entire country and like in Kosovo, there were no negative images left in these people's minds. Just a bunch of white strangers reaching out and helping, while looking for nothing back in return. Even some of the local cops tailed John and I as we walked down to a street market on the last day, not to harass us but to keep an eye on us just in case anyone became too fond of our camera gear.

Unfortunately, all things must come to an end, and it almost broke Jack's heart to come out, pick a random spot in the line and say, "No mas."

We had reached our patient level for the last day. Those remaining in the line would have to wait a year, for the next IHE mission, to be seen. Disappointed as they were, they all understood and thanked Jack and the volunteers out front. Most vowed to get in line sooner next time and then slowly walked away. Back inside, the portable dental equipment was put back into its travel bags and, as quickly as it had created, the room was bare. You would never have known that hours before, a mass of volunteers had been hard at work offering humanity to an entire community.

CUSCO, HOME OF THE SACRED ROCKS

The mission of International Health Emissaries is not only to help those with no access to health care, but also to allow volunteers from the US to travel abroad as safely as possible. They get the chance to see things that they otherwise might never have had the opportunity to see. So, on this mission our plan was to travel from Lima to Cusco, high in the Andes Mountain range. Here we could all immerse ourselves in the ancient Incan civilization and try to inhale enough oxygen to avoid altitudes sickness at its almost twelve-thousand-foot elevation. The altitude became very apparent when we walked from the terminal to the bus parked a mere two-hundred yards away. Most of the volunteers in the group were staying at a very upscale hotel right in the heart of the downtown area. I'm not sure if it was the one, where for a fee, you can have oxygen pumped into your room but it was still a very modern, stylish hotel.

John and I decided to opt for a slightly humbler location, choosing a place called the Niños Hotel & Hacienda. This turned out to be a very wise decision for two reasons. One, because it was less than half the price of the hotel in which everyone else was staying, and, two, because the Niños Hotel helped the local children of Cusco. All profits from the hotel are used to give five hundred extremely neglected children a hot meal on a daily basis, a warm shower, medical and dental assistance, and homework and sports lessons, and to support the other projects from the Foundation Niños Unidos Peruanos. True to its word, there was a basket of bread next to the front door and, from time to time, street children would ring a bell outside. Someone from the front desk would then walk over, open a smaller hinged window and hand each child a piece of fresh bread. The hotel was amazing. Once you passed through the ancient wooden door that ran parallel to the street, your eyes focused on a beautifully laid out courtyard complete with center fountain. Surrounding the court-yard were the rooms, each named after one of the street children. Each room's door opened out to the center fountain area. The building itself was very old and was originally built from stone. Then, in more recent times, it was plastered over to give it a more comforting feeling. Even the walls of our small room were about six feet thick at the base. Look it up if you ever get to Cusco. You won't be disappointed.

Cocoa leaves are everywhere in Cusco and chewing on them supposedly helps ward off altitude sickness. I'm not sure if it worked or not for altitude, but if you sucked on enough of them your mouth would tingle and you might get a mild, relaxed feeling. For the altitude I opted for a prescription of Diamox. This is nothing more than a super heavy diuretic which actually shrinks the size of your brain by reducing the volume of water in it. This allows the natural swelling that occurs at extreme elevations to happen without the added pressure between the brain and the inside of the skull. No pressure, no headaches. In a couple of days your body will adjust to the elevation and the thinner air, with its lack of oxygen, and your will breath will be just fine.

Feeling relaxed and ready to explore John and I went on a tour with the rest of the group that first evening. We learned that the people of Cusco are very proud of their heritage. Old is old, but the local tour guides seemed to think that every fucking stone, every wall and every street was sacred. They kept reminding of this us each time we leaned on something, until it became a running joke. We travel around the globe, helping strangers and being wonderful representatives of the United States and, on our first tour in Cusco, all the men in the group somehow became typical asshole American tourists— especially me. My rebellious child came out. John and I kept walking behind the guide mocking and pointing out the sacred rocks as he gave the tour.

"Hey guys, see this roc? Sacred, this one, super sacred."

"What about this one?" we would ask. We kept prodding the guide until he finally took us to the most sacred and oldest wall in the whole of Cusco. There were men there paid to blow whistles and point at you if you so as much as breathed on the sacred wall. It's twelve feet of solid granite, for God's sake. You couldn't scratch it with a Sherman tank, but, oh hell, did we ever had fun with the whistle blowers.

The tours were informative, especially if you want the Incan side of the story about how they were brutally taken over by the Spanish and forced into Catholicism. They talked about that a lot. I've heard the same story in other countries, especially South and Central American ones. Ancient indigenous cultures were decimated by the cross, and the diseases of the white strangers conquering their land. It's a gaping wound that won't heal. Maybe it shouldn't.

John and I did, however, discover this wonderful thing on the tour. It's called a Pisco Sour, and if that sounds a lot like a drink, it's because it is. And it's a wonderful drink. Pisco is a type of strong grape brandy. Add sour mix, sugar and frothed egg whites, shake well and you get a wonderful tasting libation that will damn near take the top of your head clean off. This became our drink of choice because carbonated beer at high elevations seems to never quit bubbling—even after its been consumed. To avoid the belly bloat stick with Pisco.

We saw a lot in Cusco and the surrounding countryside. Old churches, sacred ruins, markets and more ruins. We even took a really scenic train ride to the town of Aguascalientes, the beginning point of the trek up to Machu Picchu. Along with hordes of other inquisitive tourists, we took the bus ride to the ruins, paid a guide and eventually realized that our guide had no idea what he was talking about. None of the guides seemed to either, for that matter. John and I listened to three separate guides, all telling their respective tour groups totally different stories about even more sacred stones, sacred rooms, sacred effigies and small a room that, according to our guide, was the ancient monarch's toilet. Another guide called it a storage space.

Machu Picchu was a mystical and otherworldly place to visit though, truly magical. In reality, no one, especially not the guides, has a clue to what any of it means or where the inhabitants went.

This was now the second ancient wonder of the world that John and I had been lucky enough to see and, again, it was the humanitarian world that had taken us there. I implore anyone reading this to venture out to as many of the world's historic places as humanly possible. This supersedes most spiritual experiences. Just visiting and exploring these sites can really ground you. To see the evidence of past human civilizations that existed far longer than our modern, industrial society has makes you realize that we are but infants. It asks that you ponder the question, What will our generation will leave behind?

HEY, LOOK IT'S A PARADE

One of our more memorable experiences in Cusco happened on a free day, when John and I were left on our own. John and I finding trouble when left unsupervised? Never!

It was the last day of our trip and we had no set time to be anywhere special. So we slept in a bit later than usual. We took some time to repack our bags and organize our gear for the next day's flights back home. Lunchtime was coming, so we decided to venture out and explore the streets in search of a place to eat some local food. After a short time of meandering the streets on foot, we ran across quite a noisy, rambunctious gathering of locals. They were heading toward the central plaza. Here's where my sometimes childlike innocence gets me into trouble and causes John to look at me, then the sky, then his feet, then back at me with that head-tilt expression that says he wants to what planet I was born on. Upon seeing this rather large group of locals I said, "Hey look, a parade!" and I started heading toward it.

While he stood smack dab in front of the first group of singing, chanting people, John's face tightened up a bit and he loudly yelled in my general direction, "This isn't a parade Kevin, it's a protest!"

Sure-as-shit, it was, and it was a huge one too. As they chanted and marched through the narrow streets, you would have sworn that they had chosen John and me to lead them to their final rallying location. Every time we turned right or left, trying to get out of the way of the onslaught, the protest would follow us down even smaller streets. This went on until we finally rounded a corner and entered a large courtyard which, unbeknownst to us, was in front of the local government offices. At this point, we made a hard left and headed to a bar at the far end of the square. We still had a good vantage point from which to view the excitement, and we could enjoy some more wonderful Pisco Sours while we watched.

The protesters finally amassed outside the front door of the government building, and things began escalating, becoming very violent. What the protesters couldn't see was the military presence building up at our end of the square, directly behind them. John and I had no choice but to stay and enjoy the festivities. Between the protesters and the military vehicles, all the routes back to our hotel were now totally blocked. If they could have seen the open bed trucks loaded with soldiers in riot gear, rifles in hand, that were staged just out of view, around the corner, the protesters might have forgotten what they came to bitch about. Then a vehicle that said Bomb Squad in Spanish, pulled up and parked right in front of the bar, no more the twenty feet from where we were sitting. So we ordered two more Pisco Sours. It seemed the logical thing to do, given our current situation. Some poor guy came out of the government building to address the angry mob. That lasted about two seconds, and then he started running as the crowd began to attack him. Riot police started in on the protesters with rubber batons, swinging wildly at whatever was in their range until it was obvious to the crowd that this was not going to end well. They quickly retreated, leaving the square quiet and peaceful again. It was just another fun day in a developing country with Kevin and John. It did leave us with one of my favorite photos of John. He's standing in the middle of the street, only feet from the angry mob closing in behind him. A perfect Kodak moment.

By the same time the next day, we were in the air on our way back to Florida. We had a newfound respect for our dental volunteers, some amazing stories and even more remarkable new friends. Our next trip with the International Health Emissaries NGO would take in about five months and would take us to the jungles of Guatemala. We couldn't wait.

John and I had experienced so much in the past few years. Our love of humanity was growing out of control. At this point, even though Hollywood was how we made a living, we were both almost ready become full-time humanitarians. We loved advocating for those without a voice, telling the stories of the amazing people we kept meeting and singing the praises of NGOs that were truly making a difference in the world. Little did we know that this was what the universe had in store for us. And so, it seems did Cindy McCain.

Our future would show us the richness of Dubai and plunge us deep into the colors, smells and mysteries of India. As the presidential campaign ramped up, we would tour Thailand and Southeast Asia with the US secret service leading our way and guarding our backs. Guatemala would show us a new side of humanity as we followed hidden river tributaries deep into the jungles in search of a very reclusive native tribe in need of dental and medical attention. More movies, politics and humanity loomed on our horizon, John and I had only scratched the surface of our amazing adventurous life. We were ready for more!

ASIA TOUR, JUNE 2008
CINDY MCCAIN / CAMPAIGN

BACK ON THE CAMPAIGN TRAIL

WITH BARELY ENOUGH TIME TO RELAX AND UNPACK, we had to head back out to film Cindy McCain on a tour around Southeast Asia. We had been informed of our travel schedule before the Peru mission and were elated that none of the dates crossed over. The Peru trip with International Health Emissaries was important to us, but Cindy was our highest priority.

With the run for the presidency growing close to a finale and the contest now down to Barak Obama and John McCain, everything we filmed and edited about Cindy on her humanitarian missions around the globe went directly onto the McCain for President website, as fast as we created it. We were some editing fools. I believe we managed to download the tapes from Peru into the hard drive and do a quick log on the footage but that's about it.

We were in daily communications with someone from Cindy's staff about logistics and flight schedules, and when Cindy's former assistant, Wendy, emailed me to say that she would also be going along to help Teacup, I knew this was going to be a wild trip! Kosovo still might rank number one on my list of favorite trips, but the Asia tour runs a real close second.

Because we were traveling around with the woman who, at the time, could very possibly have become new First Lady of the United States of America, security was ramped up a bit. A bit, my ass! We had a huge security force, and somehow, John and I were given secret service clearance. Even as I write that, it amazes and excites me to a point that's hard to put into words. Through volunteering to help humanitarian groups John and I had somehow found our way into this secret service shit. How fucking cool is that? The person they were there to protect was the very person that we were working one-on-one with. That gave us even more super-secret, James Bond-like clearance crap.

Reality decidedly kicked me in the balls though when, about three days into the trip, I jokingly asked one of the secret service agents if he would use me as a human shield to protect Cindy.

With a Cheshire Cat grin, he looked at me and said, "Probably, I'm paid to protect her."

You know, I never really knew if that guy was joking or not.

AND WE'RE OFF

Wendy's email finally came with all the modifications to the flight schedule, and it looked like a logistical nightmare. We were bouncing around from Vietnam to Cambodia to Thailand and all over Southeast Asia—both commercial jets and official motorcades. Our friendly little group was growing in size, too. Not only was Wendy coming along but so were Cindy's daughter, Megan McCain, and two of her friends who ran a blog for Megan. There would also be two photographers from separate magazines; Melissa, who was the press aid; a beautiful young woman named Ashley, who was a family friend of Cindy's; and Mr. Frank LaRose, who was the acting coordinator and general point man.

You might recognize the name Frank LaRose. He is now

Ohio's secretary of state and served two terms in that state's senate, but on this trip, he was just plain old Frank. So now, not only are John and I great friends with the Senator of Arizona's amazing wife but we're also email pals with the current secretary of state in Ohio. That brought the number of our happy family up to twelve, not counting the five secret service members who traveled with the group. From time to time, that number would increase because there always seemed to be more of them waiting for us on the ground in every country in which we landed. As I said, the travel schedule was unbelievable. It took a bit of time and effort on my part to track down some old emails to help me get it correct.

Starting in Orlando, John and I flew to Los Angeles to start the international portion of the trip. From Los Angeles, we flew to Ho Chi Minh City in Vietnam and stayed one night at the Caravelle hotel. The next morning, we flew from Ho Chi Minh City to Nha Trang, Vietnam for an Operation Smile mission. Then we bused to The Vinpearl Resort for the night. In the early a.m., we went back to Ho Chi Minh City and the Caravelle Hotel, again staying one night. The next morning we flew from Ho Chi Minh City to Bangkok, Thailand to tour a World Food Program warehouse and then we stayed for two nights at the Mandarin Oriental Bangkok. We flew from Bangkok to Phnom Pehn, Cambodia to tour a children's school and an inhabited landfill. While there we stayed at Raffles Hotel. After two fully-packed days, John and I headed back, accidentally flying from Phnom Penh, Cambodia to Guangzhou, China, (That's a hell of a story. Be patient, I'll get to it.) and then finally making our way to Beijing, China, then to Dulles in Washington D.C and finally back to Orlando. In eight days, John and I would be in ten airports in five countries. We spent time in five hotels and one small Chinese detention room. We traveled in planes, buses, boats, and of course, in Land Rovers. Tell me that's not insanity?

ASIA TOUR, VIETNAM, 2008
OPERATION SMILE

HERE'S YOUR MONKEY

LET'S START AT THE BEGINNING OF ALL THE INSANITY. John and I had an easy flight to Vietnam from LA. I attribute this to a couple amazing margaritas in the LAX international terminal and the fact that our plane was loaded with contestants for the Miss Universe competition that was being held in, of all places, Nha Trang—one of our many destinations. Somehow, Miss Colombia walked off a thirteen-hour flight looking just as perfect as when she got on. I don't know what goes on in first class, upstairs on a Boeing 747, but as wrinkle free as she came out, it has to be something magical. I can only hope to find out one day. So all being said, the long flight way actually nice and relaxing. It's a good thing too, because as soon as our feet hit the ground at Ho Chi Minh City airport we started running and didn't stop until our flights back home some eight days later.

Having pre-bought our visas for this trip, we zipped through immigration, and made a beeline to collect our baggage and meet up with the rest of the group. John's phone started blowing up with messages as we were walking to claim our bags. Of course, he didn't have an international plan, so each time it buzzed he looked at me with mild annoyance, calculating the future phone bill that was coming. It rang again,

"Hello," John said. "Oh, hi Wendy. We are just approaching the escalators. Yeah, it was a great flight."

We were now on the escalator heading down and could clearly see Wendy standing near the bottom She waved at us but stayed on the phone.

"Yeah, I see you too," John said. At this point, I was physically speaking to her as we traveled down the moving steps, and she would respond into the phone, which John was still on, racking up the charges. As we stepped off onto the bottom floor John finally shot me the look, and said, "Okay, hanging up now."

I found this amusing only because John's fancy, new first-generation iPhone had airplane mode and my Blackberry didn't. I had just as many missed calls but, like a smart boy, I hadn't turned mine on yet.

It was so great to see Wendy again. Even though we'd kept in touch by email and phone, the last time we'd seen her was on the Op-Smile mission almost a year before. Our typical, cheerful meeting someone at the baggage carousel conversation went on for a few minutes until, the out of the blue, she said, "Here's your monkey." And she handed us each a couple of colorful, monkey-shaped luggage tags and said, "Put these on your bags so that we can easily identify them or they won't make it any farther than this." Monkey tags. This was the secret service keeping us safe. How ingenious was that? A random identifying item that no one else in Southeast Asia could possibly have, and it screamed tourist, not dignitary. Simple stupid wins every time.

From now on there would be no waiting in immigration, no baggage checks and no stupid airport security. We had just traded up to near royalty. If you ever get the chance to fly around with the secret service, do it! It makes air travel almost tolerable. Bags now tagged, Frank took our passports and we hurried out to the bus that would take us to the Caravelle Hotel.

It was a very large bus that was solely dedicated as transportation for the crew, John, me, and the other photographers and aids. Cindy usually rode elsewhere. Then off we went in our small motorcade, through the streets of Ho Chi Minh City, en route to one of my favorite hotels in the world. Had it not been for the escort of small Vietnamese men on scooters, honking and wildly waving orange flashing LED lights nobody would have ever known that we were there. It was at this point that I started to compare the differences between Bob and Tony's quiet stealth in Kosovo and the US secret service's "Get out of our way. Don't you know who we are?" tactics. It makes me lean a bit toward the Brits and their "You never knew we were here" technique.

The Caravelle Hotel awaited us like an old friend with open arms, and John and I were both looking forward to a visit to Saigon Saigon on the roof for a warm embrace and a cold beer. After a quick wash-up, the group met at the wonderful, open-air restaurant to eat some real food and reconnect a bit. The secret service had quickly begun to recognize our faces; we were welcomed members of the group. There were occasional moments of "Where do you two nut jobs think you're going?" but they were rare. If a *run down* by the SS team seemed possible, we would just be sure to make eye contact with Cindy, Teacup or Wendy, who were always close by. Never, and I repeat, never, just run up thinking that everyone knows who you are. It's a good way to end up on the ground. On the other hand, it was very entertaining to sit back and watch some innocent and unknowing bar patron get too close to our inner circle, only to be stared down by a highly trained agent of the United States secret service agency. He made it quite clear to the non-group member that there was no way they were moving an inch closer to us. It was an amazing start to the trip and although I could have stayed up on the roof for hours, just taking it all in, I knew that the morning would come early. We had to be at the airport at the ass crack of dawn to catch our flight to the Operation Smile mission location in Nha Trang, on the coast of Vietnam.

Sure enough, the morning came upon us quickly. These one-night hotel stays went by so fast that I hardly ever unpacked my bags. I just rummaged through them for what I needed, trying to disturb my original, well-organized packing job as little as possible. This works fine for about the first three hotels, but anything longer than that and it becomes hard to zip the bags back up. This was only day two, so I pulled out something comfortable to wear and stuffed my previous day's attire somewhere in the bottom to be laundered later. Each night, Frank would tell us what time to have our bags sitting outside our rooms for the secret service to pick up or give us a room number to use as a morning drop point. If it wasn't there, with the monkey tag on it, it didn't make it to the next location. Showering and breakfast was always a blur if we didn't make an extra effort to rise early, and the exact time for our second meal was always unknown. And at mission sites, meals were usually very small. So even if we had a late night, we tried to make the most of breakfast. This morning's effort wasn't a particular success, however.

Bidding farewell to the Caravelle, John and I loaded back onto the bus for another flashing light waving, horn honking, scooter-led escort to the airport for our trip to Nah Trang and the Operation Smile Vietnam mission location. The flight was only about forty-five minutes long, but the Kenny G Christmas

CD that was stuck on replay made our morning flight seem much longer than it should have. However, they do feed and pamper you very well, from take-off to landing, on Asian airlines, so that made up for the ambient holiday music and our less-than-full breakfast that morning. Even with the laughable music, it was fifty times nicer than most domestic US flights. Moments after landing we were loaded up, this time in vans, and hurried off straight to the hospital where the Operation Smile team had already been working for a couple of days. John and I were put in a lead vehicle so we could beat Cindy there and be ready to film her reunion with a special little Vietnamese girl. It was yet another wonderful story of Cindy's humanity that John and I were finding out about.

Through a contact at a restaurant back home in Arizona, sometime around 1997, Cindy was informed by a young girl's uncle that he had a niece back in Vietnam who was born with a very malformed cleft lip and palate. Cindy tracked her down and had the small girl brought to the US, covering the cost of all the medical expenses and even housing her during the lengthy procedures. This was their first meeting in almost ten years. John and I took positions out in front of the hospital to film the reunion, while Frank, with aid of the secret service, kept all other local cameras crews at bay. This was great because I hate jockeying for position with discourteous camera crews. Remember Kosovo?

Within a few moments of us getting into position, Cindy's white Land Rover pulled around the corner and stopped in front of us. As she opened the door, the little girl ran up to her revealing a beautiful smile. Hallmark only dreams that they could write a card to capture a moment like this one. The little girl stuck by Cindy's side for almost the entire visit to the hospital, acting as a living, post-surgery image of the amazing work the Operation Smile volunteer surgeons perform.

Some press had been allowed in to film Cindy as she walked through the crowded halls but, just like out front, Frank and the security team only allowed John and I, and a couple of pre-chosen others, to follow Cindy closely. You could see the agitation in the other reporters' eyes as John and I would smugly squeeze past them and enter the places they wanted to get shots of. I think that even the secret service found it amusing to wave John and I passed, while passively stiff-arming the other media members. Talk about feeling like your shit don't stink. If my head had gotten any bigger I wouldn't have fit back in the van. This went on for the first half of the day—in and out of rooms, talking to doctors, volunteers, and, on this trip, members of the Navy floating hospital ship Mercy, which was anchored off shore in the harbor. This was a joint mission between the local Operation Smile Vietnam organization and the US Navy. John and I almost got the chance to fly out by helicopter and stay overnight on the ship, which would have been so cool, but because the Navy did not want to give the impression that it was showing political favoritism toward one of the presidential parties, we were denied access. Our disappointment was short lived when we were told, that instead of staying on the Mercy, we were now staying at the exclusive Vinpearl Resort for the night. Another treat for us was running into some volunteers that we had met back on our very first Op-Smile mission in Bao Loc, over a year earlier. There were reunions going on everywhere that day.

JOHN KING'S ATTEMPTS TO HIJACK THE INTERVIEW

Of course, you know that, with all these press opportunities, this close to the election, US media were all over our tour. CNN's John King flew all the way over to Vietnam to interview Cindy about her humanitarian travels and her work with the

Operation Smile organization. Well, that's what we all hoped he would be doing. What he tried to do was make the interview a political piece and tie it to the election. Cindy kept smiling and pushing the topic right back to the Op-Smile mission.

The interview was held outside the hospital in a courtyard, which gave very little in the way of images from the mission that was going on just inside the buildings around us. I picked a place where we could film the interview without being too in your face about it. The first thing that I noticed, which I have some great shots of, was the two-foot square block of ice that was sitting on the ground next to Mr. King's chair. Placed on this block of ice was a single can of Coke. John King greeted Cindy and they both sat down, opposite each other, in fold-out camping chairs. Two cameras had set up to film the interview and there were lights galore, even though we were outside in the bright Vietnam sun. The heat and the lights added to his moisture so a makeup person kept dabbing his brow with a makeup sponge, I guess to avoid a shine on his face. Meanwhile Cindy sat across from him in her Operation Smile polo shirt and a navy-blue baseball cap with the Op-Smile logo, in white, across the front. After enough pampering, Mr. King looked up at Cindy with an innocent smile and, as he took a sip of his, he offered her a coke—with a block of ice of course. With a quick glance at the coke that he had just sat down on his personal iceberg, she smiled a sweet smile, graciously declined and sat ready to interview—no make-up crew or glamorous attire, just an oversized polo shirt and a ball cap. With one last powder puff of the brow, he was ready to start, or was he? He was quick to point out to Cindy that the bill of her Op-Smile cap was casting a shadow across her brow and the shot look better if she removed the cap. Did she mind? Keeping the Operation Smile logo in plain view was what she wanted to do. It was good press for the organization and, without it prominently displayed, the interview could possibly go anywhere. He tried his best to get her to take that hat off but, as sweetly as she declined the Coke, she kept the hat in proud display mode.

The first question was about Operation Smile and it gave Cindy a chance to promote the amazing organization and to tell people why the work they perform is so important. From the next question on, though, he went political. Each time he did, Cindy would push the topic back to the mission and let him know that her husband was the one running for office, not her. It was obvious that he had very little interest in the Operation Smile angle and was out for other stuff. None of which he got. I have the entire interview on tape, unedited and shot from my angle behind a palm tree. Again, I must say that everything she does, she does with class and elegance—even controlling an interview with John King.

After the interview was complete, we all returned to the inner rooms of the hospital to finish up our visit before heading off to the hotel for the night. As we entered one room, there was a young mother with a very small baby who had an obvious facial cleft, but because of some other, more serious heart issues the infant had been denied the reconstructive medical procedure. Cindy sat next to the woman and rubbed the baby's foot while she spoke to the woman through an interpreter. This caught the attention of the Navy's medical crew and, after a short exam, they made the decision to transport the child to the hospital ship Mercy, for further tests and possibly a life-saving surgery. Talk about being in the right place at the right time. As I preach all the time, *we are all interconnected beings contained in the same universe.*

WHERE ARE WE NOW?

The sheer number of locations that we were visiting on this tour around Southeast Asia kept us moving forward at a very fast pace. We only had the one screening day to visit the Op-Smile mission, but we made the most of it. Eventually, it was time to leave and Frank ran point to the Vinpearl to set-up everything for Cindy's arrival and that of the rest of the crew. With the secret service controlling the security, Frank always had his work cut out for him, especially in blocking off the right configuration of rooms to make the SS happy. As fast as we entered in the mission site, we exited. Cindy, with her service guards surrounding her, got into one vehicle and the rest of us piled in the vans in which we arrived. With a couple last waves to the volunteers, we were off on a short ride to the coast and to the Vinpearl.

The drive up the coast from Nha Trang into the bay is one of the most beautiful I have ever seen. Even with the large tourist influx, the coast as a whole is pristine and untouched, and the water is so unpolluted that its clarity causes you to misjudge its depth. I have seen photos of boats floating on the water, shot from below, and, from below the water's surface, they appear to be hovering in mid-air. It's that clear.

Our precession stopped for lunch somewhere around the halfway point between the mission site and the Vinpearl Resort. That was awesome because our entire herd was running on empty by now and it gave us a chance to let loose and relax for a bit. Relax I did. It felt wonderful to have the camera off my shoulder and the place at which we stopped was a beachside, open-air restaurant right on the sand. Like all our stops, lunch was short and involved the secret service strategically spacing themselves out around the restaurant and the tables where we sat. They would glace over at those of us who were downing frosty cold beers with a bit of jealousy. This still took a bit of getting use to because, on past trips, John and I had much more of a personal connection with Cindy. But the circumstances had changed, and safety was paramount on this trip. After the last droplets of beer dripped from my mug onto my tongue, and with a fun buzz going, we climbed back into the vans and finished our ocean side drive to the hotel.

When we arrived at the docks, we learned that the Vinpearl is located on an island in the center of Nha Trang bay. The only way to get to it is by boat, and not by slow-moving tourist boat. The little speedboats that shuttled us to the island spent more time launching into the air over other boats' wakes than they did traveling with their hulls in the water. We went screaming across the bay, blowing by other, slow-moving crafts and families who were trying to fish and transport goods to and from locations around the water's edge. I personally spent most of the rocket ride standing up in a hatchway that led to the back deck of the boat, camera in one hand and the other on the stair rail to help me balance and keep me from being launched overboard into the bay. I got some great footage of the Navy hospital ship, USNS Mercy, as we blew past its mooring in the bay. Of course, John and I were having a blast. I wanted to drive the damn thing but due to a lack of Vietnamese linguistic skills, I couldn't figure out how to say, "Hey dude I'm a stuntman from the US. Can I drive your boat?"

Yeah, that would go over well on a diplomatic visit. I could imagine the headline: *Cindy McCain's video crew wreck shuttle boat after ricocheting off the USNS Mercy, bisecting a family's fishing canoe.*

Bags in hand, we followed the group into the lobby of the hotel and were pointed in the direction of our rooms. Frank and the others hovered around Cindy, keeping a watchful eye out for bad guys, or whatever might give them the excuse to sneer at a curious onlooker. Cindy seemed torn between amusement and slight irritation over the whole secret service entourage. She is a woman who wasn't afraid to stand in the middle of a Rwandan war zone hospital with limited protection, so the security presence in Vinpearl lobby must have seemed excessive.

Our rooms had a West Indies tropical look and were very simple, with exception of an amazing bathroom. I have come to find out that the best way to judge a luxurious room is in the crapper. If you can sit on the toilet, control the volume of the TV, change stations on the stereo and reach the phone with little effort, all while being close enough to make a good cup of coffee, then in my book you're at a rocking place. Add to that a towel warmer and a custom tiled shower with multiple heads and you're staying five stars.

Cindy had turned in for the evening, which gave Frank and some of the staff the chance to stand down for a bit. I don't remember who it was, but one of them called our room to let us know of a great dinner buffet being held on a section of the pool deck that overlooked Nha Trang Bay. Lovers of a free seafood buffet that we are, John and I wasted no time navigating our way through the maze of hallways and jungle covered trails to locate the pool. That was step one. Actually, getting to the buffet required a few problem-solving skills on our part. We had already drained our beer stock from the mini bar and with nothing in our stomachs but an earlier lunch, that also included ample beer, you could say that we were feeling a bit happy-ish. So relying on our internal food radar, we set off across the massive, sprawling pool deck in search of our bounty—which laid at the opposite side from where we now stood. The Vinpearl has one of those free-form pools created to lead you down dead-end areas in search of just the perfect secluded place. We could see the flames of the open grill, but every turn we took led us to less deck and more pool. Even if we had jumped in and swam to the wonderful aromas. we would have had to navigate walls and bridges. I was so happy to run into a couple of other slightly buzzing hotel guests having the same difficulty guessing the right combination of twists and turns to find the food source. Finally, after being laughed at across the pool by Frank and our newly befriended colleagues, we reached the treasure and we were hungry. To this day that meal remains one my greatest food memories. Maybe it was the food, or maybe the environment. I'm not sure, but if I close my eyes for a moment and reflect, I smile, and my mouth starts to water. A blinding full moon hung right over our heads in a perfectly cloudless sky. Behind us the ocean water was so clear that the moon cast no reflection upon its surface, but the sand on the sea's floor was lit up as if a giant spotlight were shining down, penetrating the waves. There was a mild, warm breeze coming off the ocean that flicked at the flames of the Tiki torches that surrounded the buffet area, causing the smell of citronella to mix with the meat juices dripping on the hot coals. Laid out on the table across from the chefs that were working behind the grill was a cornucopia of every type of raw meat, seafood and other, unimportant, vegetable items that one could wish for, all waiting to be to be collected for charring on the grill. We grabbed a couple of plates and began sorting through what was soon to be our meal. First, I grabbed some of the most amazing prawn I have ever seen, fresh out of the ocean behind us and the size of a small lobster. Then I hit the scallops on a half shell. Scallops on a grill being cooked in their own juice—that's as close to food pornography as you can find. Of course I grabbed a couple small bacon wrapped filets to round out my selection. John and I were again flying high on life and utterly amazed at where the universe had taken us this time.

MOON LIT SWIM AT CHINA BEACH

With the delectable meal almost finished and a few more free beers down the hatch, someone had the bright idea that we should all run back up to our rooms, change into our swimsuits and go on a moonlit swim in the pool. Our judgement was a bit numb due to the dreamlike atmosphere, the feast and, of course, the booze. That combination made this sound like the perfect idea. Of course, with this group, it only took a short time for us all to get bored by the pool. So, soon-to-be senator of Ohio, Frank LaRose, egged on by John and I, led the charge down the beach to the warm waters of Nha Trang Bay for a midnight swim under the full moon. This is another one of those moments to write home about. John and I, after gorging ourselves at a gourmet dinner poolside, at the world famous Vinpearl Resort in Vietnam, were now swimming in the crystal-clear waters of Nha Trang Bay with some of the team members who were trying to help elect John McCain as president United States Of America. The sensation that was running through my body, and my mind, could not be duplicated by any pharmaceutical creation known to man.

The water was just about body temperature, so it almost felt like there was nothing around you, and, as I stated before, the water was so clear and the sand so brightly lit by the full moon that it seemed as if we were wading through clear, thick, warm air. The eight of us who were brave enough to take the plunge can probably only reflect with each other on the evening because it is so magical and hard to describe. Then as if we, a group of political professionals, were mere children, we were all run out of the ocean by a hotel security guard flailing his arms wildly and shouting something at us in Vietnamese. Like guilty kids, we all quickly sloshed our way from the sea, grabbed our towels and giggled as we ran from the person of authority that was heading our way. Running high on life seemed to be a continuing theme for John and me, and this night continued to fuel our emotional ride of experiencing the trench warfare of disparity in the humanitarian world, followed up by the luxuries of traveling with a possible first lady. It was really hard to wrap my brain around, so I didn't. I just let each day come with no expectations and truly lived in the moment.

LIVING IN THE NOW

I have often heard people use the term "living in the moment" in ways that I feel misrepresent it. I am no self-proclaimed guru, nor do I possess a degree in psychology, but from what I have witnessed in our journeys around the developing world, I feel that I have a good grasp on human connections. I have read many books on the topic of living in the moment—from those that explain it as a spiritual principle, to those that walk the realm of the absurd. I have come up with my own explanation of living in the moment, which, I believe, puts an entirely new spin on it. Yes, even Buddha spoke of being or living in your surroundings, not concentrating on what will possibly happen in the future or dwelling on what you cannot change in the past. It's very true to say that each breath comes with no guarantee of the next; it's also true to say that all the money and power in the world cannot change the fact that the breath you took a minute ago will always be in the past. It's gone and can never be revisited. However, with our modern hectic schedules of life, loaded with deadlines and meetings, we do sometimes have to live around the moment containing the very breath that we are taking.

To me, living in the moment is also living in the moment of human contact – in the moment that causes a reaction, good or bad, in one or both people, either by an action, comment or an opening of the heart.

What does this mean exactly?

Let's say that you are standing in line in a grocery store and you overhear the person in front of you tell the cashier that they are two dollars short of enough money to pay for their purchase. The moment has begun to create itself the instant you hear the comment. You now know that there is something that you can do to assist the stranger in front of you. If you do nothing, the thought of what you should have done will live in a negative place in your subconscious. If you offer to pay for the last item or give them the two dollars, what you have done will add to your collective feeling of good, peace and humanity. The connection between you and the stranger, be it positive or negative, is the moment. To me, moments are not so much lived as created, because each of these human connections is transferred from one person to the next and then can be passed along, breeding more moments. There is good and bad in everything, and to create a perfect world we can all practice creating and passing on the good moments. The moment can be as simple as pushing an empty shopping cart out of a parking lot and up to the store, just because it's not where it belongs, offering a friendly hello to a stranger, or paying the bill at dinner with friends. So, if you combine this practice with a bit of Buddha's principles of peace and being focused on present time, as much as possible, you have a good start to an openhearted existence.

If you need a simple visual, drawl a stick figure on a piece of paper. Over him draw a cone shape, like a funnel, over his head with the large side up. This is where human experience and connection pours into each one of us. Now underneath our stick figure, draw a cone in the opposite direction, larger side facing down. This is where we give our responses, our actions, back to the world, and the people with whom we connect. If the cones were to intersect with each other like an hourglass, the smallest point, the point of connection, would be the moment. This is where what come into us, what we decide to do with it and where we send it back out converge.

SAIGON SAIGON ONE MORE TIME

With each new morning the routine became easier to follow. Get up at the crack of dawn; place luggage, with monkey tags visible, in front of Frank's door and then haul ass down to breakfast before loading up into a van, bus or plane for the next destination. All the while quietly being scrutinized by the secret service guys and gals, and never totally losing the thought that, should the shit hit the fan, I would probably be used as a human shield to aid in someone's escape.

Airport routines became easier and easier. Frank would take our passports and luggage, and the security team would lead us, and follow us, to some private VIP room where we would hang out until some bigwig from the airport would walk us through security—often though a private entrance. We would then board the plane before the rest of the passengers. Trust me when I say that it's the only way to fly and will ruin your patience with basic airport procedure for life.

Since our meeting at the World Food Program warehouse in Bangkok was still one day away, the plan called for us to all fly back to Ho Che Minh City for the evening and check back into the Caravelle hotel.

Having done this, we decided to take advantage of the few hours of daylight left. The whole group, including Cindy and the secret service, went on a walk through the nearby streets of Ho Chi Minh City and then pretty much repeated the same evening that we had spent, two days before, in the Saigon Saigon Bar on the roof. We were getting more comfortable around the security team, and they seemed more comfortable with John and me. I got the feeling that they were now watching over us a bit, like we had been pulled into the inner sanctum of safety and we were walking around with a bunch of big brothers.

I had barely enough time to enjoy the expensive room, but morning came with a beautiful view of the Saigon River that ran directly behind the Caravelle. I woke a bit early, made some coffee and sat at the window watching puffs of smoke appear on the opposite river bank as locals started their morning cooking fires. As the sky lightened to a warm bright morning, I could tell it was going to be another magical day. Following the routine, we loaded up the bus and on our way to the airport in a quick thirty minutes or so, led again by the insane, arm-flailing scooter patrol. I never quite understood this; it seemed to draw more attention to us and was of no help in navigating through the swarming morning traffic.

ASIA TOUR, THAILAND, 2008
WORLD FOOD PROGRAM

BANGKOK LOVES US

BANGKOK WELCOMED US WITH OPEN ARMS and, instead of scooters, a full security force led the way to our first stop—The World Food Program (WFP) warehouse and transportation hub for Southeast Asia.

This WFP hub was extremely active at the time of our visit because it was one of the export zones for aid and supplies going into Myanmar (the country many people still call Burma) after Cyclone Nargis struck in May 2008. The storm killed thousands and left tens of thousands homeless. Cindy tried to get us all into the drop zone in Myanmar, days after the cyclone hit, but the government was so suspicious of outside help that we were denied all access—especially camera access. Here, though, the WFP logistics team was loading and sending out cargo planes at as pace as fast as they could.

We drove alongside what looked to be a long-forgotten runway on the outer edges of Thailand's Don Mueang International Airport, just outside Bangkok. To the right of our bus were immense warehouses filled with supplies that had been shipped in from all over the world. Parked on our left side were the WFP planes that would soon be delivering the tons of supplies into the heart of Myanmar's relief zone. I longed to be on one of those flights, but that just wasn't going to happen. We stopped in front of one of the warehouse offices where a very large WFP sticker proudly adhered to the glass window. Behind the window was the room in which we would spend the next hour listening to some very passionate, but very knowledgeable guys, talk about the World Food Program and their role in supporting aid deliveries from this particular location into the cyclone ravaged area.

The World Food Program is the world's largest humanitarian agency fighting hunger worldwide. In emergencies, they get food to locations where it is needed, and aid victims of war, civil conflict and natural disasters. After the initial problems of a crisis has passed, they use food to assist communities in rebuilding their devastated lives. Founded in 1961, WFP longs to see a world in which every man, woman and child can get the food needed to maintain an active and healthy life. While there are many side projects that the WFP actively sponsors, its main focus is transportation. You get it to them, and no matter how small the shipment, they will fly it into the needed location. The most amazing part is that the WFP is a totally volunteer-funded organization when it comes to disaster relief. At the Dubai location we were shown the business side of the WFP, which was just as amazing. That story I will cover in a later chapter.

After the lecture and a bathroom break, our hosts gave us a tour of the warehouse complex. I put a wireless microphone on Cindy, to capture any good conversations between her and the WFP representatives leading us, grabbed my camera gear and we were off. You could have lined up football field after football field, end to end, in this place. To call it massive would be, well, a massive understatement, and at least half of the floor space was taken up by supplies, neatly packaged and sitting on pallets, ready to be loaded into the cargo planes waiting outside. This was one of those times that spent more time walking backwards in front of Cindy than looking where I was going. From time to time, while I was focused on the conversation, John would gently, or sometimes not so gently, shove me out of the way from something that I could have tripped over, cracked my head on or possibly impaled myself with.

Walking backwards, while concentrating on framing a conversation, tends to make me lose track of time. A couple of hours had passed, and my body was feeling the effects of holding a video camera on my shoulder, when, feeling a bit cranky, I lit into another camera crew that had somehow gained access to our friendly little group.

I don't know who this guy was, what news agency employed him, or even why he was allowed to film Cindy in the first place, but he and his sound guy had been annoying me from the start. Each time I would get my shot framed up on Cindy and our WFP guide, this fuzzy microphone cover would slowly move into my shot from the bottom of the frame. Being the nice guy that I am, I would simply frame up some to remove the uninvited object from my video. This happened over and over, until I started to find myself shooting the conversation from the neck up. I would have more of the warehouse roof in frame than Cindy and the guide, and the guy holding the camera kept crowding me. After what must have been more than an hour of this invasion of my camera work, the same indignation I had when the vice president of Kosovo tried to push me out of the presidential office rushed through me. To the surprise of the entire group, right in the middle of an explanation on US aid, I hit my boiling point. As the fuzzy cover entered my shot once again, I dropped my camera to my waist and with, one quick move, turned and grabbed the guy's microphone. I spoke into it – loudly.

"If you put this damn microphone in my shot one more time, I am going to shove it up your ass, got it?"

A brief moment of quiet crept over our small tour group, as I was now the center of attention. I heard a person giggle and I was quite sure someone from secret service was going to grab me by the ear and scold me, while he walked me out to the bus. So I played it off as if nothing happened and went right back to filming the conversation, which was now resuming. On a happy note, the little bastard stayed clear of my filming for the rest of the tour.

I am still not sure just how this rogue camera guy got into the tour with us but, as the tour was coming to an end, he and fuzzy microphone guy were granted a short interview with Cindy. Short would be the operative word here, especially after his first question. The little dickhead put the microphone in Cindy's face and asked some off-topic question about one of Senator John McCain's policies in Arizona and how it would negatively affect his campaign.

She smiled politely, looked directly at him, and said something like, "I don't know. I guess you should ask my husband that question."

That's about all it took for Frank and a couple of aids to let the man know that the interview was over and his presence would no longer be needed during the rest of the warehouse tour.

I told Frank that the rogue camera guy had been getting in my way since the tour began and he said, "You should have told me sooner. I would have loved to throw him out of here."

"I will keep that in mind next time the opportunity presents itself," I said, as we engaged each other with shit-eating grins.

After a last-minute photo op with Cindy and a platoon of

US Marines who were helping to load the cargo planes with the relief supplies, we were rushed back to the bus so we could keep to our designated time schedule without running into any traffic in Bangkok.

THE MANDARIN ORIENTAL, BANGKOK

To add to our list of amazing hotels, I now present the Mandarin Oriental Bangkok. This was the first of the Mandarin Oriental hotels to be constructed in the world and its reputation and beauty preceded it. The first thing that caught my attention, as we entered the grand lobby, was the pungent aroma of flowers. Lilies and jasmine came at us from all directions because of the handmade flower leis adorning the walls. In the center of the room was a life-size statue of a baby elephant draped with a handmade blanket fashioned completely from small white flowers, thousands of them. The entire lobby was constructed of teak and mahogany and accented with the colorful fabrics of Thailand. Truly the Mandarin Oriental, Bangkok still tops my list of best hotels. There was something spiritual about it, too. This probably had a lot to do with the amazing kindness of the young Tai staff people who worked there.

Our plan was to take a couple of days to relax from our hectic schedule, to step out of the humanitarian world and play tourist for a bit. By now the whole group had become an extended family and even the secret service let their guard down around John and me. That was a good thing, because, at this location, we all stayed on the same floor and occupied an entire hallway. Cindy's room was at the far end of the hall and had a twenty-four-hour guard posted at her door. A bit farther down the hall was her daughter Megan's room, which she shared with her two friends. Then Frank, Melissa and John and me. The rest of the staff filled in the hall, right up to the elevator area. The first room, by the hallway entrance, was outfitted as the secret service command center. The door was always open and it contained enough high-tech equipment and computers to make NASA feel inadequate. In front of the elevators was a small concierge desk where our security team always had two members staged. I got the feeling that this made the concierge attendants a bit nervous.

In the grand lobby of the hotel were another two secret service members who rotated shifts throughout the day and night. So for John and me to even get to our room, we had to run a gauntlet of highly trained and ever-vigilant US service agents who were randomly changing positions. Thank God they were growing fond of us. John wandered into the command center room one day, looking for one of the female security team members. ON her down time, she had found a great place to buy local hand-crafted jewelry. His thought was to pick up something exotic for his mother, so he knocked on the door and asked to speak to her if she were around. He was told that she would be back in a few minutes and that he could wait for her as long as he didn't touch anything. Nervously, he sat on the bed waiting, but, of course, he couldn't help scoping out the room and engaging in some idle chitchat with the secret service agents who were there. He told me that there were all these computers and a ton of communications equipment systematically laid out all over the place, and every time he looked at something for too long, a security guy would, without, speaking, look at him, then at the item of his focus and then back at him with a facial expression that said, "Don't look at that." John has the uncanny ability to look nervous even when he isn't, which I can only imagine added to a bit of tension in the air. I envisioned a scene reminiscent of a guy sitting in a cold doctor's office, wearing nothing but an open-backed robe, waiting for his first prostate exam by a doctor with very large hands. Each time the doctor opened a drawer to remove an implement, he would wonder, "Just where is he going to put that thing?" After a short time John said, "Maybe I'll just wait outside."

"That's probably a good idea."

Come to think of it, I don't think we ever found the location of that store but John came away with a new respect for just how seriously the secret service takes their job. There's a somewhat safe, but unsettling, feeling about staying a couple of rooms down the hall from people who have permission to kill you if they so choose. Unfortunately, later that evening, alcohol would prevail and help us throw all this sensible caution right out the open window of rational thought.

Oh yeah, it was going to be one of those nights!

THE EVENING THAT NEVER HAPPENED

The afternoon started with a wonderful lunch and a bit of napping around the pool, before we all cleaned up and met for the most option-friendly outdoor dinner buffet I have experienced. Unlike at the Vinpearl, the magical atmosphere was a little lacking, but the selection of mouthwatering goodies was off the charts. This was our first evening without an early morning departure the next day, and, since Cindy had turned in for the night and left the staff with time to play, we all threw down our alcoholic chastity belts and drank freely— some of us more freely than others. Inhibitions fell to the wayside as we sat by the pool bar enjoying the moment. At some point, late in the evening, the small group of us that was left figured that we should try finding our way back to our super secure floor. Half way up the elevator, we decided that we weren't quite finished enjoying our once in a lifetime party experience, so we continued the party upstairs. Adding to our fun was the fact that we were now in the presence of the secret service again, and it was obvious to most of them that we were all drunk. One by one, we raided the mini bars in all the rooms to which we had access. To the amusement of the secret service, we would walk right past them and knock on a hotel room door belonging to one the staffers who had come up before us. When they answered the door to see just what the hell was going on, we would laugh our way in, grab the beers from their mini bar and then exit past the security agents who trying not to openly laugh at our frat party fun. The game reached a whole new level when, upon returning to our room, John and I found a very happy person who had decided that our bathtub was where she wanted to sleep for the evening. I won't give any names but if she reads this, I'm sure she will remember it well.

Try to visualize me coming out of my hotel room, during a presidential campaign endorsed trip, with a slap-happy individual that I had wrestled from my tub and hoisted over my shoulder. Then picture me asking the secret service guys guarding the hallway at the time if they knew where I should deposit the body. With all the commotion going on in the hall, other staffers had started to open their doors to see just what the hell was going on. Frank was having a conversation with someone just outside his door as I passed him, with the kicking person still over my shoulder.

Smiling, he just looked at me like an old friend and said, "Kevin," nodded his head,

"Frank," I replied with a similar nod and continued past him, down the hallway, as if this were an everyday event.

When I finally locating the correct room, I knocked on the door and just stood there with body still perched over my shoulder.

The door opened and, to the room's astonished inhabitants, I said, "I believe this belongs to you." I then gently flopped my lovely laughing friend on a bed.

Heading back up the hall to our room, I passed Frank again, where we exchanged the same dialogue as before.

"Kevin," he said.

"Frank," I shot back with a nod, like we were the cartoon characters Sheepdog and Ralph Wolf.

Somewhat out of breath and slightly staggering—from both the workout of shouldering a human body and the booze—I entered our room where John was calmly sitting and watching TV. With a long pause and a relieved smile, he said, "That turned out to be an interesting evening now didn't it I'm surprised no one got shot want a beer."

He said it just like that, with no pauses in between any of the words. We had lived out another scene from a movie – one that would have challenged and Oscar-winning screen writer to create.

Breakfast was served poolside and it came with a small side order of hangover—not one of those that stays around until four p.m. the next day, just the type that lets you know that you came close to making a mistake. It would not have been a good day to have a skull-splitting hangover, because Cindy wanted us all to take a longboat trip through the waterways of Bangkok in search of a specific Buddhist temple that she wanted to show us. Like I said, this was our tourist day. So we left the camera gear at the hotel and went out to have fun.

Longboats, if you have never seen them, are these very narrow, very long, wooden boats the Thai people use for transportation, commerce, tourism and about anything else that you can think of. The most easily recognizable feature on a longboat is the engine. They usually have a V-6 or V-8 gas carbureted car motor.

Instead of doing something sensible, like putting the in the boat, somewhere in the past, a creative individual came up with the idea of perching the car engine over the rear of the vessel, something like you might attach an outboard boat motor. The heavy engine is haphazardly fixed on a frame that extends up from the stern of the boat, so that it seems to almost hover in the air. The exhaust pipes, if any at all, are cut down so that they are no longer than the size of the engine block. As a counterweight to the four-hundred-pound engine, a twenty-foot-long shaft extends from the full-sized transmission drive and is armed with a dinged-up propeller at the far end. It's actually hard to describe this in writing. The driver stands or sits at the front of the engine and uses a single twist throttle to propel this rocket of a boat down the narrow back canals at ludicrous speeds. The best image that I can come up with is to think of an old canoe with an industrial weed whacker mounted on the back, and with a boat propeller set where the spool of line should be. Now imagine trying to drive ten of these canoes in an average size drainage ditch, at forty mines per hour and in both directions, sometimes making contact as you pass. Increase the size of each boat until it's large enough the hold about ten large adults and then you might start to get an idea. To turn these suicide crafts, the drivers would push down on the handle where the throttle was as if it were an oar, sending the spinning blade on the end out of the water and perilously towards whatever may be within the propeller's reach. There has to be a Thai population statistic that deals with body trauma due to getting mauled by preoccupied Longboat drivers.

This gave me a chance to cross something off my bucket list. I have dreamed of taking a longboat ride since the first time I saw the chase scene in the James Bond movie *The Man With The Golden Gun*. Of course, to one-up my own bucket list, and make it even closer to a James Bond movie, I took my fantasy boat ride complete with armed secret service members and a political celebrity. Yes, my tourist day was off to a great start and it kept getting better.

The rest of the day consisted of a bit more relaxing around the pool and, later that evening, our fun little tourist group was booked on a riverboat dinner tour. This boat was obviously much larger than the longboats and stuck to the main portion of the Chao Phraya River, which winds through central Bangkok, splitting the town, and housing most of the exclusive hotels and skyscrapers near its banks. Competing with the amazing day boat trip, the dinner excursion kept us on our toes and continually laughing. One point in particular was right out of a *National Lampoon* vacation movie.

As we sat on the top deck drinking and listening to an entertainer who sounded like— and slightly resembled—the famous Hawaiian singer, Don Ho, John and I couldn't help but notice that our vessel was approaching a very large, but very low bridge that spanned the width of the river. The guy was facing us, still singing and with the bridge to his back; we couldn't believe what we thought was about to happen. At the last minute before we went under the bridge, two guys appeared from the lower deck of the boat and started lowering anything that was taller than about five feet. This included the karaoke style speakers which were on stands, a few lamps and even some items that were on the tables where we were seated. Then they left without ever announcing that we all might want to duck. The singer never lost a beat as he continued a rendition of Elvis's *Fools Rush In* while bending at the waist to avoid being struck in the head by one of the rusty beams of the bridge's understructure. All joking aside, the top rail of the boat cleared the bridge by less than two feet. This caused everyone on the top deck, including a possible US president's wife, her daughter and half of her staff, to follow our entertainer's example and duck to avoid head trauma. This was some hilarious shit. Then, to our amazement, about a half mile past the bridge, the dinner cruise turned around and came back, repeating the same process but with even less clearance room because of the still rising tidewater. This was a great start to a very memorable evening, which included drinks at Skybar, one of the highest rooftop bars in the world, located on the sixty-first floor of the hotel Lebua at State Tower, Bangkok, and finishing up with a return ride to our hotel crammed in the back of a high-speed wheelie popping, three-wheeled motorcycle cab driven by a fifteen-year-old who thought he was Thailand's version of Evil Knievel and Jackie Chan combined. We all needed that night, because the next morning had us, once again, up at the ass-crack of daylight, bags in hand, being escorted back to the airport and soon en route to the next country, which turned out to be the most emotional draining portion of the entire Asia tour.

ASIA TOUR, CAMBODIA, 2008
WORLD FOOD PROGRAM

STEPPING BACK IN TIME

WITH BANGKOK BEHIND US, we bounced into Siem Reap for a quick change of planes and then we were back in the air for a thirty-minute flight into Phnom Pen, the capital city of Cambodia. Our hotel at this location rivaled the rest but had even more history.

The Raffles Hotel Le Royal in Phnom Pen was built in the year 1929. It was carefully restored and reopened in 1997, with modern upgrades, but the décor was kept the same to showcase the original. old-world charm. Historically Raffles was a regular destination for jet setters such as Charlie Chaplin and Jackie O. and, between 1970 and 1975, most journalists working to cover the rise of the Khmer Rouge, along with local dignitaries, found it a safe place to establish a base. For John and me it was like stepping back in time. Sleeping in the same rooms as the Associated Press had during the time of conflict somehow gave even more relevance to what we were doing now.

Later that evening, we met in the lounge for some bar food and discussed the plans for the next day. As we started to talk Wendy slipped me a piece of paper that read, "Watch what you say, we believe the rooms are bugged." That just added to my James Bond mentality. I had thought the cold war spy shit was over, but I was mistaken. It was cool though.

We started early, of course, with a quick breakfast, and we arrived to find Cindy McCain sitting on the floor packing brown bag lunches for the rest of the group. Then came a head count before we loaded up into what appeared to be Cambodia's version of a Land Rover and hit the road.

The first stop on itinerary was a children's school founded by an NGO called For A Child's Smile and aided by the local branch of the World Food Program Cambodia. From there our destination would be one of the largest landfills in Phnom Pehn, where thousands of families lived and scavenged through garbage to survive. Finally, we would tour a children's AIDS village that was created and still run by a Vietnam veteran who, after serving in the conflict, stayed to help the locals who had been displaced by the fighting. It was a lot to take in on a one-day trip and we would barely have enough time to emotionally engage with each location before moving on to the next. John and I would have to spend more time focusing on the shots that we were filming, rather than the unreal images of poverty and famine presented at every turn, but the faces and scenes we filmed that day are now, and forever will be permanently, etched into our minds.

The drive started out on the crowded roads of downtown Phnom Pehn, loaded with bicycles, child trafficking and organized crime, but soon led to the quiet, picturesque countryside of rural Cambodia. With its rice fields, bamboo village huts and water buffalo still being used to plow the fields, it appeared that time stood still here. Had we not been passed by an occasional modern car, I could have easily believed we'd stepped back into the peaceful past—long before the rise of Pol Pot, and the attempted genocide of the Cambodian people at the hands of his Khmer Rouge forces.

POUR UN SOURIRE D'ENFANT, FOR A CHILD'S SMILE

After an hour on the road, we reached our first stop. Before I tell you about what John and I experienced here, I have to explain the situation that brought this organization here to Cambodia.

For a Child's Smile is the London-based fundraising arm of Pour un Sourire d'Enfant, which is a non-governmental organization created in 1996 by Christian and Marie-France des Pallieres. This NGO, which is nonpolitical and non-denominational, works largely in Phnom Penh, Cambodia. Its objective is to care for and educate the city's poorest children, as well as those living in the local landfill.

What we were visiting was like an enormous day care center that helped to pull children out of the local dumpsite. The facility saw and fed as many six thousand children every day. Let's just start with that number—six thousand children, many without families, most of them homeless and living in the dump, all extremely malnourished and in desperate need of medical attention. From what I have read, the average primary school enrollment in Washington DC is about four hundred students. Do the math. It would take 15 primary schools to serve six thousand students. This means that fifteen American primary schools' worth of children were pulled out of the dumps and fed every day by this one humanitarian-based organization. The number is almost hard to comprehend, until you walk amid these beautiful children. John and I have.

Upon arriving, we met up with Thomas Keuster, the current Cambodia Country Director for the World Food Program. With much to see, Thomas wasted no time in throwing us right into organized chaos. Our visit was planned around the morning breakfast and exercise time for the children, just before they went off to classes. Not only did this facility feed these children, it gave them a place to bathe, to receive some dental care and corrective vision treatment (through used and donated prescription glasses), and provided medicine and nutritional screenings. There was also an exercise program and a chance to get a basic education and some trade skills, like serving food, sewing, gardening, and cosmetology.

The horrendous fact is that a child can make one US dollar per day scrounging for scraps of plastic in the dumpsite. This single dollar is the reason that many of the children's families won't allow them to leave the dump to attend the school. To help with this problem the World Food Program started paying the families with rice. For each child they allowed to leave the dump and attend the facility, they would get a pound of rice or chickpeas. Since these are both staples of their diet and valuable commodities for trade, families have warmed up to the idea and now children come by the thousands.

Walking through the compound, the first thing that you notice is the children are all wearing blue and white uniforms and that they are segregated—boys on one side and girls on another. The uniforms give the children a sense of pride and, because of the large range of ages, the segregation helps with safety. I can only imagine that it also allows the children to focus more on the education without the distractions of young hormones running wild. Thomas took us through the girl's side first. As we approached, there was a line of young women washing up in large, dented aluminum bowls filled with water. In an orderly fashion, each girl would walk down the line to an empty bowl, first wetting her hands then using soap to rid them contamination from the landfill. She would rinse and then dry her hands on a towel hung at the end of the wash basin line. From there each girl would walk over to a large serving window at the kitchen where she received a full bowl of rice, a small piece of fish and, on this day, a very large pickle. There was also all the clean, disease-free water they could drink.

Cindy wanted to spend some time with the young women, so, with the assistance of our interpreter, we mingled with the children as they sat at wooden picnic tables and ate their meal. There was one particularly beautiful young girl who grabbed Cindy's attention, and, with the girl's permission, Cindy sat next to her and struck up a conversation. She has an amazing way of making people feel safe when they are in her presence, especially children. She will be the first to get down on the floor to play with youngsters and I have never known another person so quick to gravitate toward crying babies to comfort them. This young woman told Cindy that she lived with her parents in the dump and that she enjoyed coming to the school when her family would let her. The shy girl spoke very softly, and, because of this atten-tion, the girls who sat around her would all break into infectious giggles whenever the young woman bravely responded to Cindy's questions. Upon noticing that the girl had not eaten everything she was given, Thomas explained that the children would often only eat half the food and take the rest back to their families. He also told us that, because so much of their diet was made up of bland unseasoned rice, the children would often save the protein items like fish and chicken, wrapping the well-cooked meat up and putting it in their pocket to be used later. Used being the key word here, not eaten. Later, the children would unwrap the meat and smell it while they ate more rice, often passing it around for their families to also use in the same manner. The goal was to fool the senses into thinking the rice had some kind of flavor. My guess is that this would be the opposite of holding your nose when you eat something with a flavor that you don't find appealing.

A crackling loudspeaker produced an announcement that caused many of the kids to quickly finish their meal and hurry to the courtyard just on the other side of a makeshift bamboo fence. Time for class? Call to worship? I didn't know what in the hell it was but it seemed to be creating some excitement. A few more words came through the speaker in a very high-pitched Khmer sounding language, and then, like a strange tribute to Eddie Murphy, the song *Axel F* from the *Beverly Hills Cop* soundtrack started to blare over the squawky speakers throughout the girl's side of the courtyard. Surprised as hell and still with no clue of what was going on, our little tour group took a pause to stare at each other blankly—like one of us was going to pop up with the answer to this oddity. Investigation ensued. One by one, we curiously ventured around the bamboo fence to find maybe a hundred young girls standing in neatly organized, single file lines, using their arms to distance themselves from each other to create a space large enough to do dance aerobics. Yes, I said dance aerobics. Again, the wonders of international travel had presented me with a sight to behold. In the front of the aerobics class stood a young girl with a well-used microphone who called out the out dance moves in Khmer, and she was nicely controlling the entire group of girls into one uniformed, flowing movement. These girls were right on the money and they all looked like they were really enjoying the exercise. Cindy loved it, and with a smile on her face a mile wide, she weaved in and out of the dancing girls, delighted at what she was witnessing. Thomas explained that this was all a part of the structured lessons within the school. "These children," he said, "spend so much of their lives in unhappiness and working in appalling, almost slave-like conditions that the simple act of dancing with their peers allow them to laugh and to act like children again, even if only for a short time." As we smiled at the site of the girls dancing, Thomas's words had us all fighting back tears. Once more, John and I were riding the emotional roller coaster that went hand-in-hand with filming these global NGOs.

Then, almost like he had saved the best part, Thomas said, "Would you like to see the boys?"

"Of course," we all nodded, speaking in unison and enthralled with these new visions. We followed him down a small walkway and through a fence that opened up to an even larger courtyard. Here we found quite a different environment from that we had seen only moments before with the young women.

The boys' exercise area looked like a mosh pit full of rabid wolverines at a punk rock concert. Close to a thousand shirtless, adolescent boys were moving in every direction on the compass, arms flailing wildly, punching into the air, legs kicking and jumping around. Not one of the boys in the throng could keep the beat of the music that was playing. At this moment, I understood why the school kept the boys away from the girls. They would have accidentally mangled the delicate, well-mannered young girls during morning exercises. How would that look on the records? Little Li survived ten years in the dump only to be rescued, and then accidentally pummeled by the wayward foot placement of a small boy emulating Bruce Lee. I was surprised they weren't knocking themselves out the way they were dancing. Thomas's words on poverty had us all tearing up with heartbreak up a few moments before. The sight of this flash mob of uncoordinated young men trying to do their morning workout caused us all to tear up with suppressed laughter.

Continuing on, we visited the infirmary where volunteer doctors were keeping up with the wellbeing of some of the children. One happy little girl was reading an eye chart as we walked in, so that she could be fitted with a pair of donated glasses. Behind the medical building was the nursery, where the youngest children and some infants were being cared for. And, in typical fashion, it only took Cindy a second to pick out an upset baby to hold and comfort.

The raising of the Cambodian flag and singing of the national anthem was the last daily morning activity to take place before the children found their way to their classes. With all the children in one location and well attentive, Thomas suggested that this would be the perfect time for Cindy to address the children. It was staggering to see the number of children standing in the open courtyard; to call it a sea of bodies would not be an exaggeration. This was our first view of the children, absent of the boy/girl segregation, and there were thousands, all in their blue and white uniforms, with tan skin and jet-black hair, evenly spaced apart, standing in silence. It was as if an army of child soldiers were standing in front of us, preparing to salute the flag and then march into war—minus the guns, thank God. As Cindy raised the microphone to address the congregation, I ran up the stairs of a building just behind her to film from the second-floor balcony. My hope was to get the entire courtyard of kids in the shot but even from my elevated advantage, I still could not get a wide enough field of view for the whole mass. As I filmed, Cindy talked about how honored she was to be in the presence of such brave children, how inspiring their story was and how happy she was to be able to call them all her friends. I moved from my perch and was now on the ground, grabbing some closer shots while wandering through kids as Cindy finished speaking. The microphone was handed back to a school elder and the Cambodian flag was attached to the rigging on the makeshift flagpole. The flag began to rise, and the children began to sing. The surprising sound that rose from the children was soft, angelic and unexpected. The sounds of thousands of juvenile voices blended, creating an ethereal choir-like resonance. We all became as still as the air at that moment, and we listened. The chanting faded as the flag reached its apex; there was a lengthy pause, followed by an audible command, and then the perfect lines of children became a frenzied swarm of noise and movement. Like ants when their hill is disturbed, the children moved in every direction at once, trying to get to their assigned schoolrooms. As we again followed Thomas through the chaos, I witnessed something that still chokes me up when I try to talk about it.

A child collapsed to the ground moments after we passed the group with which he was standing and other children ran to their fallen classmate, comforting him as he lay there on the damp morning earth in front of the school building. As the event unfolded Cindy looked at Thomas and inquisitively asked, "Heat exhaustion?"

His response came in only two words and was accompanied by a look that penetrated right through us and ended at the child on the ground. "No, starvation," Thomas said. In his voice was the exhaustion of man who had witnessed this so many times that he became numb to it. But this was the first time that I had ever personally seen the extreme effect of famine on a child. It is a haunting memory.

Roller coaster time again. After that emotionally draining incident, we then were treated to a lunch at the trade school's teaching restaurant. Here we were instructed to act as if we were real patrons and to let the soon-to-be waiters and hosts practice the skills that they would one day take with them into the real world. When you were raised in a dump, waiting tables in an actual restaurant is a glorious career opportunity. It was another humbling experience. Children took their turns serving food, humorously refilling our water glasses after each sip we took and carefully serving after-lunch coffees, trying their best not to spill the scalding liquid in our laps. They were all excited, by this chance to serve a meal to a group of real, live Americans. They were also nervous, and to add to their nerves, their teachers followed them around like hawks, pointing out any flaws in their serving skills and even correcting their placement of eating utensils. Their commitment to attention and detail was adorable, and I believe some of them could teach a thing or two about politeness to some servers I have had in the states.

CHILDREN OF THE LANDFILL

Our second stop for the day was the most disturbing to see, but it was the most necessary. To truly understand just how the children that we saw at the For a Child's Smile facility lived from day to day, we had to visit the place they called home, the Steung Meanchey landfill in Phnom Pen.

In the United States, we have this thing called environmental regulations. Hazardous waste cannot be disposed of in our land-fills and in order to discard bio-hazardous medical waste from hospitals, possibly containing infectious diseases, special protocols must be followed.

My own father would often take me to our local dump when I was a child. It was an adventure. We would pile up the old truck as high as we could with the rubbish and junk that he had collected, and then we would take the dirt roads to a hidden location that housed the dump, a mysterious place containing mounds of junk that others threw out. The mounds seemed to sprawl on. We would pull up to a small toll booth where the dump manager would eyeball the contents of the truck bed and then randomly pull a number from his head to charge my father to enter, but only after circling the truck a couple of times to see if there was anything back there that he personally wanted. He got the best of the best junk. As a young boy I would often tell my dad that I would like to have that job when I grew up. Then we would drive up the foothills of garbage, trying to stay on the most packed down paths to not get stuck, until my father found the perfect location to add our haul to the ever-expanding mountain of refuse. I would then jump out and wander around, marveling at the treasures that one mere kick of the foot could reveal. We always came back with new junk that either my father or I would discover and decide that we needed back home. I had some great childhood memories that came from exploring the dump, but this was different. Cambodia's dump left me with images quite different from those from my childhood.

We were told to be prepared for the odor and for the flies. The odor was how I imagined it would be. Wet, putrefied smells clung in the hot stagnant air and mixed with the methane that was rising from deep below the surface. Yes, it would take your breath away if you inhaled when a breeze kicked up. The flies, however, were more than I anticipated. Because of the constantly rotting debris, and a mere four-day gestation period for common flies, this was an ongoing insect breading cycle, and these were big flies. House fly on steroids big. If you stood in one spot long enough you would have a thousand or so swarming around your head.

Our caravan of well-equipped Land Rovers slipped and fought its way up the slimy entrance to the Steung Meanchey landfill and parked as directed in an area that would support the weight of our vehicles. Stepping out onto the ground, we were also given special instructions on where not to go and what areas were safe to walk on. Ground collapse was an ongoing problem that those living in the landfill had to deal with every day, a problem that often ended with tragic results. Garbage rots. It breaks down under pressure and heat, and this causes gaping fissures to open beneath the surface. As horrific as it may be to imagine, adults, children and entire families are sometimes sucked down in these collapsing sinkholes of garbage, where they die an unimaginable death. You can't climb back out, because the garbage just keeps falling on you as you try and it's so loud around that no one can hear you scream for help. Eventually, your body becomes entombed and you become a part of the landfill. Countless things kill the people living here: methane builds up from pressure and decay causing explosions; diseases like cholera, tetanus, hepatitis, and typhoid infect people daily; and children running to the trucks dumping fresh garbage sometimes get backed over as they try to be the first to salvage the newest trash for food and valuable plastics. Still, with all these dangers, homeless families choose to live here, making houses from the garbage, instead of wandering the streets alone. Maybe here, among others suffering the same existence, they find community in their common bond.

With the secret service team stationed all around for safety, John and I followed the guides from the World Food Program as they led Cindy down one of the trails heading deeper into the landfill. I had attached a wireless lavaliere microphone to Cindy, and our goal was to get some good audio as she went in search of some children to talk to. That is exactly what happened.

Continuing deeper into the heart of the dump, our guide led us past a crude concession stand that was run by people living in the dump, past a piece of heavy earth moving machinery, then to a cove where people were aggressively rummaging through steaming garbage, hoping to find stashes of sellable trash. As I approached a woman just off the pathway, I noticed that she had just exposed a bag containing rice that had probably been thrown out by a local restaurant. Carefully she opened the bag and removed only the rice from the center of the mound, leaving that which was in contact with the sides of the bag still resting in the landfill. Once the woman had what she wanted, she took the rice up to the makeshift food stand to be sold to the inhabitants living in the dump. Even here, a cycle of consumer sales existed.

Cindy focused on a small girl about ten years old and approached her cautiously. Because of the high rate of child trafficking for sex slaves in Cambodia, some of the children were wary of our group, while parents pulled other children back, but this particular young woman bravely agreed to speak with Cindy through the World Food Programs interpreter. She told us her name, how old she was and that she lived in the dump with her family. She sometimes attended the sponsored school we toured earlier but was needed by her parents to work this day. I had never seen Cindy visibly shaken, but the events of the day were mounting on all of us, including her, and it was obvious to me that the masses of neglected children were tugging at her emotions. Even though our tour to the dump was short, compounded with the morning visit to the school we all needed a break.

"Back to the vehicles," yelled one of the secret service

personal, signaling that our time in the landfill had ended. John and I held out to the last minute so we could continue filming as much as possible. This usually got me yelled at by someone from security, but it was always worth it—especially this time.

My stalling yielded an amazing shot. As we approached the area where we had parked the vehicles, we also walked nearer to the location in which many people chose to fabricate their garbage homes. Near there, I spotted a small girl with a somber look on her face sitting on a large bag of plastic scraps. In her hand was a small piece of twine that she continuously twisted around her index finger. Her concentration on her own actions was so focused that she seemed to be mesmerized by the movement of the twine in her hand, and she paid no attention to us. Noticing that our group was getting closer, a woman behind the small girl, probably her mother, grabbed her by her left arm and forcefully stood her to attention, pushing her our way at if she was presenting the girl to be bought. All the while, the girl maintained the same emotionless expression and continued to escape reality by focusing on the twine in her hand. Even when one of the secret service members approached her to offer her a piece of candy, the young girl refused to make eye contact, keeping her head down, emotionless. I will never know the fate of that little girl, but in my heart, I hope she has escaped living amongst the trash, as if she herself had been thrown away. I hope she and the other children we met that day have been given a chance for something better.

On our drive out, the atmosphere inside the Land Rovers was motionless and full of thought. Maybe it was that we were all trying not to think. I was deeply focused on the scene we had just left. Maybe it's because John and I look at everything through a lens; I think the images are burned into our subconscious more deeply than happens to the people who are just visiting these places, looking upon them with their naked eyes. Quietly, we drove away, away from the smells, away from the flies and the faces, headed to the last stop for the day, which would shine some light on the glum emotional state left upon us by the dumpsite. Though I can't remember the name of the last facility, or the gentleman who ran it, he was doing an amazing thing with little-to-no outside assistance.

He was a Vietnam veteran who went to Cambodia after serving in the war. He opened up an AIDS village for children suffering with the disease and for the surviving children of parents that died from AIDS. His village worked off of grants and donations and was set up to be very self-sufficient, right down to the chicken coops positioned over the fishponds. Feeding the chickens meant feeding the fish from their droppings. Children and families tended the rice and other vegetable families. school was held and there was a medical facility where volunteer medical help world came from time to time to offer checkups. Compared to the landfill, this was Shangri-La. His numbers were much smaller than the World Food Program-supported facility that we toured on our first stop of the day, maybe a hundred or so, but the children all seemed to be in good health and great emotional spirits. As this was an AIDS village, it was far out into the rural countryside of Cambodia. Death was an ever-present issue with this disease, so the village had constructed its own incinerator to discard of bodies. They had also created a shrine in which the ashes of those who once lived there were kept after they passed away. This information would have created yet another gloomy memory were it not for all the adorable, smiling kids running all over the place. The finale of our day was a singing presentation put on for Cindy and the rest of us by the children of the village. While the Cambodian anthem, sung in the morning with the raising of the flag, struck us with awe, this children's presentation lightened our spirits and allowed us all to laugh and breathe a sigh of relief. This was the perfect ending to our emotional roller-coaster ride that day. Smiles and joyous release now filled the vehicles as we made our way back to Raffles for our last night in Cambodia. It's a damn good thing the day had been laid out the way it was, or you might have been looking at a group of depressed fools who wanted nothing more than to escape the day's events in the Raffles bar. Don't get me wrong, we still headed right for the bar, but it was to celebrate the last evening of an amazing journey, not to crawl into a tequila bottle to forget.

Thomas from the WFP came to hang out and join us for a beer. He brought John and I a couple of the real classy white-collared WFP staff shirts that I asked about earlier in the trip, and from time-to -time, others would meander in and out of the bar, taking breaks from packing and readying for the next morning's long flights out of Asia and back to the states. Come to think about it, I believe Frank La Rose still owes John a half-yard of beer and a plate of nachos from that night.

SOMEWHERE OVER CHINA

Thank God Cindy's travel agent has a heart and didn't schedule us on the first redeye flight out of Phnom Pehn that next morning. We needed the extra sleep and all our mental faculties to prepare for the ridiculous flights that were about to happen. Nobody, especially not John or I, could have foreseen the predicament we narrowly talked our way out of later that day, somewhere in the heart of communist China.

With goodbyes, hugs and handshakes out of the way, we mounted our Rover for the last time and headed to the Phnom Pehn airport—without the secret service, without our point man,

Frank LaRose, without anyone that even spoke English. Once again, John and I were just ordinary world travelers. Let me state for the record that when you spend over a week traveling with all the special privileges of a dignitary, you start to feel like one— like your shit doesn't stink, and you can kind of do whatever you want. Because you really can do whatever you want. You can zip through lines, leave your bags unattended, skip the checkpoints and get a private escort to the plane, It's amazing. Then, when all this luxury is removed from the traveling process, the reality of airport etiquette kicks you in the balls so swift and fast that it will make your head spin as you cough them up. It fucking sucks, and it all started as we were standing in the heat at a ticket window in front of Phnom Pehn International Airport.

Feeling a bit like Mr. Know-It-All, I completely blew off what the young Cambodian woman was trying to tell us as we tried to check in for our flight. I mean, how could she, a simple airport worker with access to an updated flight schedule and a modern computer, know more than two guys that had just finished a tour with a possible first lady of the United States of America. We had our paper tickets and we were getting on that flight to Beijing. That was our next stop on the journey back home. Phnom Pehn to Beijing, Beijing to DC. How hard could that be, right? The young counter representative kept saying something in broken English about some problem in Beijing, but I was in a bit of a time crunch and just kept replying that we would figure out the issue when we landed in Beijing. Cindy's travel agent had booked our tickets, so I was confident that any issue we ran into would be minimal at most. After a few minutes the young woman gave us a look that said, "Here, dumbass, you think you're so smart? Get on the plane." So, we did just that. We paid our exit visa and headed to the terminal to board the flight. Within a matter of minutes,

John and I were sitting in our seats with a bit of smug satisfaction and cold beer in our hand. As the wheels rose from the tarmac, we settled in for our nearly five-hour flight from Phnom Pehn to Beijing. Had either of us spoken Chinese we would have known exactly what was about to happen.

I was almost asleep when, about forty-five minutes into the flight, we both were roused by the unmistakable sounds of a large aircraft preparing for a landing. With the sensation of descent apparent and all the announcements still in Chinese, we could do little more than sit and stare at each other in confusion. We both knew that we were nowhere close to Beijing and probably landing somewhere in the heart of Communist China, but just where our wheels would be touching down was still a complete enigma. As the plane taxied up to the terminal John and I realized that, want to or not, we were now getting off the aircraft.

DETENTION ROOM DILEMMAS, THIS IS NOT BEIJING

Entering the terminal, the first thing I saw which made me realize the extent of our situation were the full body scanners that checked for yellow fever, an ever-present problem in rural China. Clearing the health station, we walked up to the lines forming at the immigration counters. John and I were separated by a couple of rows and, at almost the same time, we reached the counters. We thought we were just changing aircraft, and, at the immigration checkpoint, the attendant was just going to look at our passports and direct us to our connecting flight to Beijing. Imagine our surprise when we were both pulled from the lines because we didn't have the proper visa stamped on our passports to gain access to China. Then we were both escorted to a small detention room, just off the main concourse. This can, and will, make your sphincter pucker a bit, especially when the country is Red China.

The room was small, about ten feet by ten feet, with a couch on one side and a few posters on the walls. Of course, all were written in Chinese. As John and I sat there I remember him looking at me with a very serious expression and saying, "Dude, this is how people disappear." His head was probably in the right state of mind, but I was thinking that it couldn't be that serious. Surely a bit of tourist stupidity could help us talk our way back to the plane bound for Beijing, which at the moment was still waiting for us and boarding. I figured that, in case someone came in to take away our phone, I would do my best to get a message out. Thank God I had a Blackberry with an international plan. If you travel internationally it's a necessity."

I shot a slightly alarmed text to Cindy that read something like, "We are held up in an immigration detention room in a town in China that I can't pronounce."

Within a split second my phone buzzed with a response from Cindy. "Have you been strip searched be any Chinese midgets?" is what her text read. I showed the text to John and he tried his best to smile at me through his mild anxiety. If her goal was to get us to relax a bit, she succeeded. My phone vibrated again.

"Where exactly are you? Would you like me to send the secret service to come get you?" If her first message relaxed me, the second one empowered me to try to figure a way out without assistance. We searched the posters on the wall and John spelled off what we thought was the name of the city in which the plane had landed. I sent one last text back.

"I believe we are in a town called Guangzhou. Let me see if I can get us out of this. If you don't hear back from me in an hour, we might need help."

Now all the while this was going on, Chinese men in military looking uniforms would randomly step into the room and look at us. I would smile back. They would scowl, while shaking their head from side to side, then leave. Each time this happened the person who entered the room seemed to have more medals and badges on their uniforms and it seemed to me that they were just as confused as we were by what was going on, because occasionally, in broken English, one would say, "Where is your visa?"

To which we would reply, "What visa? We are supposed to be in Beijing International Airport." It was quite comical, and happened so many times that, eventually, all I would say was the word "Beijing. I would then smile and point to the ground.

Finally, a younger man who obviously worked for the airline and not immigration entered the room with a person I could only imagine was a Chinese commander of some sort, due to the weight of pins on his lapel. The two rattled off something back and forth in an unrecognizable language and then the young gentleman asked, in English, how we managed to get to Guangzhou without the proper documentation. He added something about this being taken care of in Phnom Pehn. Oh, that's what the young counter girl in Cambodia was trying to tell me as I was being a total douche.

"I have no idea; I don't even know where we are. Our flight was scheduled to land in Beijing," I told him, as I pulled out my well-used copy of our itinerary, which was unevenly folded up and stored in my camera bag, and handed it to him. He and the commander squawked back and forth for a bit as he was pointing at the withered piece of paper and then he said, "May I take this for a moment?" What was I going to say?

"No, you can't have my itinerary." They had already confiscated our passports, and at least he asked nicely for this. The door was shut leaving us alone again in the room but we were starting to feel like we were making headway. Within just a few moments the young man came back in and said, "Would you kindly follow me,"

John and I cautiously got up and did as instructed. We were led past the immigration area and toward the direction of the terminals, where he stopped at a desk, opened our passports and stamped each with a one-day visa for China. We still had no idea what the hell was going on, nor would we find out until we finally made it across the country to the Beijing International Airport, but we were getting closer, so we just smiled and agreed with whatever he said. Our newly stamped passports were handed back to us and we were then escorted to the baggage screening area where our young friend shook our hands, smiled and walked away.

Communist countries are very suspicious of Americans being where they shouldn't be, especially when you're traveling with filming equipment, and, of course, our bags were loaded to the brim with camera, film, tapes, electronic gear, and microphones. This stuff lit up the screen on the X-ray machine flagging us for scrutiny and we were once again hit with a barrage of questions.

"What are you filming," the guard asked with a very authoritarian tone to his voice?

I quickly replied, "We have been in Cambodia filming the temples." If anyone had known that we were filming something even remotely political for the US, we would have ended up spending much more time in the little ten-by ten-room being questioned.

"Please wait here while I get my superior," said our new security guard friend. We looked at each other and John said, "Shit, here we go again."

Then by a streak of luck, just as the X-ray guard walked away to fetch his boss, a flight attendant from the plane that we were supposed to be on that very minute came jogging around the corner. His English was much better and, as he realized what was going on, he said, "Grab your bags and run, we are about to take off,"

"What about the security guy?" I said back to him. With an almost sheepish expression he said, "Follow me and run!" We did. We ran, and we never looked back to see if anyone was chasing us. We hauled ass all the way to the plane. The jets were fully powered up and I could've sworn the boarding ramp was moving back as we ran down it. We didn't stop to breathe until we had our butts planted firmly in the seats. Then, like any good stuntman would be, after a tense predicament, we were hit with that rush of adrenalin that made us laugh out loud, and want something that contained alcohol real, real bad.

Oh, how I would love to say that our challenging predicament ended right there with John and I drinking our way to Beijing International, but that would be too much to ask for.

The flight from Guangzhou to Beijing was quite pleasant— great food, free beer, and sexy female attendants. When we got to our seats, I let Cindy know we were fine and on our way All was well in world. Then, about two and a half hours later, we make it to Beijing. But not the new international Beijing Airport, Note my use of the word "new." Oh hell, no! John and I landed at the old international airport location that was now the Beijing domestic airport.

This would be a great time for me to explain exactly what was going on. The 2008 Olympic summer games were to be held in Beijing a few months after our little adventure. One of the many new construction projects going on was a massive, largest-I-have-ever-seen, new international hub to the Beijing Airport. This was to be used to handle the insane amounts of air traffic associated with the 2008 summer games. Instead of building this new structure near to the existing airport, the Chinese decided it would look much nicer at the complete opposite end of the city, leaving the old airport to handle domestic, in-country flights. This meant that from the moment our flight landed in Guangzhou we were now flying into a domestic, not an international, airport in Beijing. The new international facility was built so far away that we needed a one-day visa to enter the country of China just to catch a bus to it. And it would not a transport shuttle but a real number five, downtown Chinese bus. This is why we were pulled out of the immigration line. This is why we were questioned. This is why they were so interested in what we were filming, and this is why we were nearly stuck in Guangzhou. It was all because the Chinese built a new terminal for the 2008 Olympic games in Beijing.

When the wheels touched down, John and I still thought that we were landing at Beijing International. So, when the door opened and we walked down the stairs, we were kind of shocked that a major airport like Beijing would have passengers exit and walk about a quarter mile around the terminal, with only a crudely constructed chain-link fence to separate passengers from the runway. It was hot, loud, the smell of fuel pumping through jet turbines burned my nostrils and I felt the exhaust from the jets as they taxied around. Like cattle led to slaughter, John and I followed the people in front of us to finally reach the door and enter the terminal building. We still thought that this was where we needed to be to catch our flight to DC. But it didn't take long for us both to realize that something was not quite right with our current situation. First, we were the only Americans around. Hell, we were the only non-Chinese people in the entire building. Second, there was nothing written in English—no bathroom sign, no exit signs, nothing. English signs are posted everywhere in international airports. No matter where we have traveled, our language was posted somewhere. But not here. So, you have two round-eyes standing in a Chinese domestic airport, next to a few luggage belts revolving around and spitting out travel bags on the floor, and not an English-speaking person to be found. Somehow, with luck I guess, we managed to spot our bags circling on one of the belts, which again made us believe we were at the right terminal, but still there were no signs to direct us to our next flight to Dulles, and no matter how hard I tried, nobody could answer me in English. The situation was about to give both of us a migraine when I had a brain flash. Looking down to the end of the room, I saw a sign with the English words, "Lost Luggage," and made a beeline for the door.

I startling the workers on the other side of the door by bursting in and saying, "Please tell me someone in here speaks English." To our pleasant surprise, over half the room of young Chinese attendants answered, "Yes," in unison and in our beautiful native tongue. Relief flowed through my veins, and I could see John's expression perk up a notch as the group of youths working in the lost luggage room all headed our way to practice their English. When we explained our current situation to them, the room all agreed that we were at the completely wrong airport and quickly aimed us in the direction of the terminals main entrance where we would find our bus. We thanked each one of them with a simultaneous bow and handshake and made our way outside to find the city bus that we would have to take through the heart of downtown Beijing to the newly constructed International Airport on the other side of the city. It was at this point, while riding on the bus, that all the pieces of the puzzle finally fit together.

We were in China, not the airport but in Beijing. At any

of the bus's stops John and I could have gotten off and used our one-day visa to explore. We had managed to talk our way into a communist country. Mostly by accident, but we still did it. One other thing was making itself clear to us during our bus ride; that was why China didn't want international cameras around filming the pre-Olympic turmoil that was becoming extremely obvious with each mile we drove. Only months away from the opening ceremonies Beijing was in utter disarray. The air pollution was so bad that the government had implemented rules that cars could only be driven every other day, and people were being forced to abandon their homes. The land was being turned into a forest of fast-food franchise restaurants for tourist dollars. Nothing was completed. Welding sparks fell through the haze from buildings and from elevated roadway surfaces. Families and children manicured the grass alongside the highways like slave laborers, some only equipped with handheld shears or scissors. Full-sized trees, some as tall as thirty feet, were being hand carried in wheel barrels and set into holes in the sidewalk to give the illusion that they had been growing there for years. Beijing was under a huge time crunch, with a lot to finish up, and, having seen it with my own eyes, I still can't believe they pulled it off. The only building that seemed to be completely functioning was the new international terminal and it is still the most amazing structure that I have ever stood inside.

Resembling a chromed geodesic turtle shell, the inside of the open-air concourse could have easily contained five football fields. What made it so astonishing is that there were no vertical support structures to be seen. This was truly an engineering marvel, and if it doesn't collapse under its own weight in the future, it should, if you ask me, make the list as one of the Seven Wonders of the Modern World. Dwarfed by the inner expanse of the building, we made our way to the ticket counter to check in our luggage. Here we entered a near euphoric state when we were informed by the cute Asian flight attendant that our twenty-hour flight to Dulles airport was so under booked that we had the entire rear section of a 747-jumbo jet to ourselves. That flight back was the best flight of my life and absolutely made up for the rough start across the country of China. I sprawled comfortably across an entire row of seats, with the one Vicodin I had saved and a glass of red wine to make me sleepy. This Asian adventure couldn't have ended any better.

TIME TO REFLECT FOR A BIT

July came upon us fast and so did the date that John had set for his ACL surgery. This gave him a whole lot of down time to both recover and to edit quite a few segments for Cindy's section on the campaign website. I continued to pick up some stunt jobs, mostly on *Burn Notice* which was filming in Miami, and I started back up at the *Fear Factor Live* show at Universal as a day job. Most of our free time was spent at the computers, organizing videos and photos and working of our website.

Everything was still moving so fast. John and I really never had the time to stop and think about where we were taking the Karma 180 Productions platform, It was creating itself without even asking for our input. So this was a time for us to step back, to organize our thoughts, our ideas and our hard drives, which were loaded with hundreds of hours of video from around the globe. Even in his recovering state, John was and still is the go-to guy when it comes to computer stuff and electronic issues. His tenacity and his dedication to problem solving has bailed us out quite a few times. Within a couple of months, we had our editing system optimized and enough hard drive space to neatly organize all of our video files. We streamlined much of our gear and could now transport everything we needed, including multiple video cameras, in just our carry-on backpacks. Karma 180 was still expanding, but for a change it was more John and I finding groups that we wanted to help by using the contacts we made in the past.

Through a connection that I made on the Asia tour I located an NGO based in Washington called Global Action for Children and, after a couple of emails and a phone call, we were putting together a promotional video for them using footage of children that we had collected over our many journeys. It was great to be helping people and NGOs that had nothing to give us in return. It was sometimes difficult to get others to understand that we really wanted nothing back in return, and we really just wanted to give. Life was becoming very clear to me. The more we gave, either of our time or our money, the more the universe gifted us with amazing life experiences.

It's probably time to reflect on life, maybe confess things and to open up more. So far, anyone reading this has probably figured out that John and I have done some noteworthy things, but we are human. I, for one, never planned this as my life's goal. I had originally started working with the homeless as an escape from a torturous relationship, one that I was allowing to happen for some reason. I needed a place to go to get my mind clear. I needed to see that others had it worse than I did. I thought that through this, that I might start to feel better. Later I learned that a directional step like that can change the path of your life, even if the original intent is a bit selfish. It was an eye and a soul opener and it gave me the drive to be a better human being. My first documentary trip to Cambodia also started with some selfish intentions. I wanted an adventure; I wanted to be the one that people looked up to for doing something outrageous. Every time I heard someone say,

"Do you know what Kevin is doing?" my head would swell a bit. I was going where others wouldn't dream of venturing, breaking the mold of an ordinary, monotonous existence. To the women of Freedom Fields, I was this young, humanitarian filmmaker, creating a project that would have everyone talking about this group of women and their amazing cause to rid the world of landmines. The reality was that, before the first trip, I had never even practiced with the equipment that I had bought and had no idea what I was getting myself, or John, into. They were all so impressed by the way I would stand in the heat and humidity of the Cambodian countryside for hours continuously filming, but they were from Carmel California and I was from Orlando, Florida. To me Cambodia was less hot and humid than the place I worked every day, but I pretended like I was superhuman and loved the attention.

We are no angels. John and I both have our vices. I probably enjoy beer a bit too much, and I can be a hypocrite from time to time. I have never striven for perfection because perfection doesn't exist, and don't even get me started on religion. I hate people preaching at me about their God and their holy books. Religious fanaticism, and missionaries handing out food to famished people while asking them to change their spiritual views and convert enrages me. What gives them, or anyone, the right to judge and to offer aid to people in the name of something that they have no proof exists. Yes, I am far from a Christian. I used to tell people that if there is a Christian version of heaven, I didn't want to go because there would be too many Christians there. Mom was raised Catholic and Dad grew up Southern Baptist and my sister is a Bible-loving church follower. They all have great worries that they won't get to spend eternity with me because of the way I talk about the Christian faith. I believe that my intentions and my actions will stand on their own if any judgment by an astral deity falls my way. I will never put all my faith in any book that was written by the hand of man, but I have read them all, including the Bible. I log away the truths and the knowledge that I find in the words of all the world's holy manuscripts. The universe is my church and life is my God, my teacher. My God is the great mystery and what I have learned to practice is being human, loving all, judging no one because of anything that has made them who they are at the point of my first contact with them. In a short five years, I have had the world open up to me and I live with karma every day. I watch and practice balance, trying not to fall too far to one side of anything. I am no role model, even though, through what we have accomplished, people tend to look up to John and me. This allows both of us to be very open in talking about how we got to where we are, and to help others find themselves through humanity. I guess, like our name, Karma 180, I have come one hundred and eighty degrees away from my starting point.

I realized this because a friend who is going through a hard time right now just asked me, "If you could be anyone in the world right now, who would you be?" Without a thought, and even surprising myself, I instantly said, "I would not want to be anyone but me." He looked at me and said that it's very hard to find that in life.

"If someone offered me millions of dollars for the memories I have accrued during last five years of my life, taking the money wouldn't cross my mind," I said. As we kept talking, I told him that if, years ago, I had written down a list of things of the most amazing things I hoped to do before I died, none of what I have lived through recently would have even made it onto the list. s That's because what I'm doing is so far out of the realm of what I ever imagined possible.

He looked at me and said, "Would you believe that I had my entire life planned out by the age of eighteen, and every day I get depressed because I am not accomplishing it?"

My response was that maybe that was part of his problem. The day I finally let go and let life create me is the day I really started to live, and to love. It's not easy, it's probably one of the hardest things you will ever do. But it's the only way that I know to find true peace.

GUATEMALA, NOVEMBER 2008
INTERNATIONAL HEALTH EMISSARIES

RIO DULCE RIVER BASIN GUATEMALA

OUR PLANE TOUCHED DOWN IN GUATEMALA CITY in the early afternoon and we were met at the airport by a member of the local organization, Asociacion Rescate, the NGO that International Health Emissaries paired with on the ground in the Rio Dulce area. Asociacion Rescate's mission is to improve the health and education of the Indians who live in the Rio Dulce area. IHE also supports these educational efforts by funding teachers' salaries and giving scholarships to deserving students.

"By raising the education levels, in addition to improving the health of the people, we are hopeful of raising their standard of living even further," we were told by the Asociacion Rescate representative.

This was our second trip with IHE, but our first opportunity to meet Dr. Mark Bayless, its cofounder. Like Jack Faia, Mark got his start by packing his tackle box full of dental gear and flying to some jungle in the middle of nowhere to perform free dentistry. I have stated already that I am a huge fan of Cindy McCain and

Jack Faia. Well, add Mark Bayless to my list. Not only does he extend pure kindness and love to his patients, but he's a man who will go to the ends of the earth to offer help to those whose names he will never know. He is also without a doubt one of the most amazing fathers that I have ever met. His heart is equally open to everyone whose path he crosses, and I feel that he has probably never met a stranger. My life is better for knowing him.

Our small group of adventurous humanitarians found our luggage and regrouped outside, where there was a bus ready to take us into Guatemala City and the hotel where we would be staying for the night. For John and I, this trip started out much smoother than our Peru trip had, partially because we weren't standing in the airport trying to find faces that we had never seen before, without a name, number or address to bail us out. At IHE reunions, they still love to tell the story about John and me seeking out nuns at the airport in Peru. "Yeah, then there was the time that John and Kevin…." That seems to be the way many stories start where we're concerned. This time we flew in with the group. It was a good thing, too, because we never would have found the location on the river where we were staying on this trip without assistance. It was way out in the boondocks.

That night we all grabbed some dinner in the hotel restaurant and turned in early. Our morning on the bus would start at first light and the day's travels had already left us all very drained. The next morning, I woke a few minutes early to reflect, have a cup of coffee and take pleasure in the mystical view from the window in our room. In South American countries based near the Sierra Madre de Chiapas Mountain range, there is always a misty condition going on around predawn each morning. It's like a dense cloud, full of moisture, but not rain, comes down to ground level to visit. You go to bed and everything is very dry; you wake to a cool, damp atmosphere. Moisture blankets everything. Condensation gathered on the outside windows of the of our room until the weight of the droplets morphing together caused them to run down the glass in broken rivers of water. The mist that hung in the morning air caused all the lights at the street level to glistening with a starburst like affect, almost like there was something wrong with your vision. I love this time of morning because the world is still and calm, almost virginal. Everything seems to pause for reflection; so, usually, I do too. This morning I pulled a comfortable chair over to the window, propped my feet on the sill, and held my steaming cup of instant coffee between my hands, warming them as I reflected. Looking out at the mountains in the distance, partially hidden behind the concrete jungle, I once again thanked the universe for allowing me to be a part of something bigger than myself.

The bus ride that morning was a long one. It was over one hundred and twenty miles from Guatemala City to Lago de Izabal, Lake Izabal, where we would be staying and holding the dental clinic. As the hours passed, we all did a bit of seat swapping to engage in conversations with people we didn't know, and Mark and I had a chance to continue to build our friendship. After all, Mark had been my first contact with the IHE group and even though Jack and I had gained mutual respect for each other on the trip to Lima earlier in the year, this was the first time that I had actually met Mark face to face. Our route took us through mountainous jungle roads and past miles and miles of vast, fertile farmland. Our initial excitement soon turned to boredom, which in turn became sleepiness that led to discomfort, restlessness, creativity, slap-happiness and then mild insanity, which left fifteen adults acting like a bus of immature preschoolers.

Finally crossing the bridge that spanned a section of Lake

Izabal and the Rio Dulce basin was a delightful moment because we all knew we were close to getting off the bus. The last small hurdle that we had to overcome was when the bus driver got the bus stuck in a tight alleyway, right next to the boat dock. Wedged, is a better word to describe our situation and this was a full-size, forty-foot bus. As to taunt us after our long trip, we could see the boat that would take us to the island but we could not get out of the bus door until the driver pulled a pinpoint precision, twenty-five-point turn, nearly taking out the only telephone pole dockside, like an elephant trying to slowly uproot a tree. After an anxious eternity, we finally made it off the bus and with an enthusiastic gait we all headed to a shuttle boat, named, the Sledgehammer.

The captain of the boat and the owner of the Hotel Catamaran, Kevin, greeted Mark and Jack like they were long lost brothers. "Right out of a movie," is the only way to describe Kevin, boat, his bar, his hotel and his life for the most part. He was like a modern-day pirate with a modern-day African Queen, under his command. She was a blue and white, open deck boat, about thirty feet long, with a wooden canopy top to keep the elements out of the wheelhouse. This is what Kevin used to ferry guests back and forth from the docks, transport medical supplies to the clinics along the river, give tours of the local waterside areas of interest, or anything else for which one could use a vessel of this kind. With its shallow draft and wide beam, it was the ultimate river boat.

We could see the Hotel Catamaran from the dock but everything in the Rio Dulce area moved on island time, so the boat ride took a relaxing twenty minutes or so to travel across the small lake, known as the Golfete, to the dock alongside the hotel. The dock led us right into the check-in desk, which was wonderfully located in the Catamaran's Tiki bar. This bar is where we spent most of our evenings and it was pretty much the hub of communications for the entire island. No Disney pretend shit here, this place was the real deal. You could imagine Jimmy Buffet coming here to retire. The margaritas alone were worth the price of a plane ticket, bus fair and a boat trip to Guatemala. The next room over from the check-in location was a dining area in which we would meet nightly for a buffet style dinner of local dishes before we hit the bar. From there you would only have to walk a matter of feet to the pool, which also had its own bar, and then follow the trails through beautiful native vegetation to the rooms that were perched on stilts over the water's edge. These small, two-room huts were really out over the water, far enough that if the dock connecting them to the island fell away, swimming would be required to reach the shore. Cracks between the wooden floor planks along with unsealed windows kept a small, warm draft flowing through the room at night, and the sounds of the world around us could easily be heard through the paper-thin wooden walls. The only creature comforts in the room were a wobbly three bladed metal ceiling fan hung precariously over the bed, a well-used and very overworked window a/c unit and shower that afforded us with a full seven minutes of hot water each morning. Water to be bathed in only, not ingested. After all, we were still in the heart of the Guatemalan jungle. This became very obvious each morning when I drew open the nineteen seventies era curtains, covering jalousie windows from the same era, to see locals fishing from dugout canoes in the mist that hung over the lake's waters. Framed by the volcanic mountain ranges and tropical landscape, we were in paradise.

This may seem like an odd place to choose for a humanitarian mission location but it fits right in with the mission statement of International Health Emissaries, as Jack once told me in an interview.

"The mission of IHE is to help people that have no access to health care, no access. Whether it is due to poverty or location, that doesn't matter to us."

The Ketchi Indians fell into the second category. Even though these wonderful people were very poor by US standards, their needs were mostly met, and, unlike the extreme urban poverty we witnessed in the barrios outside Lima, the Ketchi lived very primitive but comfortable lives. Dwelling so far out in the middle of the jungles and mountains offered them little access to medical attention of any kind, which means that a single dental visit once a year could be the balance point between pain and no pain, eating or starving, and sometimes life or death. This is why the IHE group chose this location. Their "no access to health care" was caused by the tribe's distance from modern facilities. Just how far out in the jungle they lived is something John and I would find out soon enough.

IT TAKES A SMALL ARMY TO SET UP A DENTAL CLINIC

Sunrise and sunset on the Rio Dulce are both metaphysical experiences. One comes with coffee and the other leaves with a margarita, but both the morning and evening sky are masterpieces of celestial art. Set-up morning was upon us, but unlike some locations in which entire clinics had to be created, here there was a small clinic run throughout the year by the local Asociacion Rescate NGO. This meant dental chairs and a working air compressor to run the tools. To be more correct, I should say, a sometimes-working compressor.

After a quick breakfast under the outdoor pavilion, the group loaded the dental supplies brought from the states onto the deck of the Sledgehammer and we cast off for the clinic downriver.

Although the lake was large enough to have some small breaking waves on it, this morning the water was calm and flat. As we enjoyed the ride, coffees in hand, Mark told us how Jack found this location and all the local Indians in great need of dentistry. He was actually on vacation with his family when he met Kevin and discovered this location. The guys have been making this annual trip since 1991, and I could tell that Mark was eager to show us around. IHE had created quite a following here.

Gently pulling up to the clinic dock, Kevin bumped the Sledgehammer into reverse, allowing a couple of the locals who were waiting for us to take the ship's lines and tie us securely off. Everyone casually got up, grabbed some gear and made their way up the very narrow winding concrete path of stairs to a small house located about two hundred feet up on a grassy plateau. The actual clinic was located on the other side of a concrete wall directly behind the small house. A gate offered access to the clinic and allowed people to use the side and backyard area of the house as a congregation point for those waiting to have dental work done. The owners of the house also benefited. They set up a small bar on their porch, offering food and drinks to the volunteers, and, as in most areas like this, community was foremost, so even if there had been no monetary gain, the homeowners would have gladly offered their boat dock, porch and yard to accommodate the IHE group. We did make good use of the porch. With its bar, hammocks, foosball table and the most amazing hilltop view of the lake, accompanied by a constant warm breeze rising up from the water, it was the perfect place to escape the sounds of dentistry and the heat of the non-air conditioned sweat box clinic just behind.

Under the shade of a very large tropical tree in the side yard was the perfect place to set up the teeth brushing classes, where

Terry, one of the volunteers, taught the children how to avoid the plaque monster with a song and a wiggle dance that the children adored. Laughter is the best medicine after all, and the children never knew that they were learning. By wiggling and dancing, Terry taught them the perfect technique to get their new toothbrushes into just the right spots along their gum lines. I couldn't get enough of watching these adorable Guatemalan children giggling and trying to brush each other's teeth. They would practice on themselves, they would practice on each other, they would practice on the walls, trees, rocks and anything that would sit still long enough, including yours truly sleeping soundly in a hammock. Yep, one day I made the mistake of being so exhausted that I took a catnap in the hammock that hung from the porch overlooking the lake. Now normally this would have seemed like the logical place to slumber for a bit, and, if not for the close proximity of the cute kids practicing their brushing skills, it might have been the perfect spot. But, in my dog-tired state I slept like a rock, and I didn't feel the small lime green toothbrush enter my mouth until it was too late. Ask me where that toothbrush had been moments before entering my mouth or what was on it, and I can only answer with a shrug and a blank expression. But there it was, moving back and forth along my pearly whites. It was not so much the sensation that woke me up as much as it was the adorable giggling of the small boy holding the damn thing in my mouth. There were two boys, I believe. One was the mastermind and the other was helping with instructions and encouragement. Both were about six, one was a good half a foot taller than the other and they were both dressed in their jeans and best going-to-town button-up shirts. As my eyes slowly opened and over tiredness let me wrap my brain around the ongoing activity, I could do nothing but stare at them with a look on my face that must have asked, "Is that the same toothbrush that you were using on the dog twenty minutes ago?" To them I was the perfect practice dummy, my face was at their level and I wasn't moving. With the brush still in motion, I turned my head fifteen degrees to face the future dentist and tried to smile. He found this action hilarious because his giggles turned to full, high-pitched laughter and he and his partner in crime ran away, removing the lime green brush from my mouth with all the gentleness of, well, a six-year-old Guatemalan boy. After a couple good spits, I couldn't help but notice that my wonderful friend John Evanko was immensely enjoying the entire event as it unfolded right there in front of him.

"So remember folks, when traveling to remote, sometimes-dangerous lands it's always great to take the trip with someone who forever has your best interest at heart."

After the clinic setup was complete, we, as a group, decided to take a boat ride downriver to an Indian village partially supported by members of IHE. A couple members had financially sponsored some of the children in the village to go to secondary school, and, with help of the Asociacion Rescate NGO, a new well had been constructed the previous year to get clean water to the villagers, many of whom we would see over the next few days for dental checkups. With as many years as Mark and Jack had been coming to this area to do dentistry, the local Indians' mouths had improved from nothing but rotten teeth to wonderful smiles, many now only needing a quick cleaning. The visual proof was all around us. Hands-on humanitarian organizations like IHE can, and do, make a major difference in the world, even if it is one mouth at a time.

THE SECRET VILLAGE

Although the Sledgehammer was one of the coolest boats I have ever seen, its slower speed and lack of ability to get up on plane (get the full boat hull out of the water) made the decision to use alternate transportation to get to the village a smart choice. Asociacion Rescate had a few smaller and much faster transport boats ready for us to use. These were the typical style boats that were operated on the lakes and rivers of the Rio Dulce to take goods and people around. They were open top boats with a stand-up helm in the middle and two rows of seats near the front. Large outboard motors pushed the four-teen-foot crafts through the calm waters effortlessly. When you live on a lake or an island, you have a boat instead of a car. That's just a fact.

Asociacion Rescate owned one of the three boats we used; the other two were borrowed from local friends. Mark had told John and me about the amazing hidden entrance to the secret village, so I thought I was well prepared to film the approach. To my surprise, however, his words hadn't done it justice. Hauling ass on full plane down the waterway, our driver made a slow turn that angled our boat directly at the tree line on the south-side of the riverbank. All three boats were now heading full speed at the jungle. Still on full plane, we were quickly gaining ground on the shoreline and I saw no opening to a hidden river that would lead us to a village. I was beginning to think that we were in the wrong location but Mark just kept smiling,

"Keep your camera focused on the dark spot in the tree line," Mark yelled over the engine noise, and, after a couple more seconds, I found the dark spot in the trees that our boat aimed at. Secret river was right. I grew up running up and down the St. Johns River in Florida in my dad's old boats and I have found many small, hard-to-see tributaries to explore, but this was a true optical illusion. Even when we were only about twenty boat lengths away from the tree line, I couldn't make out the river entrance; it must have been the way the trees overlapped each other. But sure as shit, it was right where Mark said it would be. The driver backed off the throttle only about twenty feet from the wall of green and like in another scene from an Indiana Jones movie, a cave in the trees opened up, offering up just enough room for a small boat to enter into the secret river leading to the hidden Ketchi Indian village. Looking back at where we'd came from, I could now see the obvious tunnel entrance, highlighted by the lake and the sky. Turning my camera toward the bow of the boat I could see that we were now heading down a very tight, calm river that serpentined through a cavernous tunnel of trees. Into the heart of the Guatemalan jungle we drove. At about a quarter mile, the waterway ended, like a roundabout in a modern neighborhood—except instead of houses, we were surrounded by jungle—a lot of jungle. The canopy of trees overhead was so dense that it kept most of the sunlight from hitting the water.

On the left side of the murky river's end was a dock. Standing on that dock were a dozen or so Ketchi Indians who were not afraid to show their enthusiasm at our arrival. I don't know who was smiling and waving more, the villagers or the IHE volunteers. Successfully getting off the boats and onto the elevated dock was the first hurtle to cross, then came a long walk down a very nicely constructed boardwalk to the village's main center, which consisted of a very colorfully painted school and medical center, both constructed of concrete blocks. These were much more modern structure then I had imagined that I would find this far out in the jungle. Mark explained that the buildings had been built with donations from IHE and a number of other NGOs, as was the well and some fencing to contain the animals. This area served as the village hub. Conversation, hugs and introductions went on for a short time until Mark motioned for us to follow him to the more primitive area where the villagers lived. Off we went, behind the modern village area and into the jungle on foot trails. We reached the huts and this was the village that I was expecting to see in the middle of a tropical jungle. What I had not expected was the strange merging of the primitive with modern gadgetry. The first hut we entered had a single room design. Like all of the huts, it was based on a four-corner post that supported a palm leaf roof structure. Its dirt floors were swept out often to keep the dust levels to a minimum. Less typical was the very new, red Honda generator idling quietly against one wall. From it ran an assortment of electrical cords that powered some lights which hung from the roof and a television that was hanging on the wall in an adjacent hut. This second hut was filled people who apparently wanted to keep up with daytime talk shows, because that's exactly what the group was watching. *Jerry Springer* had a following that even he couldn't have imagined. Wandering around from there, we entered a couple more huts where Mark would do his best to communicate with the families inhabiting them. The language in this area was a mixture of Ketchi and Spanish, but the language that Mark spoke best was laughter and kindness, which is spoken and understood in even the most remote locations on earth. I have yet to mention that Mark's second passion is magic and this made him easy to find. All you had to do was listen for the sound of children laughing and follow it to Mark and his magic bag of tricks. Like the Pied Piper, Mark would walk along the trails, followed by the village's children. The farther he walked, the larger his following grew.

What I have witnessed with humanitarian volunteers everywhere, especially with the IHE group, is that they have truly found the fountain of youth. No excuses, no regrets, just openly given love, and the love they give away propagates and flow back at them tenfold. This compounding effect of a human being's greatest need acts like a fountain of youth on the body and the soul. Grow younger by giving to the underprivileged people of the world. I believe this is another part of the meaning of life that people search for.

After Magic Mark had made a lifelong impact on almost every child in this particular village, leaving them all giggling to the point of tears, it was time to go. Many more villagers than before now followed us back down the boardwalk and then stood on the dock waving and yelling broken-English goodbyes as our three boats started back through the shadowy river canopy to the secret entrance. Now, the opening in the trees was blatantly there, like a brightly lit beacon. It looked much larger heading back out then it did when we entered, until the point that we breached the tree line and returned the boats to full plane. Then, within a matter of moments, the jungle swallowed up the dark entrance again, leaving a solid wall of green in its place.

Our next stop for the day was the town of Livingston, in eastern Guatemala, at the mouth of the Rio Dulce in the Gulf of Honduras. To reach this destination we ran the entire length of the Rio Dulce River starting at Lake Izabal and ending at the Caribbean Sea. The trip down river was breathtaking. The sides of the gorge rise up to 300 feet on either side and are covered with teak and mahogany trees. In places, sheer white limestone cliffs rise right out of the water. If there were a place on earth in which monster hunters should spend some time searching for a giant sea creature, this would probably be the location. As rivers go Rio Dulce isn't particularly long, but it is deep, with the sea at one end and a massive freshwater lake at the other. Who knows what type of unknown, hybrid aquatic creatures dwell in its dark depths? Through sections of the waterway where the mountains kept the wind from reacting with the surface of the river, the water was as calm and glassy as in an undisturbed bathtub. Reaching the beginning of the river and the location of Livingston, Mark had the crafts pull a short distance into the Gulf and pointed out that we were sitting right in between Belize and Honduras but still in Guatemalan waters. This is one of those places where you really don't want to cause an international incident, because you never know who is going to be the first to either start shooting or to detain someone. Personally, I think I would start swimming for Belize. If you ever get this far out, Livingston is a must to see, if for no more reason then the massive amounts of pirate history in the area. Actually, the entire Rio Dulce River is rich in pirate history. you can close your eyes and with easily imagine large wooden ships slowly sailing up the river to the inner ports around enormous Lake Izabal. Right past the bridge, near the entrance of the lake, is the Castillo San Felipe de Lara, a fort built by the Spanish when this area of Central America was an important staging point for transcontinental shipments. Early in the sixteenth century, trade was recognized between the inland colonies and Spain by use of the river. Frequent attacks by pirates and privateer incursions into Guatemala through the Rio Dulce made it crucial to protect the entrance to Lake Izabal, a location in which warehouses had been established for goods entering from or leaving for Spain.

The trip from the Gulf back the fort was the last thing we did for the day, and it was a brutal twenty-six-and-a-half mile trip back upriver, with the sun directly overhead. It sucked the last drops of energy from our fatigued bodies. So, we replaced the missing energy with ample amounts of beer. If not for those ice-cold beers that we had acquired for the journey back, I believe it might have been unbearable. Again, cold beer came to our aid when we needed it most.

BOATLOADS OF INDIANS, FIRST DAY OF CLINIC IN GUATEMALA

Day one at any clinic is usually a time to wrap your head around just what you're going to deal with and how it's going to work. New sounds, smells, languages, and experiences reveal themselves every first day. Here in Guatemala, however, many of the volunteer dentists were familiar with the location and the people; a number of them had made the pilgrimage to this very clinic multiple times over the past years. This allowed for a very smooth start. There were three rooms equipped with donated dental chairs that ran the gamut from brand new, right out of the box perfect, to an older one in the back room that had a mind of its own and would decide to rise, lower and buck at variable speeds without warning. This particular chair was a source of constant humor. One time, hearing a commotion coming from the room, I peered in with the camera to see one of the two dentists occupying the room on his tiptoes trying to reach a young boy, and, in broken Spanish, reassure the small child, who had a death grip on the cushion, that everything was okay. If only the child had understood Spanish, he might have thought the ride on the bucking chair was fun, but this Indian kid had no idea what was going on. He probably couldn't understand why everyone who looked into the room contracted the same fit of uncontrollable laughter. This is another reason that these volunteers choose to come to places like this—adventure. Anyone can pull a tooth in a hygienic office in downtown New York City. But try it in the middle of a jungle where it's so hot that your sweat is rolling off your forehead into your patient's eyes, where insects that you have never seen before are crawling up the wall next to you and the generators fail, leaving your head lamp as your only source of workable light. All while twenty dirty children stare at you through a dust covered. chicken wire window as you try to hold a person down in a chair that is duct taped together. Then pull out a rotting tooth with a failing suction unit. Now that's dentistry. All joking aside, this is one reason that the dentists and doctors come and do these missions. It's real down and dirty work, and some people are not cut out for it. The ones that are leave with the biggest sense of accomplishment and pride. Not pride in the conceited sense, but pride in knowing that they went above and beyond the call of duty to really help people in need, and they did it under inhospitable conditions.

Another thing that was different, here in the Rio Dulce, was the way the villagers arrived at the clinic. Again, boats played a huge role in the locals' lives, but these weren't like any boats I had ever seen before. Custom to the area, the boats which would randomly pull up to the dock in front of the clinic were sometimes as long as thirty feet. but no wider than five feet. This made them resemblance monstrous canoes. The vessels had a small flat bottom, and most were wide open, without the addition of seats. This caused the older villagers to sit up on the sides of the boat, filling in the floor space with the younger children and the elderly. If this sounds like a large number of bodies to have riding in one boat, you're visualizing the scene correctly. Sometimes as many as fifty men, women, and children, none of whom could swim, would pack themselves into the handmade wooden boats like sardines in a can. The lot would all be dressed in their best clothes—boys in jeans, collared shirts, and boots; the young women in dresses— and they would slowly make their way up the Rio's tributaries from their secret locations, until they reached the dangerous lake crossing. With the driver half sitting on the stern of the awkward boat and propelling it forward with a small, underpowered fifteen horsepower outboard motor, if anything was going to go wrong, it would be on the lake. The design of these boats was ideal for narrow river use, but in open water, one smack from a wayward wave would capsize the craft sending its collection of non-swimming Indians into the deep water, where most would drown. Even if they managed to cling to the overturned boat, the plywood and board construction was not meant to stay afloat upside-down. Still, they came by the hundreds, dismissing from their minds all thoughts of the dangerous trip to make the once-a -year journey to the dental clinic. Sometimes this meant the difference between teeth or no teeth. The results outweighed the risks.

Seeing just how much interest that John and I had in the villagers' travels to the clinic, Louisa, our local NGO contact, approached us with an idea.

"How would you two like to accompany me on an early morning trip to a village deep in the jungle?" How the hell do you turn that offer down? Even with all the trips that Jack and Mark had made to the Rio Dulce, neither had ever gotten the opportunity to make this journey.

"Of course, we would love to," John and I replied, slightly overlapping our sentences through smiles that wouldn't seem to stop.

"It's set then. We will pick you up on the dock at the Hotel Catamaran at three in the morning." The three in the morning part wasn't going to win any awards with us, but the chance to visit a tribe in the jungles of Guatemala quickly pushed any negative thoughts of no sleep from our minds.

MOTORING INTO THE DARKNESS

Three o'clock in the morning came, as one would imagine, way too early. Even though we tried to turn in at a decent hour, the excitement of the coming morning's events kept me awake and staring at the wobbling ceiling fan over my bed for way too long. Grabbing our camera gear, we left our little stilt room and walked through the dimly lit paths to the dock at the other end of the island. Waiting for us on the dock was Louisa. Standing beside her was the small, barefoot Indian man who was to be our guide and boat driver on the adventure.

The morning air was damp and cool, and, looking out at the lake from where I stood, it was hard to tell where the water stopped, and the night sky started. It was a seriously shade of darkness out. Louisa smiled, said something to our guide in Spanish and then made a motion for us to get in the boat. I glanced down to what was tied to the edge of the rickety wooden dock and my eyes came across something other than what I was expecting to see. Parked there, awaiting us, was a twelve-foot, flat bottom johnboat with sides low enough to make us feel like we were sitting on the water. This was going to be one interesting trip. Johnboats are wide, flat bottom boats with very low sides and squared off front and rear ends. Duck hunters frequently used them as floating platforms in small lakes Not something that you usually see in deeper, rough water, at night. Carefully we climbed down in the boat, found a dry spot to stow our electronic gear and with a shove of a shoeless foot we were off.

Within moments of pulling away from the island we were totally immersed in darkness. Johnboats don't come equipped with running lights so the little barefoot Indian pulled out his trusty flashlight and aimed it in the direction we were heading. The darkness swallowed up the beam from the handheld spotlight a mere six feet in front of the boat, but it's not as if there were anything to really see in the middle of the lake. Still, it might keep anyone else who happened to be out for a 3:00 a.m. cruise from broad siding us during our crossing. The plan was to keep heading out into the open water for a specified distance until we hit the headwaters of the Rio Dulce. From there, we would continue down river until the Indian guide located a small tributary that would take us deep into the jungle, to a trail that would lead to the Indian village. Things became a bit unnerving when I realized that, in order to find the small, unmarked canal entrance in pitch black darkness, our guide was standing up in the boat and trying to locate a specific porchlight hanging on a house clear on the other side of the lake. That was his beacon to make the left-hand turn toward what he hoped was the shoreline. Thank goodness the homeowners kept up with light bulbs or God only knows where we would have ended up. All this was, of course, happening while our vessel shot through the water under full throttle, and let me tell you, a twelve-foot johnboat with a fifty horsepower Honda outboard motor on it, will haul ever-loving ass. At one point I turned to John and told him to get out the small camera and film me in night-vision mode. I looked into the camera and said,

"So here we are, in the black of night, in a small johnboat, driving across a huge lake in Guatemala. We are being piloted by a barefoot Indian who is trying to find a light on

a house on the far side of the lake with a handheld spotlight,
so that he can figure out where to turn to then take us up a
river to then meet a tribe of Indians deep in the jungle. Are
we insane?"

John agreed that, yes, we were both a bit insane. The little guy proved to know his way around the waters extremely well, though; it only took him a couple of attempts to locate the correct piece of shoreline that held the entrance. There were no markers or lights, or even a homemade sign, just a patch of darkness that was a shade darker than the tree line to aim at. This was our left turn.

Scrubbing down the speed to an idle, we proceeded to head down the narrow tributary. In places it would open up to about fifteen feet across, but mostly it was narrower than ten, and because we were still riding in total darkness, idling was as fast as we could safely go. At one point we were visited by a school of very surprised pinfish who for some reason decided to jump from the water into the boat, startling the four of us. It was like an eerie omen telling us to beware of what lurked ahead. Well, not really, but on a dark river, in the jungle, your imagination plays enough tricks on you without the help of stupid fish committing suicide in your boat. Each time the handheld spotlight illuminated the trees at the water's, edge I could imagine hostile villagers hiding in the overgrown vegetation with blowguns aimed at our boat. These thoughts were really going through my head, which made it transparently obvious to me that I had watched way too much television as a child. I wasn't scared, but the whole scene was a bit creepy. At one spot we almost ran into a fishing net spanning just below the surface of the river, but the little Indian guide came through again, somehow managing to chop the throttle and raise the outboard from the water before we bound it up in the propeller. Mile by mile we rode, as the sky slowly brightened to a dusky shade of gray, allowing our eyes to adjust and view our surroundings without the need for the spotlight. The timing couldn't have been more perfect for the sky to lighten up, because at one bend in the river the water became so shallow that our driver had to jump out and pull the johnboat along by hand until the water deepened. This same process happened a couple more times, due to fallen logs, sandbars, or other obstacles, until we were finally back to our regular speed of a slow idle.

It was about six in the morning when we rounded the final bend in our river journey, and our guide steered the craft to the right bank of the river and slowly beached it alongside a couple of the very long, narrow-style river boats—the ones that would be used to transport the villagers to the clinic site later in the day. From here we went on foot. Up the slippery mud slope we climbed, using exposed roots to aid our ten-foot ascent. At the top of the slope, we paused to admire our jungle surroundings and to let the barefoot Indian guide find his boundaries. With a quick glance back at us, as to say, "Okay, follow me," he turned and disappeared down a small jungle trail. John and I had no choice but to keep up. Louisa might have been able to find her way out, but we two white boys would have probably wandered around there for weeks. We were deep, deep, in the Guatemalan jungles and now we were hoofing it even deeper into the unknown depths. So, we walked, leaving the river, our only identifiable landmark back to civilization, farther and farther behind us.

Daylight brought songs from dozens of species of exotic birds, and dew formed into larger droplets on the wide tropical plants, with aid of the warming sun, which also woke up the jungle insects. The quickly rising temperature and the aggressive morning hike suggested that I shed my light jacket, I tied it around my waste and trudged on, and within a short time we came to a road. Not a paved road, not a dirt road, but somewhere in between, and I have no idea how it magically formed this far out into the jungle. But there it was, and it would lead us to the village. There were, in fact, two separate Indian tribes that were meeting up together, to kind of carpool in the boats to the clinic on the lake. One of the tribes, which lived far up in the mountains, would take an entire day to make the journey from their mountain village to the lowland village, staying for the night. The collective of villagers would then rise early the next morning and start the lengthy walk to the river, load up into the transport boats and make the two-hour river run to the lake, ending up at the IHE dental clinic on the shore at the opposite side.

About twenty minutes down the road, John and I started to run into random villagers walking by themselves toward the river. Moments later, we were passed by small groups, then came the mass exodus, filling the gravel road five-wide with children and families. This, we decided, was the perfect stopping point. We really wanted to see the primitive village, but these natives were not planning to wait for John and me to sightsee around their dwellings. They were all hastily scampering to the river for their annual boat ride and their appointments with the Gringo Dentists. Mark summed it up best when he remarked that most of them couldn't care less about the dental work, but they knew that, once they were seen, the next room to visit was the store from which they could pick out a free gift from the shoes, hats, clothing and, especially, toys on display. For the chance to head home with a Mr. Potato Head Doll, I can almost promise you that and of these kids would let you pull out a tooth, even if they weren't in pain.

The closer we got to the river, the faster they all walked, until there was an excited sprint covering the last fifty yards to the boats. I relate this to my own youthful excitement when I found myself in eyesight of the main gates to Disney's Magic Kingdom in Orlando. I guess when you live in the jungle, a boat trip is as good as a monorail ride.

Even John and I had to run down the road a few times to keep ahead of the group and to line up good shots of the village children. They were nimble little things. Reaching the water's edge, they wasted no time scrambling over the high sides of the blue wooden boats and finding their appropriate position, either up on the rail or down on the floor. One by one, they piled into the boat until there was no room left. It was a disturbing number of bodies in one boat, at least fifty, if not more. I quickly maneuvered myself down the sloping embankment, until my feet were touching water, and hoisted my camera into position, but, with robotic precision, the children had filled the vessel so quickly that I was lucky to get that last few on tape as they climbed over and sat down. With speed equaling that of the village children, a young boy of no more than fifteen, wearing dress slacks rolled at the ankle and a white button-down shirt, holding his good shoes in his hand, made his way past and pushed the boat off the shore. His bare feet sunk into the river bottom as he managed to free the craft from the suction of the mud against the keel, sending it floating free into the river. Now hanging off the back of the floating boat, trying to keep as dry as possible, he clawed his way onboard. Others grabbed his arms or whatever they could reach and dragged the young boy into the boat where he began violently yanking the start cord on the outboard motor that was bolted to the stern. One, two, three pulls, four, five, six, and the motor sputtered to life. By this time the bow of the thirty-foot long canoe boat, along with the first twelve passengers, was nicely lodged in some low hanging tree limbs. Both fighting with the undergrowth and helping to hold the boat in place, the villagers seemed to find the humor in their quandary. What I filmed next looked like an optical illusion. While standing on the shore videoing the boat from the rear, I saw the passengers, with aid of the outboard in reverse, push the boat out into the middle of the open river. At this point, the young boy, driving slowly, turned the thirty-foot boat one hundred and eighty degrees, pointing the bow in the direction of downstream. The illusion came from the fact that the boat seemed much longer than the river was wide, and, from my vantage point on the shore, the craft seemed to start at four feet wide, then grow to the width of the river and then shrink back to the four-foot wide boat, just facing the other way. Probably mysterious jungle crap. Then, with a twist of the throttle, the overweighted craft slowly built-up speed, and then it was gone around the first bend.

Now accompanied by a mother and a small child, we took our time loading back into the johnboat, figuring it would be effortless to catch up with the villagers given their small head start. Boy, were we wrong. Even with the weight of two extra bodies in our boat, we over powered their homemade wooden monstrosity, and, if average weight of each person was only sixty pounds, the fifty people in their boat had a combined weight of over two-thousand five hundred pounds, plus motor and the weight of the boat. Yet, somehow, we never caught up with them. Their young driver must have known the river like the back of his hand. Try as we might, turn after turn, we never laid eyes on the villagers in their boat until we hit the open water of the lake, which was rough enough to slow them down to a crawl. I guess we should have told the smiling boatload of Indians that the whole reason for our three o'clock in the morning venture was to document their journey to the clinic. What we got instead was a video of a group of excited Ketchi Indians running past us and the ass end of an overloaded boat full of the non-swimming natives disappearing down a narrow waterway. Don't get me wrong, it was an adventure of a lifetime, but we only ended up with about five minutes of usable footage and a great urge to come back later and try it again.

Managing to overtake their boat in the open waters did give me a couple of really nice moving shots at a very close distance, and we did make it to the dock at the clinic before them, but not by much. As we came off plane and floated in the last few feet, I grabbed my gear and leapt from our johnboat to the dock. Puttering up only seconds after us, the assemblage of excited, giggling children gave me only moments to position myself on solid ground and film their chaotic, yet somehow organized, disembarking from the boat. Out of breath from trying to stay one step ahead of them as they ran up the steep flight of steps to the clinic, I somehow outmaneuvered the pack and caught them heading around a concrete wall, en route to the teeth brushing classes. I could tell how amusing I was becoming to the group. They had their very own gringo to play chase with. I really didn't mind, though. More than the filming, more than the giving, more than the dental or medical procedures, the bonding and friendships made between different cultures left everlasting memories of peace and love on both sides. That, after all, is why we really do this.

BAD TEETH INVADE OUR LAST DAY

The next couple of clinic days were very mellow. Because of the annual IHE trips, some of these children were getting dentistry that rivaled children living in Beverly Hills. The proof was in the teeth. Day after day, child after child only needing a cleaning or a superficial filling elevated the pride level in this volunteer group, as it rightly should. Sure, they came down to the jungles to remove some teeth and take away pain, but they had been doing this for such a long time that the lessons were sinking in. Because of the dedication to humanitarian aid by the IHE volunteers, the native people were now passing down the knowledge and practices to their children and their children's children, and teeth, along with lives were being saved.

"A small group of thoughtful people could change the world. Indeed, it's the only thing that ever has."

–Margaret Mead

As smooth as thing were going, you just know that fate has to throw a monkey wrench in the works somewhere. Our monkey wrench came on the last day of clinic, during the last hours of the day, and in the form of an Indian boy about nine years old. Mark called me into the back room at the clinic,

"You might want to film this," he said. In the room with him was the young native boy, about three dentists, and a man that I can only image was the boy's elder. The earlier dental checkup had shown some strange discoloring and softness to the boy's four upper front teeth, and this led to the need for a more extensive examination.

"I think we need to use the portable x-ray machine," I overheard Mark say to one of the other dentists. I had been on this trip from the beginning, and I knew what most of the equipment we had brought along did. My father worked in the radiation department at a hospital in Orlando, I have seen what a portable X-ray unit looks like, and I was very certain we didn't have one. As I was about to laugh at what I thought was Mark's joke, someone walked over to a regular sized travel case and removed what looked like two blue rechargeable batteries, the type that would power a portable drill one would find at any hardware store. From the same case the batteries were in, someone else removed a device that looked like a cross between an oversized Nerf gun and something an astronaut would use for protection against alien attack. It was the Nomad Pro Handheld X-ray Device, and I was about to get a lesson on how high-tech was merging with humanitarian aid. Weighing a bit over five pounds, being totally handheld and easily interfacing with a laptop computer, this device was more valuable than gold to a dentist in a remote location. Like the portable vital sign monitoring equipment that I have seen used in Operation Smile missions, or the self-contained communication centers that the World Food Program offers to members in the field, modern technology is bringing amazing new equipment to the humanitarian world. In our circumstances, it gave us the ability to look inside the teeth of a person located in a jungle in Guatemala, at a site that barely had running water and power.

With batteries inserted into the devise and the USB cable run to the laptop, all that needed to be done was to convince the young man that the old gringo dentist wasn't trying to do him any bodily harm, but he wasn't having any part of it. Standing erect against a wall, the boy clamped his jaw so tightly that it took two people to pry it open while one brave volunteer had to insert a small X-ray film into the boy's mouth, pressing it against the backside of the upper front teeth. It was quite the undertaking. Of course, everyone was trying to hold the boy up against the wall because there was no way to get him to lie down in what he must have seen as a torturous dental chair. This kid was almost a wild jungle child, one who had rarely come out to the more civilized world, and he was proving it. After a battle that seemed to last an eternity, Mark looked up at the computer screen and said, "Hey, I think we got one." And we did.

We walked to the laptop computer half hanging off a fold-out card table and Mark showed me how great the X-rays were that his portable gizmo took. Using the images on the screen, Mark pointed out the problem with the boy's teeth. It appeared that he had never seen a dentist before and, from years of sucking on the local sugarcane plants, the enamel on the front teeth had totally worn away, leaving nothing but exposed dentin and, in some spots, just pulp. These were the boy's permanent front teeth and Mark wanted to save them. Had they been baby teeth, he would have just removed them, but, in this case, he had a different plan. His hopes were that he could drill away all the damaged area of the teeth and permanently bond then with a porcelain filler, leaving the boy with pearly white, strong, usable teeth.

"Want to film it?" Mark said. I figured I would give it a shot. I had filmed extractions and facial surgeries before. How bad could this be? By now you have probably figured out that when I end something with, "How bad could it be?" it's not going to be pretty. Yeah, this was one of those so-ugly-that-my-knees-almost-buckled situations.

Through the interpreter, we gained the young boy's trust, or at least he didn't think that Mark was going to cut out his heart and sacrifice him. Multiple injections were given into the upper gum line surrounding the teeth to be worked on and Mark gave the numbing agent ample time to take effect before cranking up the drill. He showed me how he poked at the area around the teeth to make sure the boy would feel no pain. Satisfied, he began the procedure. I don't know many technical terms for dentistry, but, to me, it looked as if he was trying to hollow out the inside of the boy's teeth. After a good amount of time Mark looked up me and quietly said, "You might not want to watch this anymore."

I could tell by the almost queasy look in Mark's eyes that this was not going to end the way he wanted. Because of years of damage to the internal structure of the boy's teeth, from essentially soaking them in sugar, they had the consistency of children's playdough. There was nothing Mark could do but extract them. This would leave the young boy with a four-tooth wide gap in his upper palate, exactly what he was trying to avoid, but in the long run it would probably save the kid's life and save him years of agonizing pain from infection and tooth rot. They can't all go well.

As it was the last day of clinic, we shut down early, leaving ample time to pack everything back up in the cases and prepare the gear for shipping back to the states. As for the volunteers, we all headed back to the Hotel Catamaran for one last night of well-deserved margarita drinking. It had been a rewarding but exhausting week, and we had a long day of traveling ahead of us, starting at very early the next morning. As with most IHE missions around the globe, the first half is designated for the clinic time and the second week is set aside to, well, to unwind from the first week of dental work in merciless surroundings. Here in Guatemala the chill-out location was the historical town of La Antigua. The name La Antigua means The Old Guatemala and it was the third capital city of the country of Guatemala. Now a tourist town, much of the city's architecture was ruined by a 7.4 magnitude earthquake that hit Antigua on September 29, 1717, and again by another earthquake in 1773. Three years later, Spain ordered the location of the capital to be moved to a safer setting. At that time this location was known as the Valley of the Shrine. It's where present-day Guatemala City now stands.

Like most Central and South American tourist towns, the

streets are safe by day, but   require a bit of caution after dark. Markets and trinket shops, where you can find the same shit from store to store, line the streets, but the historical value here well outweighs the shopping hassles—especially if you're into early Spanish architecture. Antigua is also surrounded by active volcanos, making it very prone to earthquakes. This gives you a bit of an uneasy, jack-in-the-box feeling while you're touring around the old cobblestone streets, but, for me, it added to the excitement – particularly when I stood by near ruins that had been damaged by an ancient, massive quake. As a group, we had an amazing time here. But of course, with Mark, Jack and the rest of the International Health Emissaries family, we could have fun in even the most dismal locations. I know this for a fact because we have.

Our final bit of adventure in Guatemala was a day trip to the Mayan city of Tikal. John and I could add this to our collection of visits to ancient ruins, and it give us some location shots for Guatemala to go with the Machu Picchu stuff we had filmed in Peru. Tikal is known to be one of the largest archaeological sites of the pre-Columbian Mayan civilization. It is also known to house thousands of pyramids, but only a handful have ever been unearthed. Its modern claim to fame is when George Lucas hauled a crap load of camera gear to the top of Temple One and shot a scene for the rebel base in the original third movie of the *Star Wars* trilogy, *Return of The Jedi*. To me that was almost as amazing as the Mayan history stuff. Almost.

With this footage from the Rio Dulce trip, added to the Peru footage that we filmed earlier in the year and some shots from one of their missions to Cambodia, we now had enough footage to edit together the mini documentary that we had promised Mark. He made John and me promise that we would continue to travel around with IHE as often as we could—a promise that we have gladly honored.

HOW WE WERE MAKING A DIFFERENCE

November was flying by, and yet there was still one more commitment that John and I had to honor. Veronica, an active board member with the Freedom Fields USA nonprofit organization, contacted me. She needed a new video for their annual fundraiser to be held in our home-away-from-home, Carmel, CA. We had only a week to put the new video together before the event, so we dropped everything else and gave it top priority. Weaseling our way out of a week's work at *Fear Factor*, we chose to hand deliver the finished product to Carmel ourselves and take that opportunity to attend the fundraiser and catch up with some of our old friends. Mark, whom we had just parted ways with on the Guatemala trip, graciously offered his house to John and me while we were in town. Never ones to miss a chance to hang out with Mark, we graciously accepted his offer. The event went great, and it was so gratifying to see firsthand, people's response to our work. The video we created was designed to take a person, with no prior understanding, through what it was like to walk through a live mine field. Freedom Fields exceeded their financial goal within an hour of showing our video and I gained a new level of respect for just how much documented images can affect people's minds, when it comes to opening their wallets to give. Energized with this new boost of passion, John and I finished out the year working on the IHE documentary and set our sights on the fresh year to come.

The holidays came and went and soon we were living in

the year 2009. With the new year came a new chance to help yet another NGO. Through a contact that I had made on the McCain campaign trail, I had been introduced to Global Action for Children. GAC was a global child advocacy group. They supported a range of children's issues and Angelina Joli and her Joli Pitt foundation had recently presented them with a one-million-dollar grant. As they were a smaller, more grassroots organization, they had never come across the right people to produce a marketing piece for them. Until now.

Let me break it down. If Joe Ordinary from something, something, global nonprofit group searches the Internet to find a production company to film a documentary, or even a marketing video, the prices that he's going to get quoted will make him gasp in disbelief. On average, every one-minute of finished video cost about a thousand dollars to produce. This is the combined rate of camera and gear rental, operator fees, and post-production costs like logging tapes and editing. You also have to consider that the quote is also based on filming in a controlled environment—like a wedding or a training video shot at a nice, cushy, air-conditioned studio. If a global NGO contacts a production company inquiring about filming on location in a possibly dangerous, developing country, you're going to get a quote closer to three thousand a minute, plus travel costs extra expenditures. Plus, they usually want to take way too many people. Camera guys, audio guys, assistants, producers, directors and that extra guy who always sits around doing nothing. A friend of mine that works with Autism Awareness contacted a video group to film a simple Walk for Autism event and was quoted an amount of over ten thousand dollars. This is why we started Karma180, to help NGOs get the multimedia and video pieces that they need, without taking the needed money away from the causes these humanitarian group support. With GAC, we offered to create something for an event using existing footage that we had of children we had shot in locations around the globe. It turned out great, and this opened our eyes to doing even more to help NGOs based out of the states, NGOs that may never even make it to the global locations they are trying to aid. We would act as their eyes on the ground, pairing up their organization's information with our images to create a personalized marketing piece to be given free, and used however they wanted. I have found it harder to convince people that we really don't want anything in return for our services than to try to ask for money—especially after they have received pricy quotes from numerous other production groups. But that's what John and I are about—giving. Freely giving to create a better world. In my heart, I truly believe that, if we could take greed from the human conscience, we would be one step closer to healing the planet. Take one instead of two; hand a homeless person a couple dollars instead of having that next drink; donate money and things that you worked hard for to someone that has very little. But do it from the heart, and don't look for anything in return. Karma likes this.

When people hear what John and I have been doing and where we have been, they are sometimes amazed when they realize that we have really accomplished all of this. All this knowledge, all these spiritual journeys, the global travels, and the unbelievable adventures started when I was thirty-five. Do I wish I had gotten an earlier start? Of course. But this was the time when the universe thought my mind was ready for these experiences, and I was open enough to understand how to give back.

THE BEGINNING OF MY SPIRITUAL QUEST

I can't remember how old I was, but I must have been somewhere in my early twenties. I was chasing down stunt work and more than likely collecting unemployment from previous jobs. I had a lot of time on my hands with very little on my mind, and I was a blank spiritual slate. For some reason, unknown to me, I woke up one day and had the urge to go to the local library. I can't imagine why—I never read anything and didn't even have a library card—but there was some strong force pulling in that direction. So, I just went. No question, no reasoning with myself; I just got up and drove there. Once inside, I awkwardly meandered around a bit, like a shark circling around searching for an unknown meal, until I found myself standing in front of the rack containing the library's selection of audio books. (They were called books on tape then. We hadn't yet entered the CD era.) Still not sure what the hell I was doing there, I began to thumb through the plastic binders containing books that I could listen to. I must have made a dozen passes over one particular audio book before I pulled it from the shelf. Again, it was almost like the damn thing was pulling me in, the same way I was pulled to the library in the first place. For some reason I didn't put the stops on anything that day. I patiently read the title and then flipped it around to read the description on the back side of the well-handled plastic case. *Anatomy of The Spirit*, by Carolyn Myss was the item that I was now holding in my hand, but I still had no idea why. The funny thing is I never even tried to put it back, even though it looked like something that I would have absolutely no interest in listening to. I just held it in my hand and blindly continued walked around. Then, to add to the strangeness, I applied for a library card and checked the tapes out. I sat there in my truck for a few minutes, just staring at the title on the cover, before opening the case and inserted tape number one, side "A," into my cassette player. I couldn't stop listening to it. It was astonishing. *Anatomy of The Spirit* explained exactly why I had gotten up off my couch, climbed into my truck and driven to the library to find this exact audio book. This was the point at which the universe decided to open my eyes to why we humans are on this earth and what life is essentially all about.

How do I explain this? The book covered many topics, including the points of energy that flow through the human body that in Eastern thought are known as chakras, and how Caroline was able to match these energy points on the human body, each having their own message, to the sacred rites in Catholicism and the Judaic Tree Of Life. All this I found interesting, but the overall message that I personally took away from the book was about moving forward into the unknown, bravely walking into the unfamiliar through the doors that open up in front of you and letting go of where you think you are supposed to be, and what you want to do in this life. Let the universe guide you and don't question it. She said that we really can't make a wrong decision, because that decision served our needs at the time it was made, and that God doesn't need our help to plan our lives— whether we believe in God or not. In one chapter, she told a story of a gentleman who worked for a limousine company. One day, when he had the limo parked at his house, a group of neighborhood children asked him if they could have a ride. Reluctantly, he finally said, "Fine, you can all have a ride, but you all have to ask for your parents' permission first." The children did and, before long, he had a limo full of happily laughing kids and even a couple of parents too. The man had no idea why he said yes to the wishes of the children. This was an uncharacteristic thing for him to do but to his surprise, he did. At first, he kept thinking, "What am I doing?" but after a short time, even he was finding the children and the ride enjoyable. Sometime later, when the man had saved enough to buy his own limousine, he decided to throw caution to the wind and open his very own limo service. A parent of one of the children to whom he had given the ride to turned out to be a highly paid executive for a major corporation. Remembering the man's generosity to the neighborhood kids, he hired the new limo service and recommended it to some of his other highly paid business associates. Within a short time, the man's new limo service was booming with more clients than he ever imagined. The simple act of not saying no to the children who wanted a free ride changed his life. The universe gifted him for following the path of moving forward through the doors that opened for him. This is the way the life is supposed to work. If he had gone in another direction that first day, his life would have followed a different path—not necessarily in an unsuccessful direction, but on a course that might have taken him longer to achieve his goals, or possibly, led him to another career altogether. His correct decision was to not question the doors of the universe, but to flow with them. Allowing life to move faster—this is our purpose. To allow life to let us live our existence how it sees fit.

People like Carolyn Myss, Paulo Coelho and Eckhart Tolle have all listened to the universe. They have opened their minds, bodies, and souls to all the world's religions, philosophies, and possibilities. They all speak openly and walk through the doors that open to them. As did Gandhi, Mother Theresa, Jesus, Mohammad, Buddha, Lao Tzu and too many more to name.

Why do we still speak of these people? Because they all understood that a life is intended is to be lived. We are all human and we all have an ending date. You reading this, the rest of the world and I will all cease to exist one day. Slightly led to a prophetic state by some very delicious sake, I recently opened my own mind and realized just how little time we have on this earth. If you live to the ripe old age of eighty, you will have roughly 29,200 days in which you can breathe, walk around this world and spread peace. To put that in perspective, the current poverty level in the United States is around $22,975, depending on the state. So, if you think about these two numbers, you can see that we, the human race, live our days in numbers that almost rival poverty levels.

It's an eye-opening thought. 80 years, 960 months, 4,160 weeks, or 29,200 days is all we get. Looking at the days, weeks and months, it is much easier to see how time slips away from us rapidly, and unlike money, we can't make another day. With this rather depressing though brought to mind, how could you possibly spend your life without going forward in search of newness, of adventure, of love, forgiveness, trust, and compassion. It's not too late. Walk through the doors, travel an unpredictable route, communicate with a stranger, see where it leads. It can be life changing.

THE GEORGE CLOONEY CONNECTION

The *Fear Factor* show was running full tilt and John and I were still fully engulfed in our mental high from the previous year's events and ready to continue the ride into 2009. I had so many new thoughts and perceptions of the world roaming through my mind, I had really become comfortable with who I was. With the talk of a possible new foundation being formed by Cindy McCain, we kept in frequent contact with Teacup about the possibilities of future events and how we would play a large role by heading up the video and photo division of the multimedia-based NGO.

Darfur had always been a hot topic with Cindy and, with our earlier attempt thwarted because of the campaign the previous year, the location was now back for open discussion. John and I had been included on a few email chains, so we had a small idea of what was going on. In one of the emails, there was mention of a conference call with someone who had all the logistics of this possible upcoming journey into the heart of one of the most volatile war zones in Africa. No dates were established yet, but this was enough to get our blood flowing for some more adventure, and with a brief call from Teacup with the time, date and access codes to enter this very discrete phone conference, my brain went to a spot between anticipation and anxiety. This is a dangerous place we are talking about, and there are many stories about seasoned aid workers coming home traumatized by what they saw and experienced. I wasn't sure that I was ready for it, but at the same time I was eager to go.

The conference call was scheduled for January 8, but as a precursor of things to come, Cindy and Teacup wanted to catch me up on what we might be getting into and provide some basic information that had been communicated to them up to this point. So as instructed by an email, I called Teacup and we caught up for a couple minutes as we waited for Cindy to patched into our little three-way chat. A moment later I heard a slight click in the receiver and then, "Hi Kevin, how are you?" Cindy said with an energetic cheerfulness in her voice. She always puts me in a good mood when we speak, but there was something extra in her tone on this call.

"I just wanted to give you and John a quick heads up on the Darfur trip," she said, and then Teacup jumped in with the information that they had accumulated so far. It seemed that the United States had frowned on its citizens traveling into Darfur, or any of the surrounding warring countries for that matter, so our first stop was to be Paris, France. I guess the French government is much more lenient about such travel scenarios. This would put us closer to the African continent. We would buy tickets from Paris to a country, or province, on the west side of the African continent, (near Cameroon, I believe), and work our way into the country of Chad. Here we would meet up with our contacts who would travel with us to the backside of Darfur. This could all change—it was a work in progress – but, as planned, it would keep us out of most of the civil and border wars that flanked Darfur. To me, that looked like on all sides, but I guess our contact had a safe way in. Our security would be minimal and would mostly consist of traveling quickly, in between curfews, and never staying in one spot for too long. The less attention that we drew to our party the safer it would be for us all. Yet another reason for heading in through Paris.

"We will all get more information during the conference call on the eighth," Teacup clarified. Cindy said her goodbyes, leaving Teacup and I still in conversation so she could give me all the access codes and the proper numbers to call. She told me to say hi to Nancy, or Sally, or whichever nickname she gave John, and then she sternly repeating one last thing before exiting the call.

"Speak of this call to John only, no one else, It's for our safety." It took a few minutes for me to hang up. I just stood there with the phone to my ear listening to the droning hum of the now voiceless call while trying to decipher the notes I had crudely scribbled on a yellow pad in front of me. Once more I was asking myself just how I managed to get involved in another amazing situation.

The eighth was only two days away and John and I were both scheduled at the *Fear Factor Live* venue, so we knew that we were going to have to play hand off with the phone if the call happened during the middle of one of the shows. Murphy's law of course made sure that this is exactly what happened. Two o'clock came around. This was the discussed time for the conference call and two o'clock was also the start time of our third show of the day. With permission of the rest of the crew, we set things up so that one of us could be off stage at a time. This would assure that at least one of our voices was interacting with Cindy and the rest of the group during the call. We were there more to listen in than add to the conversation but, from time to time, Cindy or Teacup would say, "You two get that," and we wanted one of us to be able to respond back with at least a simple, "Yep."

Two o'clock came around. Setting the phone to speaker John dialed the number and, when prompted, he punched in the security code and stated both our names. Seconds later, we were patched through and were announced to the rest of the conference group. Almost at the same time, our two o'clock show was starting, so while I was attending to the contestants, John found a semi-quiet location backstage on the second floor for us to continue eavesdropping on the call. John was in the back up position, which meant that he had more time to be on the phone, so poised with his notepad he took down as much information as he could. Meanwhile, I was stuck in a show position, but I would run over to him as often as I could so he could fill me in on what I was missing. At about midpoint of the show, I ran past him in between stunt segments, it was written all over his face, something real cool was going on. Waving wildly at me to get me to come over to the phone he excitably said, "Kevin, just shut up and listen to who's on the call with us."

I removed my show headset, leaned in close to the phone and listened as a familiar sounding voice spoke up to explain to Cindy just how we were going to travel into a refugee camp deep in the heart of Darfur. Then it hit me, I knew who this was, but before I could say anything, I heard someone address the mystery voice as George." I froze for a moment, staring into nothingness, and John could see the gears in my brain trying to grind out thought.

He covered the speaker on the phone and said, "We're on a fucking conference call with George Clooney!"

I have been in the film industry for many years and so has John. We are so far beyond the level of getting starstruck. It's just something that happens after the newness of the movie business wears off. Actors become nothing more than people doing a job, but when normal life includes a movie star in a non-Hollywood film environment, that puts an entirely new spin on things. An example is that when I was working on the feature *Striptease*, Demi Moore always had a kind of untouchable presence surrounding her, somewhat larger than life, but she was just another actor to me. Until, while on set one day, her cell phone rang and I heard her answer and say, "Oh hi, Bruce, how are you?" Demi Moore was standing next to me talking to Bruce Willis on the phone. It was so normal that it brought her down from star level to ordinary, making her much more approachable. Not like I walked over to her and said, "Tell Bruce I said hi," or anything like that, but in the oddest way, I became more starstruck over the action of a common phone call then of the fame of the person making it. This is exactly what was going on with the Clooney conference call. In person, on a movie set, I could be performing a stunt fight with him, and it would have been routine. This, however, was a phone call about humanitarian efforts in Darfur, and George Clooney was talking to us as if we were all equals. He was using his knowledge and connections to help get us in and out safely. Of course, on our side, to add to the insanity of the situation you have two stunt guys in the middle of a live *Fear Factor* show, with audio calls about catching rancid octopuses resonating loudly from the stage, huddled in a badly lit backstage area in full rigging harnesses, trying to scratch down information that could possibly save our ass, and do it before the final pyrotechnic explosion went off—which would have certainly deafened everyone actively involved in the phone conference. Does life really get any stranger? Not in our karmic world.

The call ended just before the two o'clock show, John and I went back into the break room to try to make sense of what he hastily scratched down. This trip had us jumping from Paris to Chad, somehow avoiding all the border wars around Darfur, flying into the desert, and staying one day at a refugee camp housing over forty-thousand people and driving out to a safer location before the evening curfew, when the area became very dangerous. There was a day at a women and children's shelter being run by an NGO called CARE and a day zipping around to a few other humanitarian-based centers, never staying in one place long enough to draw attention to ourselves and always traveling before nightfall. This mission would have been mind-boggling, and the dangers of traveling around Darfur might have trumped all of our previous adventures if it had come to fruition, but it didn't. Our second attempt was also unsuccessful. Unlike the first time, the campaign didn't cause the failure of the trip. What did was that too much information leaked from one of the NGOs that we were to visit, causing the security team to pull the plug on the whole thing. Too many people knew we were coming, which raised the risk of possible attack. Even though we all love adventure and humanity, Cindy wouldn't knowingly put out happy little band in direct line of fire.

DUBAI, JULY 2009
INTERNATIONAL HUMANITARIAN CITY

WHAT CAN I SAY, IT'S DUBAI?

I CAN'T LIE, the disappointment of the Darfur cancellation was a huge mental blow. John and I were really looking forward to it. You get used to the roller coaster ups and downs when you work in the movie industry, but when it comes to the humanitarian trips the disappointment seems somewhat more personal. You're not just going out to do a job, you're going out to try to make the world a better place.

As karma would have it though, our disappointment was short lived due to a well-timed phone call from Teacup.

"Hey Kevin, are you and John available for a trip at the end of the month?" She barked out in her playful, sarcastic tone.

"Of course we are!" I spouted back, trying to keep my cool as usual. "Just where are we off to this time?" Teacup's answer was that we would be going to a couple of locations on this trip. We would start out on an Operation Smile mission in India and from there we were to fly into Cambodia to visit a landmine field actively being de-mined by The HALO Trust.

A couple of days later, Cindy's travel agent emailed John and me the travel itineraries, revealing the trip in its entirety. My heart skipped a beat at what I read. It seemed that Teacup forgot to mention the first stop on our journey, or maybe she just didn't know about it at the time of our chat. Either way my adrenalin spiked again.

Like on all of our Cindy trips, as soon as our travel information was emailed out my brain switched to pre-school mode, and, while I was still ogling over the words in the email, the voice of reason in our two-man video crew called me. John was almost as excited as I was.

"Kevin, did you see where we are going first? Dubai!" John said. I could hear the same kid-like anticipation in his voice that was going through my head.

"Exactly where is Dubai?" I asked. I knew it was near a desert somewhere, but I couldn't pinpoint it on a map.

"Dubai. It's in the United Arab Emirates. It's on the Arabian Peninsula. Kevin, it's one of the wealthiest places in the world! Remember the Travel Channel shows about the island being created to look like a palm tree, and the hotel that looks like a giant sail that's also built right on the water?" Travel Channel, Palm Island, late night TV images were swimming through my brain, "Holy shit, John we are going to the Middle East!" I belted out.

"I dreamed about going to this place for years!" John said, followed by, "Did you see the rest of the itinerary? This is going to be an unbelievable trip!" John was right. This was an amazing trip schedule.

We were to go from Orlando to DC to Dubai. Leaving Dubai, we were to head to Mumbai and then to Guwahati, India for the Operation Smile mission. Post mission we would fly from Guwahati to Delhi, Delhi to Bangkok and Bangkok to Siem Rep, Cambodia, where we would meet up with the HALO Trust guys to tour a minefield. Heading back home we would go from Siem

Rep to Phnom Penh to Seoul, Korea to Atlanta and finally back to good old Orlando. That is twelve cities in five countries in just under eleven days. This was sheer insanity, but the more insane the trip was and the worse the conditions were, the more John and I always seem to enjoy it.

FIRST STOP, THE MIDDLE EAST

Landing in Dubai International was something to behold. Clean, modern, no expenses held back to accommodate for luxury, as you would expect to find in one of the wealthiest locations on the globe. Damn, I wish we'd had time to explore the intricacies of the airport, but my phone started to go off as our plane touched down. It was Teacup. They had already landed and were waiting for us with our transportation to the hotel, "Get a move on it guys, time's a wasting" she said lightheartedly. For a country on the same peninsula as Saudi Arabia, immigration was a breeze to get through. Hell, I have had a harder time getting back into the United States through JFK in New York than we did here.

Dashing through customs, I called Teacup from the luggage carousel to find out just where we were to meet them. Here is where I should have known this would be no ordinary trip. Our instructions were to grab our bags and find the passenger pick up location just in front of the main airport entrance. She said to look for the two four-door BMW seven series town cars. They would be there waiting to transport us to the hotel. Ours was the BMW in the rear.

John, not hearing the call, kind of looked at me with an inquisitive expression on his brow as I lowered my phone from my ear to about waist level and stared at it quietly for a moment. This action of mine had become very familiar to John while I was engaged in phone dialogues with Teacup or Wendy, before or during one of these trips. Then it's usually followed by me slowly turning to him in disbelief and beginning my next sentence with something like, "You're not going to believe this," or "Shit, this is going to be cool." Following suit as normal, I turned to John, shrugged my shoulders, smirked with a little sarcasm, raised an eyebrow, and said, "Wow, wait till you see what's waiting for us outside."

Gathering our luggage we exited the climate-controlled environment of the airport and were hit by the hot, dry desert conditions of the Middle East. We were also met by the grace, luxury, and an ostentatious view of the Dubai skyline, along with two superb specimens of the flagship of BMW's armada—the 740i. As I spot the women, Teacup waved us over and Cindy popped out of the lead car for a quick hello and a hug. Then, with the assistance of our driver, we entered our car and were immersed in opulence. Before pulling out from under the airport breezeway, our driver turned and offered John and I ice cold towels that smelled of mint to wash our faces, sparkling bottled water and leatherbound menu of songs from which we could choose to add to the enjoyment during our drive to the hotel. We both laughed a bit at the lavish treatment, but I took the song menu and chose Andrea Bocelli for our listening pleasure to accompany us on our drive. As if I had just ordered a two-hundred-dollar bottle of French wine, when I handed back the list to the driver he agreed, with much emotion, that I had selected superbly. Off we drove and the amazement began.

Let me first start by stating the fact that John and I both thought that we were staying at a Hilton hotel. I had looked it up; even by Dubai standards, it was very classy, but, in contrast to the US, it was marvelous. This already excited us. As we were chauffeured from the airport to the hotel the driver gave us the two-dollar tour, describing the history of Dubai and pointing out some unbelievable architecture, like the 2,717-foot tall Burj Khalifa—the world's new tallest building. At the time, it was still in its last days of construction. Our driver answered as many questions as we managed to throw at him. We passed the Dubai mall, where for a nominal fee you can go snow skiing at Ski Dubai, indoors, in the middle of the desert, at the mall. Then, a few moments down the road we saw it, the Burj Al Arab Hotel. Constantly voted the world's most luxurious hotels, the Burj Al Arab has had more National Geographic, Discovery Channel and Travel Channel specials filmed on it then any single hotel ever built, and the closer we got, the more unbelievable it was. With one last right hand turn we were now driving parallel to the sea and closing in on our left was the Burj. Such elegance and remarkable architecture. contrasted by the blue sky and the ocean, its white sail structural design managed to just seamlessly float there above the waters of the Persian Gulf. Driving a bit farther, we approached the intersection of the highway that paralleled the ocean and the entrance road to this mega-hotel. Stopped here by a red light I had a clear view to see down the drive, which eventually became a bridge separating the Burj Al Arab from the mainland. It was on its very own, man-made island. Totally enamored by this favorite star of the travel shows, John and I both tried to take as much of it in as we could before the light turned green and this colossal monument to hotels entered the BMW's rear view mirror and faded away like a memory. Then, with one purposeful motion of our driver's right hand, the game changed in our favor.

The left turn indicator of our car had been switched on, we were preparing to turn left, left onto the bridge leading to the Burj Al Arab. It was only then that I noticed the custom metal plate adhered to the dashboard engraved with the same name as the hotel. We had been riding in the hotels private BMW shuttle cars all along. This luxury was no coincidence, nor was the fact that we were approaching the guard gate leading to the beginning of the bridge. We were not staying at the Hilton Hotel. John and I were soon to be guest of the Burj Al Arab Hotel,

STUNTMEN IN THE BURJ AL ARAB

"Well, this is one hell of a surprise," I said, just kind of speaking out loud to whoever in the car was listening. At this point John and I both expected, one hundred percent, that our car would turn and take us to our pre-selected Hilton hotel after dropping Cindy and Teacup off at this palatial retreat. I was wrong again. Coming to a stop behind Cindy's car, our driver quickly exited the front and signaled to a troop of bellhops and other hotel staff who excitedly ran to help us out of the BMW and escort us up to the front doors of the hotel. Clutching my camera backpack like I always do, I got out of the back and headed up the steps to the lobby.

Cindy just looked over and smiled at the sight of John and me as we tried to stifle our childlike exuberance, and Teacup just looked at her feet and shook her head while motioning for us to keep up. Entering the lobby, our group was met by a personal escort who would take care of us during our stay. There was a beautiful young lady standing there to welcome us with a silver tray full of dates and next to her was another beautiful young woman with a large brass Moroccan style lantern containing incense. Her job was to walk around us and make the air smell good.

The reason for our surprise trip to Dubai was for much more than a luxury stay in a sensational seven star rated hotel. The purpose for the stopover was to visit the World Food Program's warehouse located at the newly created International Humanitarian City in Dubai. Ideally positioned within five hours flight time from Egypt and most of the Middle East, this is the perfect location for such an outpost. Not only does the International Humanitarian City (IHC) house a World Food Program distribution center, but also within the village, as it's called, is an office for The United Nations Children Fund (UNICEF), The United Nations Refugee Agency (UNHCR), The International Islamic Relief Organization, (IIROSA), SOS Children's Villages, World Vision International and a host of other global humanitarian organizations. This tour would be the business at hand on our second day in Dubai, but for now, it was time to unwind and enjoy the splendor of our hotel.

Our room was close to three thousand square feet, much larger than my house back in Orlando. It had a marble staircase with a rod iron railing that curved eloquently up to the second floor where the bedrooms were located. I took the smaller of the two and John graciously stayed in the master suite, complete with its own spacious walk in closet and secret emergency exit. We never did find out where that went. On the first floor was a lush living room connected to a very spacious meeting room that finished out with a fully working kitchen. No mini fridge here; this was the real deal. The office area was just inside the entrance door, it contained the bar. Like the refrigerator, this bar was full size and loaded to entertain.

From our suite on the twenty-sixth floor, looking to the left we could see the famous Palm Island. This is yet another man-made island but this one is, as the name states, in the shape of a palm tree and it's large enough to easily be seen on Google Earth. In the distance beyond this was a second larger version of Palm Island. This left me guessing that the first one was just for practice, to make sure they got it right. To the right we could see the soon-to-be finished Earth Island, again this is just as it sounds, a manmade island in the shape of the Earth. Why the people of Dubai insist on filling in the ocean when there is so much open land laying around is a mystery to me. It's a desert. How hard could it be to build a massive palm-shaped resort on land? I guess they do it because they can.

John and I were way out of our league in this hotel. The place was so far away from the depths of my imagination that even though I have stayed there, my mind still perceives it as a dream. Realizing that no one would believe this, (Hell, we barely believed it.) we figured that it would be a good idea to create a video tour of the entire room. So as to not bore anyone with an entire written rendition of our video tour, I will only mention some points that I found funny while re-watching the footage a year or so later. John performed a masterful impersonation of Robin Leach, from, *Lifestyles of The Rich and Famous*, lecturing on the finer points of the multi-function room remote control that allowed him to open the curtains and raise the television out of the dresser from the comfort of his bed. He also seems to remember me picking up a uniquely shaped piece of decadent chocolate that was left on my pillow and presenting it to him as The Tears of the Desert, then trying it and realizing that it was only a crunch bar melted to look like a fig. We often laugh at my innocent ignorance., Now, I have been in a ton of interesting bathrooms around the world from beautiful to downright scary, and although this was not my favorite, it was the most lavish, and to walk in and film John's laundry strung between the gold-plated shower head and the ornate gold door handle was priceless. You know what they say: You can take the stuntman out of the trailer park, but you can't take the trailer park out of the stuntman.

Neither John nor I were raised in a trailer park but maybe

you can see where I am going with this. Again, the pursuit of humanitarian aid had taken us to a place we never thought that we would see. This experience was no more inspirational than being in a landmine field in Cambodia, taking a private Jet plane to Kosovo or walking down a Guatemalan jungle trail but it was happening because we just kept following the directions of life's flow without throwing up any barricades.

To continue the special experiences on our first night in Dubai, reservations had been made at one of the world's top rated seafood restaurants. Located on the ground floor of the Burj Al Arab is the Al Mahara. It is like dining at your own private Sea World. Surrounded by a giant aquarium while you feast, you are literally submersed in a man-made ocean. John's meal was the topic of conversation for the night, he had Golden Risotto which was a mushroom risotto covered in a leaf of gold for dessert, we had chocolates coated in gold. There was real twenty-four carat flake on and in his food, and the only reason that I am even bringing up such splendor while describing a humanitarian mission is to show the stark contrast between the beginning of the trip and where we would end up in India two days from this very meal. It was quite the opposite, I assure you. Sometimes seeing the extremes in distance from the super wealthy to the super impoverished helps you to find that all-important balance between the two. You can't know good without knowing bad, without hot we would not have a definition for cold and without day we could not understand night. I find the same importance in this world of opposites when it comes to the understanding humanity. It helps me to create a balance in my mind, as I always try to know both sides of the hand that someone has been dealt. That person in the dump or sleeping in the gutters could have been John. it could have been me, or it could be anyone reading this.

"There before the grace of the God go I."

That night I pulled a chair to the window of my bedroom. I sat and reflected like I often do. I had come so far at this point in my life that my talks with the Universe expanded from questions like, "Why me?" and "How did I get in this amazing situation?" to a simple prayer of thanks and of peace. Staring out into the darkness of the Persian Gulf, I could see the lights of boats passing in the far distance. At times I felt as small as one of those lights being swallowed up by the blackness of the sea, but I also felt enlightened. I knew a secret of life, and I was a living example of it.

Morning came with an amazing breakfast buffet served on the open deck overlooking the Gulf. Cindy and Teacup joined us, and we went over the plans for the day. The big-ticket item was the visit the World Food Programs new headquarters and distribution center located at the International Humanitarian City. This would be followed up with quick trip to the Dubai mall and a brief run through Ski Dubai. When in Rome.

We were given the order by Teacup to finish feeding our faces and go grab our gear, as the transport van would be waiting down in front of the hotel in about twenty minutes. I made one last run past the buffet table armed myself with a small to go box and then hurried to catch up with John at the elevators, stuffing maple bacon into my mouth as I ran. We time checked ourselves frequently as we changed and inspected our gear, to not leave anyone waiting on us. Scurrying back out to the elevators we made our way down through the lobby, past the smoking hot girls waving the incense to the front drive area where of course, Teacup was standing, looking at her watch and shaking her head as usual.

INTERNATIONAL HUMANITARIAN CITY

It was a short drive by car to the IHC location from the hotel, and the route took us directly behind the worlds new tallest building, yet another plus. Although we did not have the comfort of driving around all day in those sweet BMW's we did get the benefit of traveling with a representative of the local World Food Program and her English was much better than that of the driver who picked us up from the airport. She also wasn't afraid to speak of some shadier information surrounding Dubai, like the competition of the super-wealthy sheiks who were continually trying to one-up each other by creating the most ridiculous mega skyscrapers their money could buy, mostly for bragging rights. She also let us know that while this grand infrastructure was creating many jobs, most of the workers laboring on these monstrous buildings were uneducated, underprivileged people who traveled long distances away from their families and villages only to be housed in what she described as slave labor camp conditions. It was much like being shanghaied onto a pirate ship, only this ship was a mega building in the desert, and your cabin was a barbed wire encampment guarded by armed men whose job was to discourage anyone from wandering off. This is the Middle East and things are done differently here.

As we drove up to the WFP center the first thing that I noticed was the fleet of brand-new vehicles parked in long lines in an open field next to one of the warehouses. There were Toyota trucks, six-wheel transport vehicles, water tankers and a group of Land Rovers, all painted white, most with the blue WFP logo painted on the side and a few with UN emblems. I have seen and ridden in vehicles much like these in many countries around the globe, but I had never seen a fleet this large and impressive.

This piqued my curiosity. Continuing past the guard gates we followed the drive and parked in front of a building with a very well-manicured landscape. This was the main office for the WFP Dubai program.

Entering an NGO's center of operations with Cindy McCain is a very fun experience. Her name is well known in the humanitarian world, but people who have never met her don't know what to expect. They always line up on their best behavior, nervously waiting for their turn to be introduced. She enters a situation with elegance and grace but wastes no time getting to business—asking questions, and creating so many smiles that, within a short time, everyone eases up and relaxes around her. I guess it's her nurturing side that comes out when she is in the presence of the needy. Cindy has seen it all and completely understands the importance of international aid.

The tour started, as most do, with a couple of informal meetings about the NGO, what it does and its effectiveness within the humanitarian world. This gave me the opportunity to inquire about the fleet of vehicles I had noticed earlier. The answer I received provided some information on an element of the World Food Program that I didn't know existed. One of the representatives, while leading us around the compound, explained that while the WFP will ship anything brought to them from NGOs, charitable organizations, religious groups, and even private citizens, for free, to any disaster area currently being supplied, they also have a business based side. The fleet of vehicles were for sale. As I would see on our tour, there was a fully-loaded vehicle fabrication shop that would turn any auto-mechanic green with envy. NGOs can buy as many vehicles as they want, or as few as one and have their purchases fully customized to suit their needs in whatever environment they are working. At present there were two white four-door Toyota pickup trucks being retrofitted for an NGO currently working in the Sudan. The suspension had been beefed up, extra fuel and water tanks were added, modern global positioning system and radio equipment installed, and shrapnel resistant floor wells had been created to help protect the occupants from explosions due to accidental landmine contact while driving. These vehicles were obviously headed for a hostile work environment. The WFP is trying to make it very easy for global humanitarian groups, large and small, to have access to such equipment, and the WFP makes a profit from these sales. Not only are vehicles available, but groups can also obtain communication equipment; portable, freestanding warehouses; security gear, such as helmets and flak jackets; and medical packages. Everything was well organized and boxed up to go anywhere at a moment notice. Once the equipment is paid for and customized to the buyer's needs, the entire lot is transported by WFP planes to the NGO's specified locations. How amazing would that feel? To be a grassroots NGO, working in some developing nation, and to see a couple of fully customized Land Rovers, loaded to the hilt with medical equipment, two-way radios and other gear, roll out of the back of a C-130 cargo plane that had just landed on a dusty, over-used runway in the middle of nowhere. That image is reality, and it's happening all the time thanks to this sector of the World Food Program.

The tour continued for a couple hours, leading us through warehouse after warehouse where food and supplies were either being stored for future use, or being prepared for shipment to. The WFP had pulled together an amazing operation and the key to their success was the ability to organize and coordinate complex logistics. The International Humanitarian City itself was a marvelous idea; bringing so many top-ranking world relief organizations together, under one umbrella, is ingenious. It helps to merge individual NGOs think tanks into a monster of communications and improves the speed of international aid delivery. If this were to be used as a working model and emulated on a global scale—with humanitarian cities in key countries, all working on the same information platform—so much good could be accomplished, with so little waste. Maybe one day.

While John was finishing up with a group photo of Cindy and the staff, set nicely in front of the main entrance just below the massive WFP logo, I decided to have a walk around. I found myself standing in the middle of an unused road just outside the WFP guard gates. Rotating in a slow circle, I just took it all in from the ground level. Looking out the window of a luxury hotel can give you a false perspective of the world. It makes you feel safe and untouchable. Here, though still in a very safe area, with my feet touching the dirt, Dubai felt much more real. Facing the growing skyline, I could see the future. Tourism for the rich and famous, and spectacular, climate-controlled monuments, rising into the heavens, to which the laborers who built them will never gain entry— much like the great pyramids. However, facing away from the grandeur, I could see the desert; I could taste the dust contained in the hot dry wind that circled around me. Out there was the true Middle East. Saudi Arabia was within driving distance;.Iran lay just across the Persian Gulf; and we were still involved in a conflict one country away. I was standing close to a literal line in the sand that marked the collision of the old and new world. John came over after he finished taking the phone and we talked about how unbelievable this place was. We took a couple photos of ourselves with the skyline in the background and just spent a few moments in silence taking it all in.

Our peaceful moment of reflection was broken by the toot

of a horn and Teacup waving us over to the vehicle. John and I climbed in the back seat and got situated. We all talked for a bit about our amazement at just how well-run and organized this entire compound was and how this hub would increase the humanitarian aid output to future disasters zones within the Middle East and surrounding areas. "That was a great tour. Thank you again for involving us," I said, before following up with, "What's next? Anybody else hungry?"

As if on cue, Cindy spoke up from the front seat, "Let's go check out the mall." Pondering her words for a second, we all spoke at once.

"That's where Ski Dubai is," John said. Teacup chimed in with, "I'm game," and I ended our group run-on sentence with, "I could definitely use a Starbucks." So off we went to check out the Dubai mall and the attached Ski Dubai; get a glimpse at some indoor downhill snow skiing in the middle of the desert; and snag a cup of familiar coffee.

Malls are malls wherever you go. This one was super fancy and very expensive. At one end, we ran into walls of windows that separated the comfortably cool shopping area from a frozen winter wonderland. Standing at the glass was like looking into a life-size snow globe and it only took Cindy a couple seconds to say, "Do you guys want to go in? I want to go in. Come on, let's check it out." Who am I to argue with such a fun suggestion?

"Why not? Let's play with snow in the desert," I said. We didn't go as far as to ski—being from Florida, John and I both are more at home on the water than on ice—but we did all suit up and wonder around the lower level, which housed the ice caves, kids play area and the hot cocoa bar. I can just say that if you do ever find yourself in Dubai and want to a good laugh at just what copious amounts of money can create, check this place out.

Exhausted from the morning's events, we came to the unanimous decision that a nap and a bit of down time would fit in perfectly before we met for dinner later that evening. The nap turned into quite a few hours of relaxation. Our room was just too amazing to not enjoy we'd had no word from Cindy or Teacup. It seemed as if they were in no hurry to do anything either.

The phone finally rang at about seven o'clock and Teacup said that Cindy wanted John and me to come over to her suite to discuss the remainder of the trip.

"Copy that, be right over," I replied. In Cindy's room learned that there were some pressing matters back home in Arizona and the trip was going to be cut short. Cindy and Teacup's trip, that is. John and I were to continue to India and Cambodia without them. Because the filming on this trip was more focused around the actual NGOs and not as much on Cindy's interaction with them, we could still manage to get some great video footage for her new foundation. She did not need to be there while we were filming. This actually is the position that Cindy had envisioned for us all along. John and I would visit global NGOs that would possibly be associated with the new foundation. We would shoot small video segments about each organization and, while doing this, we could feel out the groups and give our personal opinions of them to Cindy. The new foundation was in its infancy stage, but we were open to helping in any way we could. Here was a chance to start.

Cindy and I sat down and discussed what shots and information she wanted from both locations in India, and Cambodia. This Operation Smile group was the first mission ever to go to Guwahati, India, which is located just south of the Himalayan Mountains, in an area called Assam Province. Here we decided to focus on the newness of the location, and the stigmas children with facial deformities face growing up in such a superstitious and mythologically-based culture. After a few days, we would fly to Cambodia, where we would document the progress The HALO Trust was making in their efforts to clear some landmine fields in a mountainous region of the K-5 mine belt. The area was accessible only by helicopter.

This was going to be quite a task. Even though John and I now had many international trips under our belts, I won't lie. I was a bit nervous. But I didn't let it show to anyone in the room, not even John. Finding two nuns in a small airport in Peru is nothing compared to finding your way from the Middle East, through Mumbai, India, to Guwahati—located 2,254 miles away in a province infamous for smuggling and human trafficking. Then add making it from Guwahati to Siem Reap, Cambodia— another two thousand miles away—and finish with the trek from Cambodia to DC trek. All in all, it would be a journey of just about nine thousand miles. Really, though, it wasn't the distances that concerned me, but transitioning through all the Third World airports. This would really put our lessons learned over the past five years to the test.

"Have fun. You guys will be just fine," Cindy said as she turned to John and handed him some money to cover any extra expenses we might encounter.

"I'm not sure how much is there, maybe four hundred. It just came out of the ATM that way," she joked to John who thankfully accepted the wad of folded bills.

"Do you think that's enough? I can go get some more if you like," she added.

"No, thank you. That's plenty, Cindy," John replied.

In a motherly tone, Cindy replied, "Well, if you're positive, and make sure you save all your receipts from anything else that might pop up and send them to me." She made us promise that we would.

Because she and Teacup would be taking an early flight out of Dubai the next morning, the two opted out of dinner, but Cindy recommended that we try the buffet style restaurant in the lobby for some traditional local cuisine. We said our goodbyes at the door, where Teacup made sure that we had all the numbers that we could possibly need to get us around—or out of—any situation that might arise.

"Give us a call when you get back home. Have fun and try to stay out of airport detention rooms this time," she said to me, with one last hug.

Thinking about it now, I realize that, the last time we left a country without Cindy, it only took John and me two hours to find our way into a Chinese detention room. That should have been an omen had I thought of it then. Which I didn't!

The dinner buffet was as simply amazing, just like the rest of the meals we ate at the hotel, and we followed it up with a bit of fun at the wonderfully loaded bar in our suite. With a light, intoxicating numbness running through my head, I filled up the three person Jacuzzis in my bathroom and bubbled away until I nodded off.

Our flight out the next day was not until 11:55 that evening, but rather than explore the town, John and I decided to lazily lounge around our three-thousand-foot spacious suite and enjoy it for as long as we could. It was one of the most relaxing days that I have spent in my entire life. We had already set up everything with the hotel for a shuttle ride to the airport that evening, giving ourselves plenty of time to arrive at the Dubai airport, clear customs and get a relaxing start to the second half of this journey.

This surprise Middle East excursion had dropped John and me into the center of a land that we never imagined we would see, and it had expanded my knowledge of the World Food Program by showing us its many venues for assisting global NGOs. Don't even get me started on the Burj Al Arab and the meals fit for a sheik. That level of luxury has to be experienced to be understood. My words cannot do it justice. Now, we were about to leave it all behind and head to another magical place—a country with a population that dwarfs much of the world's by comparison; an ancient world shrouded in superstition, effigies, offerings, gurus and spices, and where Mahatma Gandhi spoke his words of peace.

Be the change you wish to see in the world.

Staring out the little window over my right shoulder. as we were flying out of Dubai, the image of Gandhi's face hung in my mind, I closed my eyes and. within seconds, I could feel sleep taking over my consciousness. The visions in my head faded from Gandhi to a scene of Indiana Jones lowering a weathered fedora over his eyes and settling in for a long flight in an old, twin engine, silver cargo plane, the sun just disappearing behind some ancient Tibetan Mountain range. Mystery was on the horizon and my imagination was working overtime.

GUWAHATI INDIA, JULY 2009
OPERATION SMILE

GUWAHATI, INDIA

THE GREAT THING ABOUT AN EVENING flight out of a country is that you spend most of the trip fast asleep. The bad thing is that you sometimes wake up a bit disoriented and in some strange locations. This evening journey incorporated both factors.

I woke up to the smell of food—food being passed out around me. This meant that I had slept through the young woman asking me if I wanted meat or vegetables and woke during the serving process. Food being served on a plane usually signifies that the flight is either just getting started or getting close to the destination. It was almost four in the morning. We had been in the air for a little over three hours, and we were closing in on Mumbai, India. I was half awake and all I could smell was curry. Groggily, I captured the flight attendant's attention and asked her for two black coffees—one for me and a second for John, who was in the same semi-comatose state I was. A short time later. the internal cabin lights flickered on, and the announcement came from the cockpit that we were on approach to land in Mumbai.

Somehow John and I both managed to stagger out of the plane and clear immigration. It's something we are both accustomed to, but at four-thirty in the morning, with only a couple hours of cramped sleep fueling us, it wasn't an enjoyable process. Heading out into the main terminal hub to find our connecting flight to Guwahati we spotted a man holding a paper sign with "Cindy McCain" written on it. John and I paused to look at each other,

"You suppose we should tell him Cindy's didn't come?" I said as John looked at me and gave a shrug that was accompanied by raised eyebrows.

"Maybe he's here for us too," he countered. This sounded plausible to me, so we casually headed in the direction of the man holding the sign.

"Hello, we are Cindy McCain's video team. This is John and I am Kevin. I am guessing that no one informed you that Cindy had something come up and she had to travel back to the states."

"Miss McCain is not coming, are you sure?" The man replied. His statement sounding annoyed and confused; it wasn't actually a question..

"You're certain of this." he said again, his annoyed tone becoming even more pronounced. Pulling out his cell phone, he dialed a number. While it rang, he gave us one last, "You're sure!"

We just nodded yes. He relayed the news to whomever answered his call and, without even a look back at us, he stormed off, leaving the two of us standing in the middle of the terminal snickering at his aggravation and still looking for our connecting flight.

"I guess no one told him," John said with a smirk. We were both still too tired to really care, I, for one, just wanted to get my ass into a seat on the plane and attempt to get some more sleep. With most people in India speaking fluent English, it didn't take us long to find our gate, board our plane and take to the air. Another three hours and we would be landing in Guwahati. That's what was printed on our tickets, and all was going according to plan on the second leg of the flight, until the captain's voice came over the cabin speakers in a singsong sounding Indian dialect.

"This is your Captain speaking. Ladies and gentlemen, we will be diverting from our current flight path to pick someone up in Calcutta, after which we will then return to our original flight plan into Guwahati. Thank you for your patience." Like we had a choice. I have seen some strange things happen in and around air travel, but I have never seen a pilot land a commercial Boeing 777 passenger airliner, in an unscheduled stop to pick up someone. This curious comment kept both of us awake for the remainder of the flight, and I believe that's about the time we started ordering beers.

We made good time, even with the unscheduled, touch and go landing in Calcutta, and we were both feeling nicely buzzed by the time we reached our destination, which was probably a good thing. From the air the Lokpriya Gopinath Bordoloi International Airport in Guwahati looked very small and there's a good reason for that. It is small, crudely laid out, extremely cluttered and home to more than one sacred cow and a herd of goats.

Our landing was more of a direct flight into the ground then a pleasant touchdown. The plane impacted so hard that every one of the overhead compartments burst open, allowing carry-on baggage to freely fall into the aisles and onto a couple unfortunate passengers' heads, I just attempted to maintain control of my cup of coffee and enjoy the E ticket ride. Once we came to a complete stop and the doors were opened, it only took three steps down the boarding stairs for me to have another one of those, "Toto, I don't think we're in Kansas" moments.

Guwahati is in Assam Province. If you are looking at a map of India, Assam Province is a small land-locked peninsula located at the far eastern edge of the country. Surrounded by Bhutan, Nepal, Tibet and China to the north; Bangladesh to the south; and Myanmar to the west, this small province is a smuggler's paradise and, with the diverse ethnic cultures that surround the peninsula, it's a prime location for terrorist activities. Armed soldiers, carrying some form of automatic weapon, patrolled the streets by the thousands, and because Assam is a military run province that wants to become its own country, we were informed that all phones, Internet and two-way radios were prohibited because the government owned all the airwaves, creating a communications lockdown.

Scott Snider, an old friend of ours, picked us up at the airport. We had first met Scott in Vietnam two years earlier, when he was in charge of an Operation Smile mission, but on this Guwahati trip he had just come along to be an extra hand, without as much responsibility. John and I became close friends with Scott because an unfortunate Vietnam chicken bone incident.

We arrived at the Bao Lac hospital in Vietnam one morning to find Scott in the recovery room drowsy and coming out of anesthesia. It seemed that one of the surgeons had persuaded him to let them remove a small bone fragment that had lodged in his throat during the previous evening's dinner. Finding this somewhat humorous, we filmed it. Scott finally awoke to find Cindy McCain holding his hand and thanking people for enough donations to help this young man back to a healthy recovery. Then, as any good friend would, we sent the video to his boss at Operation Smile headquarters and we have been friends ever since.

Finding the luggage proved to be calmest part of the beginning of our India excursion. With English still a widely used language, even in this part of the country, our passage through immigration was nothing more than a friendly hello and a smile on our part, and a kind of head bobble movement and grin right back at us from the customs official, followed with a hand gesture that said, "*Thank you. Go now.*" I can't tell you how glad I was to run into an easy country admission. This had been a succession of very long flights, my body was cramped, and my back was still aching from our plane's hard smash into the landing strip some forty-five minutes earlier. At this point I needed something simple and painless.

Now legally in the country, we made our way outside past the men with guns to the small pick-up area in front. There waiting for us, next to a little van that had apparently lost its last battle in local traffic, was Scott. Never one to be oversensitive, he thrust his arm out, greeted both of us with a handshake, coaxed the mangled sliding door open on the van, hopped in the front seat next to the driver and started giving him directions to the hotel where we would be staying. Scott is an amazing team leader, a no-nonsense type of guy that gets things accomplished, but he has always seemed to have a low tolerance level when dealing with Third World van and bus drivers. For one thing, Scott always knew where he was going even when the drivers didn't. It was like he had a built-in global positioning system for back roads in developing countries.

In only a few sentences he told us a bit about the area, but mostly he kept his eyes on the driver, correcting him from time to time, when he would attempt to aim the van in a direction other than the one in Scott's head. John and I, still suffering from economy seat cramping, just sat in the back of the van quietly taking it all in.

CULTURE SHOCK INDIA STYLE

Culture shock in any developing country can take you by surprise, but India is a monster all its own. Add to that the fact that we were in a remote location that even people who lived in the larger cities in India never went to, and you get mega culture shock. We were in such a remote location that many of the local people had never seen a white person before. With India boasting the second largest population on the planet— 1.21 billion people—getting from one place to another is like constantly being stuck in line for Space Mountain at Disney World during the peak of summer tourist season. People were everywhere. Another difference that took me by surprise was the number of soldiers in the streets. As I said earlier, Assam Province was governed by the military and the rumor was that the province wanted to secede from India and become its own country. This was partly the reason for the massive build-up of soldiers. We were told that, because of the high military presence, the streets were extremely safe. The men with guns were there to influence locals, not to engage in violent acts upon each other, and especially not toward any tourists who might venture away from their hotels to explore the street life. Open sewers and public urination are something else that will catch you off guard when you visit parts of India. Not just men urinating off the side of the road, but crudely constructed concrete dividers that run along the walls at the sidewalk's edge, stained yellow from years of urine. If you are walking down the sidewalk and feel the urge, just turn away from traffic and relieve yourself. It all flows right along the broken concrete at your feet into an open sewer system. Then it makes its way to the nearest river where children play, people fish and everyone bathes. With these many contrasts of culture to deal with, I believe the hardest thing for me to get used to was the Indian peoples' lack of personal space. Maybe it's because of the hordes of people inhabiting the country, or maybe it's just that we in the United States over-value our spatial distance from other bodies. I'm not sure, but what I do know is when you get in a conversation with a person in Assam Province, expect a lot of head bobbling and almost nose to nose contact as they speak to you. To an outsider, it can be quite awkward when a stranger comes in so close to talk that you start to wander if he's going to kiss you on the mouth. Of course, as you start to back away from the conversation, they keep moving forward until you either get pinned against a wall or trip over something.

My personal fun experience with this cultural practice happened during an event thrown for the volunteer doctors on our mission by the Ministry of Health of Assam Province. This Operation Smile mission was a huge deal to the region. No other group of volunteers had ever come in to aid to the people of Guwahati before. So the entire team was treated with much love and respect, even John and me. Preceding this grand event of chanting, dancing and ceremonial activities, the Minister's special security team came out to conduct a thorough bomb search. John and I clued into what was going on when an old mama Doberman Pinscher with six saggy teats walked past and sniffed the couch on which we were comfortably resting. In an extremely polite tone, the dog's handler looked at us and asked would we please stand for a moment. To our surprise, a second man, garbed in all black, ran a small metal detector over the cushions we had been sitting on and then lifted the front of the couch to perform the search to the underside.

"It's okay," he said, and he gave us a thumbs up and a goofy smile before following the aging dog to another couch to check.

As I stood there, laughing to myself at the idea that I just been sitting on a couch rigged to blow up, another man approached me. He was dressed in an all-black suit, and it was obvious that he had something to do with the security operation at hand. He was tall, with very dark skin; his hair was jet black and well groomed; and he had a moustache that would make even the Mario brothers envious. It was like someone had glued a tar brush to his upper lip. I looked over and cordially acknowledged his approach with a friendly smile and a nod. The man seemed very focused on me; he just kept coming closer and closer until his moustache hovered inches from right cheek bone. Talk about feeling uneasy.

"Are you enjoying yourself in our country?" He had a thick Indian accent, with a strong vibrato. This was followed with, "Is this your first time in India?" To my relief, he was just making small talk, trying to be friendly to a visiting volunteer, but his accent was so thick that I had to decipher his words before I could respond. The longer I took to answer him back, the more he felt the need to get even closer to my face as he spoke, which in turn caused me to move ever so slowly in the opposite direction. I don't know what he thought was causing me to gravitate away from his friendly conversation but his response to my movement was to place his hand on my opposite shoulder and gently pull me back closer to his face, where we could talk. This seemed to amuse John, who stood at the opposite side of the stage smirking at my nervous predicament. After what seemed an hour, but was probably only a couple of minutes, the conversation and the dark man's grip on my shoulder ended.

A tip from me to you. When traveling to obscure foreign locations, don't fear contact or communications with the locals. Most people are just as curious about you as you are about them. Many people do not have the rights to travel outside their homeland as we do as US citizens, or the ability to travel. You may be the first outsider they have or will ever meet. Be calm, be friendly, speak with peace, and remember that smiles work everywhere.

Back in the van ride from the airport, Scott's directions were spot on and within a short time we were pulling up in front of our hotel, home for the next couple of days. Surprisingly the accommodations were not too bad. It was a reasonably clean building, with a white marble entrance way and a very slow, but usable wireless Internet signal broadcast throughout the lobby. For a change, John and I were booked in separate rooms that were of moderate size for a hotel in this part of the world where space is at a premium. Everything in the bathroom worked, a rarity for us, including the hot water, which, to me, adds two stars to the rating of any hotel. Were it not for the mothballs that covered the sink and shower drains leading down to the open sewer and prevented a rank odor from permeating into the room, I would have thought I was in a hotel back in the states.

This fleeting thought left me as I paused to admire the view from the windows that lined the hallway outside my hotel room's door. India was vast and over built. The sun was hovering just below the skyline, causing the aging building that fought for space to cast odd, angled shadows, and backlighting the light, misty smog that always hung in the Indian sky. From my side of the window, quiet and still, it was like viewing a mystical painting created by using only shades of gray. Located just on the other side of the fragile sheet of glass, deep in reality, were the smells, the textures and the personal connections to Guwahati. After allowing ample time for the vision to create a memory, I moved three rooms down, knocked on John's door and we headed down to the lobby where Scott was waiting to take us to a team dinner and to introduce us to the volunteers on this mission.

As the three of us made our way out to the busy highway that ran in front of the hotel, Scott turned to me and asked, "Walk or ride?" Usually, I am never one to pass up a good walk through the streets of an exotic country, but I was glad to see Scott glance at his watch and say, "Better we catch a ride, we're kind of late." The only reason that I was hesitant to walk is because we had only been in Assam province for a few hours, it was now dark-thirty and, on the short ride from the airport to the hotel, it seemed to me that every tenth man standing on the roadside was holding an assault rifle. I still wasn't quite sure just who they were there to protect.

While I was looking in the parking area for the same van that we rode in earlier, Scott walked out into traffic, held up his hand and started signaling for what I assumed was going to be a cab. Not quite what you would call a cab pulled up in front of him and stopped. It was a green, three-wheeled death trap driven by a shoeless thirteen-year-old boy wearing only a pair of shorts. It reminded me of the back half of a nineteen-seventies VW Beetle, with hood and front wheels cut clean off, and retrofitted with a single go-cart tire and a set of motorcycle handlebars. I couldn't help but laugh at the expression on John's face.

"I don't think we're all going fit in that thing, Scott. I'm not even sure if I can fit through the door." John said only half joking.

"Sure we can. They're cheap," Scott said with conviction.

In my description of this vehicle, I left out the observation that the passenger compartment was centered over the rear wheels and directly behind the driver, who sat in front of a half partition on a makeshift seat over the single front wheel. The steering and throttling of the death machine was controlled by the motorcycle handlebars.

One by one we packed in like sardines. I went first, followed by Scott in the middle position and finally John squeezed in.

My shoulders and John's spanned the width of the vehicle's inside, almost touching in the center and causing Scott to lean forward, slightly pressing his head into the back of our grinning juvenile chauffeur, who was probably smiling because he had three Americans in his cab-thing. After an awkward moment of silence, and remember that we were still sitting in the center lane of flowing traffic, Scott looked up at the driver and said, "Well, can we go now?"

Still smiling, the driver turned the key over, twisted the throttle and the little green vehicle shot to life—for about one hundred feet. Then it gave a sputtering cough and rolled to a stop. The teen jumped out with a long screwdriver in hand, ran to the back of the cab and started pounding on something. He jumped back in, cranked the throttle a couple of times and we started to move. Proudly, the boy glanced back at us, and then, with another grinding clunk, we were sitting still again in the middle of the active highway. Again, the boy leapt from the cab with his screwdriver, but this time he was trying to push the vehicle down the road while he worked on it. With a slow momentum built up, he hopped back into the driver's seat but this time he put his feet on the handlebars to steer so he could tinker with the inner electrical workings beneath the dashboard. Slaphappy from all the travel, John and I started laughing hysterically but Scott was increasingly getting irritated. What the young driver did next caused him to almost completely snap. Like something right out of a Three Stooges movie, the boy, while still steering with his feet, grabbed Scott's right hand, placed it on the throttle, cranked it wide open, smiled at Scott and motioned for him to not let go. He then jumped out and pushed the cab from behind. The three of us were still sardined in the back seat of the driverless vehicle and Scott, reaching over the partition, now had total control of it while the driver pushed us down the road. Of course, we all knew what was going to happen next. The tiny cab came to life and accelerated past the running capability of the young Indian boy who was left chasing after us down the center lane of the highway. You can't make this stuff up. Eventually, Scott let go of the throttle and, by the time the out of breath barefoot boy caught up with us, we were nearly at the other hotel where the rest of the volunteers were. A mild insanity had crept into Scott's brain by this time. "Out" was the only recognizable word he spoke that I could recognize., as the three of us fought to exit the little green machine. Of course, this was the introduction story we told the rest of the volunteers over dinner that evening. It seems that, wherever we go, life gives us some off-the-wall conversation starters.

THE MORNING BRINGS A DIFFERENT LIGHT

After the previous evening's hilarious activities, John and I were ready to get the day going and see what else India had to offer. Breakfast was not too bad. Even though the inhabitants in the area was almost all vegetarians, the hotel did its best to offer some Americanized dishes, which we gladly devoured while waiting on our bus ride to the hospital.

Most of the volunteers were at another hotel, but there were a few staying at our location and it didn't take us long to find each other. We all stood out. Our small group made its way to the roadside, where we only had to wait for a few minutes for the bus carrying the rest of the volunteer Operation Smile team.

Daylight gave India an entirely different dimension and, on our bus ride to the hospital, I could see the overcrowding that plagued the country. I had been to many interesting global locations, and seen many overcrowded cities, but it's hard to find the word to help someone who hasn't seen it understand how dense

India's population actually is. The traffic in Assam Province wasn't as bad as I expected it would be, but the sheer number of people on the streets took my breath away. It was at this point that I was told that all the young men, dressed in military uniforms and toting the assault rifles, were there to keep the peace. The local government wanted more tourism, and they wanted it to stay free of street crime. One of the nurses, whose world traveling puts mine to shame, told me that, despite the intimidating state of the streets and the extreme poverty, this was one of the safest places to walk, day or night. The people here were Hindus; they were more likely to come up and smile at you than attempt to rob or harm you. That would be bad karma. This was great to hear.

It took less than a half hour for the bus to make the trip from the hotel to the hospital. Each road we turned down was unmarked and looked exactly like the previous road. I couldn't help wondering how people could find each other's houses, or how teenagers could get together and hang out or date. But the expanding population is proof that they find a way.

We did make our way down one contrasting street, however, and I found that street fascinating. Maybe it was because the bus just barely fit, often scraping the wooden flower stalls that lined the right side of the road, but mostly it was because of the flower stalls themselves.

The streets were filled with effigies and religious monuments where people stopped to pray and make offerings. So flowers were in great demand, and the flower of choice was the marigold. Thousands of hand sewn, orange and yellow garlands, some as long as five feet, could be purchased from the flower vendors on this block. From the elevated height of the bus windows, we had the perfect vantage point to witness this spectacle of floral color being created each day. Other than the brightly colored fabrics worn by the women, these flowers were the only color visible against the background of the well-used, dirty gray streets, dirty gray buildings, polluted gray water and the polluted gray sky. Three more turns after this road and we closed in on our destination.

Pulling up to the hospital, I was not surprised to see more young men with guns, and an ever-growing crowed of curious people who passed by to just what all these white people were doing wandering around an old hospital in Assam Province, India. This was the first Operation Smile mission ever to come to this location, and, with rumors that Assam wanted to become its own country, the local government was bending over backwards to both accommodate the Operation Smile organization and to prove to the people who called this area home that their government cared about them.

My first impression of the location was, "Wow!". The local government did an amazing job and created a section of the hospital dedicated solely to reconstruction surgeries of cleft palates and cleft lips. To walk into an old, very well-used hospital in a developing area of the world and find a brand new, state-of-the-art surgical center just seemed odd—especially when the wards down the hall, and the rest of the hospital, were somewhat below par, by US standards at least. It would be like putting a gourmet kitchen in an abandoned double wide trailer. Since finishing touches were being put on the beautiful, marble-walled operating rooms, the patient screenings would take place in the courtyard, inside a building that could easily be confused with a barn or large storage shed. That is probably what it was before the volunteer team got hold of it. Now it was being outfitted with medical stations and readied for the next morning's inundation of surgery applicants.

WILDEST SCREENING DAY EVER!

Inundated is exactly what we got. The local government had announced this first-ever cleft lip surgical mission by US doctors over radio and television, in newspapers and on the Internet. By the time our bus pulled up in front of the hospital, on this first of the two screening days, there were over five hundred people waiting. To our surprise, most of these people were not children. Hundreds of teenage boys and girls, and adult men and women were standing in front of us. Of course, there were children too—infants in their parents' arms, small toddlers wandering around and juveniles. There were just more older people then I had ever expected to see.

Since this was the first medical mission to openly bring attention to facial deformities, many of these people had never seen another person afflicted with a cleft lip or palate. Many thought they were cursed and to see so many others with the same deformity instantly created a feeling of comfort within the ever-growing crowd. For the Operation Smile team, however, this was going to be an emotional and busy couple days of screening. With such a huge turnout, not everyone would make the cut for surgery on this first mission. That's why the screening process exists.

Although they are as susceptible to emotion as anyone else, the mission staff has guidelines to follow when it comes to choosing the right candidates for acceptance as patients. Factors such as age, health and possible complications from the procedure, set against the number of possible surgeries, all play a role in the decision process. With the procedure time for a lip being usually less than an hour and cleft palate surgeries sometimes lasting over three, it's easy to see why the team, especially on a virgin mission like this one, would choose to perform as many lip surgeries as humanly possible.

At one point the nurse in charge of scheduling walked up to the microphone on the stage at one end of the courtyard and said, "I know that there are many you still waiting to be seen, and we will get to as many of you as possible. You must understand that three doctors cannot see four hundred people in one day, Many of you will have to come back tomorrow, and I am sorry to say, even then, many of you will not make it to surgery on this mission. But we will be back."

When the interpreter finished translating the nurse had said, people seemed in disbelief. Even with the military presence, parents kept coming up to the head nurse, or any volunteer they could find, holding up their numbered pieces of paper, with a look of dismay in their eyes. I took my camera and started to meander through the sea of people, capturing as many ill formed faces as I could. Here, that wasn't hard to do. On other missions John and I had been on there were always unique faces to film, but here in Assam they were all amazing. Maybe it was the culture, or the age of most of the candidates, or the overwhelming need, but behind each set of eyes was a hardship story waiting to get out. With each pivot of my head, I would see another deformed face. There were so many that I started having a hard time remembering who I had already filmed. To me, the teenage boys were the hardest to see. I can't imagine what it would be like to live your entire childhood regarded as a monster. And that, I found out, is exactly what happens to these children.

CULTURAL EFFECTS OF FACIAL DEFORMITIES

Somewhere late on the first day I was able to film an interview with a gentleman who was working to assist the Secretary of Medicine on this new section of the hospital. The local government had vowed to make Assam a cleft free state and I believe that to date and with help from the Operation Smile International teams, over seven thousand cleft surgeries have taken place in Guwahati, India, Assam Province.

Finding a semi-quiet room, we set up the cameras and John started to ask the dignitary questions. What we were trying to get was some information on the psychological issues that these children, these people, with such openly visible defects, face in an area in which religious belief is so steeped in mysticism and lore. Eager to talk about this very topic, the gentleman spoke eloquently as if he were pleading his case to the world.

These are his words:

"What I find is that children who are born with this problem, particularly in our villages, because of superstitious beliefs, because of religious beliefs, these are supposed to be people who are, in some formal manner, afflicted with an evil spirit, hence the facial disfigurement. Therefore, they are normally not involved in social activities within the family. In the Hindu culture there is a ceremony called the head shaving ceremony, where the male child's head is shaved. It's a very auspicious kind of activity, but these children normally are not allowed to come into that place because the parents do not want the evil influence falling on this auspicious occasion. So that is one. The other is when there is a wedding or something in the family, these children are usually hidden away. They aren't allowed to come to the forefront. It has, to my mind, a severe impact on the child—depression, loneliness, withdrawal—so along with the physical deformity that the child has been unfortunate to be born with, he gets loaded with certain amounts of mental challenges as well."

He paused for a moment and then he started to speak about what the families experienced.

"When they hand over the child to unknown faces, some of these people have never seen a formal hospital before. When they are able to hand over a child to our surgeons and our team of doctors, and you see the trust with which it is given, it's amazing. I have had the opportunity to see two parents, at least, who saw their child after the child came out of surgery. The look—words were not necessary—the look on their faces, the gratitude on their faces, every time, brings a tear to my eye. It's fantastic. And some of them, in their own way, say that you corrected something, which even God did not bless us with.

Again, he paused and emotionally said,

"That smile which the child gives you once their face has been corrected—no amount of money in the world can buy for you. It is, it is just amazing.'

His words stuck in my head and merged with the images that I had been filming all day, and with the faces that were still around, gazing at us and waiting for a chance to be seen by the doctors.

Thinking about it now, another comment comes to mind, something Mark Ascher, a good friend and the main photographer for Operation Smile, said to me after a long, stressful day on a recent mission to Rio De Janeiro, Brazil. Over a few beers he revealed a thought to me, one that had been slowly building in his mind mission after mission. He said that if you watch a family with a child who has had a cleft lip repaired walk away from the hospital and down the city streets, you will see that no one looks at them. They become invisible. Invisible to scrutiny, to awkward glances, they blend in with everyone else on the streets around them. In a world of people trying to stand out in a crowd, to be known or famous, what Operation Smile really does is nothing more than grant a child's wish to be normal, and, for once in their life, unnoticed.

This really put everything into its simplest perspective because most international humanitarian organizations, no matter what their cause, try to accomplish the same feat. They want to bring equality and balance to people's lives/. If the needy are starving, NGOs try to give them enough food to live a normal existence. If they need clothing or shelter, groups try to clothe them and help them to find a place out of the elements so that they can raise their family in a normal environment. If the needy are without schools or education, groups exist to aid with learning, and if medical attention is needed, there are NGOs that help to make people healthy enough to live a normal life.

No nonprofit or nongovernment organization strives to help students obtain master's degrees or seeks to provide families with excess amounts of food, name brand clothing, cosmetic surgery or houses too large to be useful. We, as humanitarians and global aid groups, are not trying to put the needy in situations better than the ones in which we exist. We are trying to make them self-sufficient, capable of caring for themselves and able to live as normal, unnoticed, competent individuals. The children and adults in Assam Province may still retain some of the emotional problems that they had before the Operation Smile surgery team came in, but they will look like the other non-important, unnoticed people walking down the dirty sidewalks, This will be a huge improvement in their quality of lives.

UNEXPECTED NEWS

That night, after the first day of screening, as I relaxed back at the hotel, I received an email from Teacup. She wrote that the last portion of the mission had been canceled. If you remember, after leaving India, John and I were scheduled to fly to our beloved Cambodia, where we were to helicopter into a remote minefield location with The HALO Trust and film the progress of the landmine removal for Cindy. While she still insisted that we go, the US Embassy had asked the local HALO crew if the Ambassador to Cambodia, Carol Rodley, could visit and tour a minefield in Siem Reap. Since Cindy could not make this trip, Miss Rodley would be the substitute. There was no need for John and me to come. Seconds after I read the email, there was a knock on my door. Behind that knock was John; his expression clearly read, "That sucks."

"Did you read the email? He asked, despondently.

"Yeah, I read it. Sucks." I pouted back. The trip had already been a long one, but we both love HALO and adore Cambodia. The excitement of going to a minefield that was only accessible by helicopter had elevated our adventurous spirits. Oh well, we both agreed, at least we would be getting back home a bit sooner, which would be restful. If we had only known what was ahead of us, we would have walked to Cambodia and forgotten about getting home. Teacup's email also asked that we finish up the trip, through the first day of surgeries as planned, try to get some patient aftershot and then depart from India on our scheduled flight. Sherry,

Cindy's travel agent, would adjust the rest of the itinerary to get us back to the states. All's well that ends well, right?

Day two of screening produced more of the same. Hundreds of faces needed of attention. John and I worked our way through the throng of people for most of the day, filming and taking note of interesting stories to follow up on later. The second day is usually half or three-quarters filled with actual patient screenings. The last bit of the day is devoted to the posting of names of those accepted for surgery. Here the names were posted on the side of the barn where the screening had taken place and, like always, this was the most emotional part of the mission. Watching parents franticly search a posted list for their child's name in a desperate crowd of others doing the same will turn your heart inside out. The experience here was no different, with exception of the large number of adults that were also looking for their own name. Among the tears of happiness and the tears of dismay there are always a couple of stories that stand out.

Here in Guwahati the heartfelt story is about a grandmother that brought her granddaughter to the screening. Both grandmother and grandchild had been born with cleft lips. While searching the posted list of names, the grandmother saw that she had been chosen for surgery but that her granddaughter had not. With the heart of an angel, the older woman gave her surgery slip to her grandchild, saying, "I don't want you to have to go through the same difficulties in life that I have had to experience." One of the nurses witnessed this act of compassion and dragged both generations back in front of the doctors, singing the praises of the grandmother and making sure that an extra surgery spot was created. Lessons in humanity were learned by all, and both grandmother and grandchild walked away from the mission with brand new smiles.

Since medical procedures begin the next morning, it's tradition to have a team dinner on the night of the posting of names. It's always something different and held somewhere that displays the local culture and flair. It's a time to let your hair down and relax before a stressful week of surgeries. That night the team had scheduled a dinner cruise on the Brahmaputra River. The Tsangpo-Brahmaputra River, as it's also known, means transboundary river, and is one of the largest rivers in Asia. Almost eighteen hundred miles long, it starting in Tibet and ends at the Bay of Bengal. John swears that I ate pigeon all night on the boat, but I have no idea if that's true. I couldn't tell you half the stuff that I ate on the India trip. I just stopped asking. He just might have been right that night, but with enough Kingfisher beer and local spirits to wash it down, I probably would have eaten rat. Who knows, maybe I did.

Why the first surgery day always starts at the crack of daylight after a night of relaxation has always perplexed me, but who am I to attempt to change tradition. As predicted, morning came way too fast and we all met in the dark, in front of the hotel, to wait for our bus to the hospital. No doubt more than a few of us wished we'd gotten to bed at a suitable hour, but the patients were waiting. John and I had gotten up extra early to pack our bags and check out of the hotel, so we were extra tired. We weren't hungover, but we both had that feeling you get when you realize you partook of a few too many adult beverages the night before. We were off to a great start for our upcoming forty-eight hours of international travel. Our day would consist of getting to the hospital and filming as many shots of pre-ops and surgeries as we possibly could before we had to jump in a van and rush off to the airport to catch our 4:30 flight into Delhi.

OUT OF INDIA CHAOS

The first day of surgery started out without a hitch and, as usual, the Operation Smile volunteers were in amazing form. I really wish the John and I could have stayed for the entire mission to see the result of all this hard work, but time was not on our side; we eventually had to call it a day and leave for the airport. We packed up our camera gear and made our rounds, saying goodbye to all our new friends. Leaving every mission is like stepping back in time and leaving summer camp when you're a preteen. On these missions, I always find myself surrounded by other people who think like I do—humanitarian minded people who are willing to take time out of their lives to help strangers. Believe it or not, it is sometimes very hard to get others, who don't think with a humanitarian mind, to understand just why we take the time to travel across the globe to aid the less fortunate and do it without being paid. On missions, though, everyone understands, and every volunteer has the same question running through their mind. "Why don't more people think the way we do?"

India is always hot and humid, and, at this time of the year, it was well over one-hundred degrees. Because we had no time to change or freshen up before heading to the airport, John and I had both chosen to wear the most comfortable, hot-weather clothes we could find that didn't actually stink. I threw on the pair of jeans that I flown out in two weeks earlier, and a thin, button-up, short sleeved travel shirt. John found a semi-clean pair of quick dry-pants and a colorful cotton T-shirt from a previous Op-Smile mission.

Pushing our departure time as long as we could, we finally loaded up the van that was sent to deliver us to the airport and, with a last handshake with Scott, we were on our way. Off through the dusty streets we went, our driver maneuvering down roads as if he had a couple of dignitaries in the back who were late for a UN meeting. He stopped only to allow a random cow to walk across our path. I had always thought the cow thing was over-exaggerated, but traffic grinds to a halt at the sight of any sacred cow that happens to be lazily strolling right down the center lane of any given motorway. Then, we saw a dead body, neatly wrapped in a bright red sheet, just lying on top of a low concrete retaining wall that ran along the sidewalk. His or her cell phone, wallet and keys were neatly laid out on the wall, about where the head should been, and pedestrians walked past like it was an everyday occurrence—which it probably was. I couldn't even get a single word out of my mouth as I pointed at the body and turned to John. He just glanced back, as if he'd had enough of India, and casually said, "Yep, I saw it."

After only another two or three stops to avoid wayward bovine that were half in the road, we made it to the airport. It was the same airport at which we had nearly crash landed, but from the departure side it reminded me much more of a small-town bus station. As we pulled up under the overhang, the breaking of our tires in the gravel unloading area sent an orange dust cloud into the air, coating the unattended packages sitting outside the terminal with yet another layer of grime.

"Okay. Thank you," our driver said with a big smile and a back-and-forth wobble of his head. He got out to walk around and help us remove our bags from the sliding side door of the van. John and I climbed out, our driver set our bags on the gravel road and then, without another word, he climbed back into the van and drove away. By the time we turned around to thank him for the ride, he was halfway out of the parking lot, leaving John and I standing there in yet another lingering cloud of dust, and next to a couple of goats that were tied to a wooden pallet. There was a very lengthy moment of awkward silence as we both tried to comprehend what had just happened. Still standing there in the dust cloud, we looked around for some type of assistance, but there was none. It was about this time that I realized we were going to have to find our way back home all by ourselves.

Grabbing our bags, we walked towards the terminal building and, as we approached, I noticed a small glass window with a softball size circle cut from the center allowing you to speak to the woman seated on the other side of the window. Other than doors leading inside, this was the only opening on the building. Up until now, we had not given much thought to any issues we might have with our new flight schedule. We were just going on the information in Teacup's email, which said that Sherry would take care of any adjustments to our travel itineraries. So up to the hole in the window I ventured, with the paper copy of the old itinerary in my hand.

"Hello, can you help us?" I said as passed the paper through the opening. She smiled, and she spoke English—both good signs. As American customs would suggest we do, John and I backed our faces away from the window so we wouldn't be of any annoyance to the young women who was now typing on the keyboard of a very slow, very old computer.

Cultural idiosyncrasies decided to interject themselves into our calm little situation when an Indian gentleman, who had recently walked up behind us, figured that, since we had backed away from the window hole, it was now his turn to have a go. When I say we had backed away, I just mean that I didn't have my face stuck halfway through the small round opening. We were still well within arm's reach. But apparently, sticking your face into the hole was the sign that it was your turn, because this is exactly what our new friend did. Then he started yelling something in a local Indian dialect to the young woman seated only a couple feet away. As we took a step even farther back from the conversation, we were flanked from the other side by a second man that we hadn't seen approach. This gentleman also found it necessary to insert as much of his face as possible through the small circle and he started up a second, very chaotic conversation with the young woman. My attempt to inform the two men that I was not finished yet was met with nothing but smiles and shoulder contact, as the three of us all battled for the attendant's attention. The poor young woman was bombarded by papers, hands, words and entire faces – all shoved through the hole., Finally through the middle of the opening, a small hand burst—tightly gripping a crumpled piece of paper aimed at us. The two men paused for a split second, smiled, and nodded at us as to say, "All right, good for you." I honestly thought one guy was going to shake my hand, but they went right back to their cheek-touching conversation through the small circular opening.

For the second time in only a half hour John and I stood in front of the dusty terminal building, speechless and slightly confused by what had just happened.

Thank God the lines were short inside the terminal, and, because we were traveling to New Delhi from Guwahati, the flight was domestic. That meant that we didn't have to deal with immigration, which gave us time to mentally regroup for the next leg of our journey. The bad part about flying on a domestic flight in India was that we were flying on a domestic flight in India. We were the only non-locals on the plane, or in the entire airport for that matter.

Security was a bit strict; there were many checks and many

men with guns doing these checks. If you think airport security in the states can be a pain in the ass to get through, it's probably because you're doing something stupid or being an obnoxious airport patron. In India, like many other locations, you have no rights. If you piss someone off, you simply don't get to board the flight. No refund, no rebuttal, no "I am sorry." You are just left standing there, until you make a big enough scene that the men with guns escort you outside, or worse.

After the last security check, we found ourselves in a large room resembling an American driver's license office. Flight numbers were called once, maybe twice if you were lucky, and signs with the flight numbers were written by hand and posted near the doors leading out to the tarmac. Eventually, our number came up and we made our way out to the shuttle which drove us out to our waiting plane. Soon thereafter, we were in the air and heading to the New Delhi domestic airport. Yeah, another domestic airport, and, oh yeah, it's a good story.

Since the flight time to New Delhi was only one hour and thirty-eight minutes, we decided that we would save our beer consumption for the much longer flight from New Delhi to Chicago. There would be plenty of time to relax, get somewhat sloshed and sleep it off on that flight.

We should have started drinking earlier, maybe even at breakfast, because our only sane moment, for the rest of the trip back to Orlando, was the short walk down the boarding ramp from the plane and into the terminal in New Delhi.

Now I can't be certain, but I believe Cindy had someone from the local government checking up on us throughout our return, because not more than fifty steps into the domestic terminal, after getting our bags, we were met by a very well-spoken gentleman who approached us like he knew exactly who we were. He might have even said something about us being Cindy's guys. This informative man then told us that the shuttles to New Delhi international airport were shut down because there was a hijacked aircraft inbound and headed our way. In fact the entire domestic airport was on lockdown; we were our flight had been given permission to land.

"You should take a prepaid cab to the international airport as it's across town," he told us. Then, like many people seemed to be doing around us, he just disappeared into the crowed without as much as a backward glance. For the third time that day, and I was starting to keep count, John and I were having another awkward moment of silence.

"I wonder where we are going to find a prepaid cab," John said as he scanned the insanity building in the airport. The news of the lockdown was spreading.

"I have an idea; follow me," I said, and I walked right up to the closest guy dressed in a military outfit with a gun slung around his shoulder.

"Excuse me sir" I inquired, " would you know where I might get a prepaid cab to the international airport terminal?" It's almost as if Indians are afraid to commit to a yes or no answer the way they bobble their heads up and down and side to side while they contemplate answering your question. Even this military guy did that. He took so long that I think I subconsciously began to mimic his head movements, which probably only exacerbated his already irritated mood. Finally, he pointed over his right shoulder and said something that all ran together about hurrying if we wanted to get a cab out.

I smiled at the man. John gave me that look that he gives me when I gravitate towards armed individuals, and we quickly made our way to the prepaid taxi counter.

It was very simple and cheap to get a ticket. Our instructions were to go outside, stand in line number ten, wait for our cab, present the ticket to the driver and then be on our way, It sounded easy enough. Awkward silence moment number four came the minute we took our first step outside, to the front of the airport where the taxis were. New Delhi itself is always overcrowded and insane, which made the airport twice as insane—just as it does in the states. Compound this level of insanity with a hijacked aircraft preparing to land, the simultaneous cancelation of hundreds of flights and the media frenzy that surrounded the airport entrance and you get ultimate India chaos. To say that there were ten thousand people clamoring around the airport and spilling into the streets would not be much of an exaggeration. They were congregating into masses, the largest of which was about half a football field's length away, to our right. But the angry amoeba of humans was slowly expanding our way. We kept following the signs to the prepaid cab area—thank God, it was clearly marked and just at the edge of the road that ran in front of the terminal building. Yellow lined lanes, separated by railings, much like a ride entrance at a theme park, ran to the sidewalk, each having a number painted on the ground that identified the lane and corresponded with the ticket purchased at the counter inside. The system was very organized; even with the escalating situation at the airport, the lines and cabs were moving at a steady rate. We found our numbered lane and were quickly standing at the head of the line waiting for our cab to stop. Within moments, a nicely kept yellow cab pulled up and stopped in front of us. "This is going way too smoothly," I thought. "It's too easy."

That was the thought going through my head when two Indian men shot past us, jumped into our cab and sped away. I set my bag back on the curb and we both looked around to see if we were in the wrong line. Maybe we hadn't figured out the system as quickly as we first thought. We watched as other cabs pulled up at other numbered spots and, each time, the people at the head of the line walked up, got in and drove away. We had the system right but something odd was going on. A second cab pulled up at our number and again, by the time the wheels had come to a full stop, someone other than us was jumping in our ride. This would go on all night if we didn't do something. So, like any red-blooded American trying to catch a cab I showed my colors.

As the third vehicle pulled up at our number ten spot, I could see two men with their luggage in hand starting to move for the cab, I looked up at John, said, "When in Rome," and headed off to intercept our line jumpers. Indian people are not violently physical, but they will push their way past you at the drop of a hat.

"Oh no you don't," I said to one of the two men while stiff-arming him in the center of his chest. "This is our cab; back your ass up." Normally I wouldn't have been so abrupt, but it was late and it was becoming obvious that the cab drivers didn't care who was loading in the back. Surrendering to my action, the two men smiled, wobbled their heads and jumped in front of someone else. Rude is just a way in India. Sometimes international travel comes down to a kill or be killed mental state. This was one of those times.

THE DEATH CAB

Let's get back to the cab that pulled up—not the first, well-maintained yellow cab, nor the second, also neatly kept cab, but the third cab, our cab. The one that the universe decided would take us to the international terminal on the other side of town, that cab. First of all, this was no cab; it was barely a clown car. The tires were small enough to be used on the the front of a wheel barrel and the number of dents and crumples in the body made it look malleable. I think it started out as a micro van, but I still can't validate that thought with proof.

You guessed it; awkward silence moment number five came after we had crammed ourselves into the backseat of the mangled death-ride machine. As soon as the door closed, the cab peeled out from under the overhang of the airport and rocketed neatly through the crowd of travelers and media people that had now grown large enough to partially block the exit road. This was no accident or near miss; our driver aimed at them and laughed as we launched over a curb and climbed up a small embankment that led toward the highway entrance. Forget awkward silence moment number six; we went straight to not being able to speak and barely able to breathe. At the first red light, our driver did a partial slowdown, then shot through the intersection and cut the wheels to the right so hard that I think two of our tires lost contact with the road by a few inches. John, I and our luggage were thrown to the left side of the back-seat area with the g-force of a spinning carnival ride. Our concern changed to laughter as we both knew that we were in for one hell of a cab ride.

Just outside the airport exit, our driver finally did decide to come to a full stop at an intersection – but only to pick up a police officer who had just gotten off duty and needed a ride home. The officer ran around from the driver's side, opened the door and hopped into the open front seat. The two exchanged a couple words and then the officer turned to us, smiled and, of course, wobbled his head, before returning to his conversation with the driver. We must have looked like two dumbfounded tourists; our eyes had to be as large as saucers. Physics still had us in a heap, slid to the left side of the backseat, John looked like he was about to jump out and walk, but then, as if it had been launched like a pinball from a slot, the cab was at full speed again and tearing down the highway— ricocheting off any vehicle that blocked its path. At each intersection, we nearly missed the crossing traffic and we sideswiped at least one car, if not more. These were not slow-speed sideswipes either. They more like glancing blows that sent us veering off on a different trajectory with each collision. It was dark out and all I could see was dust and headlights, so I don't know how far out of our way we went to deliver the officer, but it was a prepay so it really didn't matter to the driver. At his destination, the officer jumped out quickly, because we just pulled off to the side of the highway to let him out. He glanced in the back, probably to see if we were still alive, shook the driver's hand and trotted away.

Our driver looked back, smiled and repeated the same pinball maneuver, instantly accelerating from zero to whatever the cab would do, but this time he veered through oncoming traffic and found himself stuck behind a semi-truck. With gridlock to the right leaving him no option to accelerate, he turned the steering wheel hard to the left and headed once more into oncoming traffic in his attempt to pass the slow, overloaded truck in front of us. Blindly, we came around the left side of the semi, only to be met by the headlights of a second dump truck style vehicle heading right at us. With no option other than head-on impact with the vehicle bearing down on us, our driver jerked the wheel again, and the cab continued left—over a curb, down a dirt median and onto a gravel road that ran alongside the main highway, still heading into oncoming traffic. Our driver held his ground for a few moments, causing other vehicles to split to the right and left of us, until he found what looked to him like a good place from which to re-enter the highway, ahead of the slower moving semi-truck. His entry point turned out to be more of a dirt ramp then a drivable surface. All four wheels of the cab left the ground, sending us air-born into the congested traffic on the highway. If you are reading this and thinking, "Yeah, right,", I can only assure you that, if anything, I am downplaying this event and not exaggerating it.

Finally exiting the highway into a slower, urban environment filled with streetside businesses, Mario Andretti, cab driver, lifted his foot from the gas pedal so he wouldn't kill any of the people meandering around in the middle of the roads. We were now starting to think that we just might make it to the airport in one piece but, as one issue left, another one seemed to present itself. At every stoplight, large groups of children would charge the cab from all sides, forcing their hands through the half open windows and yelling, "Money, money, money." This absolutely stole my ability to reason; I didn't know what to do. They were like zombies, relentless and starving. John and I now found ourselves pushing together, trying to take refuge in the center of the cab where their arms could not reach us. Our driver, obviously prepared for and used to this, started hitting the little hands with a piece of broom handle until the light changed green and we could pull away. It was yet another new experience for my mind to grasp; reality is so much more impressive than anything even the greatest Hollywood screen writer could devise.

ANOTHER AIRPORT RUN AROUND

After only a couple more minor collisions, we made it safely to the passenger drop-off area at the international terminal. John and I climbed out of the cab, which now had more dents to add to its collection, pulled our luggage out and stood there laughing at the fact we had survived, I almost kissed the ground. The driver quickly exited from behind the wheel, looked right into my eyes and said, "Do I get a tip?" I believe these were the only words that he had spoken to us the entire ride.

"Do you get a tip?" I yelled excitedly. "Of course, you get a tip. For the experience alone you get a tip!" I started digging through my wallet,

"You can have everything that I have on me," I said. It wasn't that much, but I gave him all the US dollars I had, along with the rest of my Indian rupees and even some paper money that I had left over from Dubai. The man smiled from ear to ear as he gladly took all that I gave. Then he shook my hand and rocketed away to find his next victims. The ride left John and me almost speechless. The best either of us could manage was the occasional laugh, followed by, "Holy shit"

When we had gained enough composure to continue, we grabbed our bags and went to find the entrance to the terminal building. As we walked closer to the sliding glass doors, I noticed that there was a guard standing outside inspecting passengers' tickets. Neither John nor I had a ticket. We had been allowed access at the Guwahati airport with an electronic ticket and the printed copies of itinerary we had received from the young woman through the small round window. Here, however, we were denied entry until we could present an actual airline ticket. We were instructed to go to the United Airline office, where we could get this sorted out and get our tickets. I have now lost count, but it was time for another just-stand-there-speechless-and-look-at-each-other moment.

"Just how are we supposed to get to the United Airline office?" John frustratedly asked the guard at the door.

"Follow the sidewalk that way," she said, pointing in the direction of the end of the building. "Take the stairs down to the basement under the parking garage and look there."

These were her instructions. It was fortunate that the cab driver had gotten us here in world record time, because, if we were going to get out of India this night, we would need every second we could steal.

Off we walked in search of a United office in the basement of an international airport. We followed the sidewalk to the stairs, descended the stairs into the basement and then hunted madly for something neither of us really thought existed. After a couple of wrong turns, we started asking anyone who walked past us if they knew where this possibly mythical office was. Finally, one very helpful airport employee walked us through a couple doors that led us back to the sidewalk, and then he pointed to the door to an unmarked room with a glass window front. He motioned for us to go inside and smiled. We both enthusiastically shook his hand, to almost an annoying level, then went inside and stood there. We were the only two people in the tiny two-hundred square foot room.

"Hello, anyone?" I yelled, and to our surprise, a woman who appeared more Caucasian then Indian came out from a back room. We informed her of our problem and, while she was looking into it, we unloaded the evening's travel experience so far. She spoke great English, was sympathetic to our situation and, within a short time, she handed us two tickets and our boarding passes.

"This should be all you need to get past the guard. Don't wait in line; just walk right up to the door," she said. Then she showed us a quicker way to get back up from the basement. Following her instructions, we walked right up to the guard, flashed our tickets and went right inside. From there it was a harmless trip through immigration and we made a beeline for our boarding zone. Where we were informed of the current, six-hour layover. At that point we were elated to find a vendor selling beer—good beer with a very high, eight percent, alcohol content. We drank. All was now well in our world.

FINALLY! CHICAGO BOUND

I don't remember that much about our fifteen hour and for-ty-minute flight from New Delhi to Chicago. Exhaustion, the strong beers and just knowing that we would soon be back home helped to lull me into a deep sleep for the about the first five hours of the flight. That left ten hours for inflight movies, Bloody Marys, airplane meals and more sleep.

February in Chicago is cold—not nicely cool, but freezing, snowy and sometimes even deadly cold. India in February is hot, really hot. It had been over one-hundred degrees when we started this adventure, twenty-four hours earlier in Guwahati, and we were both dressed for and fully prepared for India's heat. What we were not prepared for was a Chicago winter at 5:00 a.m. in the morning. Of course, the spot in which we landed had no gangway, and no climate-controlled tunnel leading from the plane to the terminal. Oh, no. We got to walk across the jetway to the building. There was a light, fabric covered tent to walk through; its purpose was to keep the snow and subzero winds from blowing directly on us during our journey from the aircraft to the warm terminal building about seventy-five yards away. Two steps down the stairs leading to the tarmac and we might as well have been standing naked in the Arctic Circle. Even that short walk made all my joints ache and each time the wind penetrated through a tear in the fabric, it felt like a thousand needles ripping into our flesh. Even inside the airport it was cold and we were probably the only two people in the entire airport without jackets, or even long-sleeved shirts. At least fifteen people must have asked, "Where did you two just come from, dressed like that?"

We were very happy that we only had to wait two hours for our connecting flight to Orlando. At least we were until we attempted to get through the security checkpoint and the TSA

Agent informed John that the name on his ticket did not match the name on his passport. His name was not misspelled; it was an entirely different name, first and last. I think this was our final and most dramatic long, awkward silence moment. We just kept looking at the ticket, hoping the name would miraculously change to read "John Evanko."

"How have you managed to travel across the world with someone else's plane ticket?" I asked out loud, more just throwing the question out to the universe than expecting John to have an answer.

"The woman in the basement at the United office must have given me the wrong ticket for the connecting flight. But they checked it in New Delhi. I didn't even think to look at the ticket." John conjectured.

"What are we going to do? Do you want me to come with you or go and try to hold the flight if you run into a problem?"

"No, you go ahead," John said. "I will call you if I can't get this figured out."

"Don't worry, I won't leave without you." I yelled back as I moved further through security.

Moments before I was getting ready to beg them to hold the flight, John came jogging up to the gate.

"Beer me!" John said with a smile.. It hadn't taken long to figure out the problem, but it left us wondering the predicament of the poor individual whose ticket John had. Standing in line on the gangway, we just had to laugh at each other, Each time the wind blew, snow would find its way through the space between the plane and where we stood, way underdressed for winter in Chicago. Oh, how I love the wonderful world of international traveling.

The flight home was peaceful and, after our harrowing

adventure, it seemed brief. Soon we were back in our own town, in our own homes, sitting in the comfort of our own living rooms and reflecting on what the hell the past two days had given us. It still amazes me that, no matter where I go and how long I stay gone, time stands still back home. Within moments of entering my house, I notice the stack of late bills that need to be paid, the magazine on my coffee table that is still where I left it and the sticking doorknob that still needs repair. The dogs look at me and want to be fed. It's almost like a time warp. Friends are still complaining about the same pointless issues and I have another wonderful view of the world. There is nothing tangible to show what I went through, but my mind and my soul are loaded with new memories and new stories to recite. I have accumulated another file of visions to keep me up at night and leave me in a mad love affair with my country.

No matter how bad we think we have it in the United States, it's still the best place in the world to call home.

Once, while we were sitting around a table in Ecuador, with a group of volunteers, John looked up and said that he wished everyone in the United States would just leave the country. Just get a passport and leave. Go see the world and come back a changed person. I agree with him.

One of my favorite things to do, when I get back from a mission to a developing country, is to get stuck in traffic on our amazingly well-maintained highways and watch others around me get road rage. It makes me laugh and smile uncontrollably. I love to go to a grocery store, shelves loaded with every type of food you want, and stand in a line behind someone checking out who trying to use a coupon. I like to witness the impatience of the people around them— some of whom get physically upset by the minor inconvenience of a momentary wait. Just seeing the shallowness of people, but not being affected by it, makes my soul glow inside. Most people just don't know any better; it's really not their fault. I am not saying that I am a saint. Trust me, after a few months back, I can be just as shallow and impatient as the next person. But it never takes me long now to take a deep breath and snap back into a humbler state of mind. Maybe if others ventured out of their comfort zones from time to time, the world would be kinder, or at least a more patient and forgiving place.

BACK TO REALITY, LIFE GOES ON

I took a few days to recover from the insanity of our return voyage from India, to clear my head, relax and adjust my sleep patterns before I jumped back into my the regular, bill paying *Fear Factor* job at the studios. But wouldn't you know? Shortly after I returned to *Fear Factor*, we were informed that, due to the bad economy, the show would be shut down in late March until at least until the peak of summer season. While this was tragic news to any of our friends, the break gave John and me plenty of time to download video and to reconfigure our hard drive system to store the massive amounts of footage that we had been accumulating. Our office needed a good house cleaning as well.

As promised the *Fear Factor* show started back up. Along with it, the film business, which had also dropped off in a knee-jerk reaction to the economy, started to show signs of recovering too. In June, John and I both picked up a stunt gig in New Orleans, working for a good friend of ours on a film called, *Jonah Hex*. While the movie turned out to be another box office flop, we had a great time working on it. Period pieces are always fun to be do.

Who doesn't want to get dressed up as a cowboy, run around on antique locomotives and ironclad steamships, and be paid for it? Especially when you get to do all this around Megan Fox, John Malkovich and Josh Brolin.

This is still what we are doing today, we are still working on movies as professional stuntmen, we still pick up shifts at the studios when we are needed and we still chase down humanitarian organizations that we can help out.

Since I started to write this book full of stories of amazing adventures, John and I have traveled with the IHE group to Ecuador. Operation Smile sent us to Columbia, Bolivia, Paraguay, Rio De Janeiro, Brazil and on one fantastic mission to Mexico City. In Mexico we got to document Brooke Burke, her husband, David Charvet, and two of her amazing daughters. We were given the opportunity to hang out of the back of a US Air Force C130 and film the space shuttle before one of its last launches, and then go float in the ocean while the US Air Force 920th Reserve Pararescue Unit quick roped or jumped from helicopters that hovered no more than twenty feet over our heads and splashed down in the water around us. Multiple medical and anti-human trafficking missions to Haiti left me with enough unbelievable stories to fill a second four-hundred-page book. And I can't leave out the unbelievable mission to the Philippians with a telemedicine NGO a mere week after typhoon Haiyan decimated the island chain in 2013.

It seems everywhere we go people, just appreciate that we want to help. John and I have, for the most part, turned into good will ambassadors. The volunteers and dignitaries that we meet on humanitarian missions are enamored with our stories about movies and stunts, and all our friends in the stunt business are so amazed by our tales from the humanitarian world that many have volunteered to go with us—if for no more reason than to help carry our gear and to see what we're talking about with their own eyes.

LAST THOUGHTS

FOR OVER TEN YEARS, every day, in some way or another, I have thought deeply about humanity and tried to live by moving forward without fear, and without allowing myself to fall into a complacent, comfort zone. If you go to college for six years you receive a master's degree; that's what I feel like I have—a master's degree in humanity, with a minor in how to love people. Each time that I go to a mission location and film a VIP, celebrity, or even just someone who is new to this world of humanity, they ask the same question.

> *This is so very important to understand and it took me many, many missions to comprehend the essence of this question and to learn the real answer.*
>
> *How can I help them all?*

This is the question that has also kept me up for countless sleepless nights. How can I help them all?" The simple answer is that we can't! No person, group, state, NGO, government or country can help them all. It's an imposable task. But as I have told so many, that's just not what humanity is. Humanity isn't helping them all; humanity is about helping one person. Humanity is simply one hand reaching out to another hand in need. That's it. There's nothing more. It's that plain and simple. Don't look for anything in return. Don't expect the universe to bless you or even to get appreciation from the person you just helped. Do it because you can and because it's right!

If you take nothing from this book other than that last statement, and the urge to explore life beyond your personal comfort zone— to peek through the doors that open in front of you every day, even if you are too afraid to fully commit to stepping through them, then I have succeeded in my message. Remember, the world loves the bad boy; the universe appreciates a renegade soul, and humanity can always use a few more people with the heart of a stuntman.

EPILOGUE

2017 WAS AN OMINOUS YEAR for weather in the southern half of North America and the Caribbean. Hurricane Harvey plowed through the Texas coastline, flooding inland towns as far away as Houston. Irma was the next storm that the tropics threw at the US and she came in with a vengeance! After skipping her way over the Caribbean, she made a hard right, cutting a trough across the Florida Keys, just below Largo. Islamorada and the Middle Keys looked like they had been through an atomic war. She remade landfall over Marko Island and continued to terrorize the peninsula, passing over Tampa, skirting Orlando and flooding Jacksonville's riverfront areas. She finally faded out past Atlanta, with remaining wind gust strong enough to topple trees and close businesses in the peach tree state. The triple threat was Maria! While Irma only edged Puerto Rico, Maria decided to take the island out with the direct force of category 4 and 5 winds reaching continual speeds of 130 to 150 miles per hour. To say that hurricane season hit us hard is an epic understatement. And let's not forget the 7.1-magnitude earthquake that hit Mexico City on Sept 19th.

Hurricanes, typhoons and earthquakes are the great equalizers. They don't care if you're wealthy or if you live in extreme poverty; they strike without prejudice, sometimes leveling entire towns, sometimes choosing a single random house in a neighborhood. Young and old, rich or poor, it matters not to the forces of nature. And since I am writing about disasters, I have to include an attack on humanity—the senseless mass shooting from the Mirage hotel in Las Vegas on October 1st

Of all the locations affected by the storms, including my own home city of Orlando, the Florida Keys moved me the most. From 2015 through 2017, by a lucky happenstance, I was given the opportunity to stunt double the lead actor of a Netflix show based near Key Largo. The show was called *Bloodline* and the actor was Kyle Chandler. *Bloodline* was a dark, film noir drama based around a family full of secrets. Each member was running from their own past. Our show had wrapped for good in early May of 2017, after only three seasons, but that was a long enough run for it to build up a large following and to propel Kyle even farther into Hollywood leading man status. The series added to both the local economy and the tourist industry of the Keys. Many tourists took sojourns to seek out the locations where we had filmed—the Rayburn House and the log where John killed his brother Danny being the two most popular. Kyle and I became good friends, and to my surprise, at the Bloodline wrap party, he asked if I would continue to work with him as his stunt double on a future project—the two-hundred-million-dollar summer blockbuster *Godzilla King of the M*onsters to be exact. Trying to contain my excitement and maintain a macho stuntman image I smiled, calmly grabbed his outstretched hand and accepted his offer with a firm handshake, while repressing the giddy child inside.

We parted ways for a little over month when out of the blue, a friend of mine asked me to double Kyle on yet another small feature starring Jason Bateman and Rachel McAdams. It was called *Game Night*. This comedy was also being shot in Atlanta, not far from the locations in which we would soon spend four months filming *Godzilla* together. *Game Night* gave Kyle and me the chance to work together on a very detailed and somewhat slapstick fight scene that worked its way through five rooms of a house and took four grueling days to film. It intertwined the actors and stunt doubles in a ballet of throws, punches, kicks and ground pounding moves, and it was a perfect reunion for Kyle and me before we headed off to something much large in scale.

It was early June when I got the call from the stunt coordinator of *Godzilla*. My start date just a couple weeks away and I was excited to get to work on such an iconic feature film. The show was a dream job! And after twenty-five years of hard work, I was finally getting treated with the respect that had eluded me for so long. I felt a bit of pride in this accomplishment. About six weeks into shooting, while having dinner and cigars with Kyle one night, our conversation grew from onset chitchat to a heart-to-heart talk, the kind that good friends would have. With the wine and cigars doing their thing nicely, we uninhibitedly talked about our lives, past and future jobs, our families and to my surprise, humanity. It turns out that Kyle and his wife are donors to Operation Smile. I inquired if he and his wife had ever been on a surgical mission and that I could reach out to the founder, Doctor Bill Magee, if he wanted. This is usually the point in a conversation where people stop talking and give me that head cocked, deer in headlights stare. It's usually followed with a remark like, "You're joking right" or "How do you know so much about that subject?" This is also the point in the conversation that I usually hop up on the soapbox start talking for hours about so many aspects of humanitarian groups that it will spin the head of even the most focused listener. This booze driven evening would prove to be no exception! After telling my Operation Smile mission stories and describing children's cleft palate and facial reconstruction surgeries in detail, I moved on to humanitarian landmine removal in Kosovo, sex trafficking in Haiti, child soldiers and the global dental NGO's I'd traveled with. As many do when I go on a humanity whirlwind speech, he listened attentively and when I paused to breath, he asked questions. We also spoke of our love of the film industry but how its superficial side sometimes blinds us to the real situations that go on around us every day. We talked about the international tragedies and global conflicts we will probably never have to live through and about creating a better world for the children. I halted my bantering because my jaw muscles began to ache and my tongue felt too large for my mouth. This is also something I am used to when I preach about humanity like a minister at his pulpit during a rapid-fire revival sermon. Staring deeply out at nothingness, we both took a sip of wine, followed by a long pull on our cigars, without speaking for some time we let the whole moment sink in. The lead actor of one of the biggest budget movies being filmed at present and his stunt double engaging in a dialogue about humanity and giving, not Hollywood and fame. Kyle could see my passion!

"But how can you help everyone? I mean... It makes you feel kind of helpless" was the sentence that broke our silence. On a mission to Puebla Mexico with Operation Smile, I had sat at a bar in our hotel with a hedge fund millionaire and heard the exact same question. The answer, which had taken me over ten years, thirty countries and countless NGO mission to figure out was the same answer I gave Kyle that night. "You can't!" I told him, "And it can be emotionally damaging to think you can!"

You see, the truth, is that humanity is nothing more than one hand helping another, reaching out in need. It's one single person acting human to a stranger who has fallen on hard times. It's giving only what you can, when you can and realizing that the heart of giving is the heart of humanity. It is impossible to personally help each of the hundreds of thousands of refugees fleeing Myanmar right now. Or find a way to help each and every person in the Caribbean displaced by hurricanes Irma and Maria. Thinking that you can help everyone will only cause you sleepless nights and can send you spiraling into depression. Trust me, I know! It happens to most people who devote themselves to a life of empathy. We start off needing to heal everyone, until we grow, we understand and we learn how to help one.

Evil also rears its head during times of misfortune. The looters, and scam artist who attempt to relieve an elderly woman of her insurance money or FEMA checks are just as revolting as sex traffickers who pursue children fleeing storm ravaged lands. But during times of calamity while there is evil, there is also goodness— lots of goodness. Never do the seeds of humanity sprout stronger shoots than when a stranger comes forward to help his fellow man during a global disaster. Just watch the news. Every other image and story is about people that are now being called heroes. Heroes opening their homes up to strangers, heroes giving their money and personal belongings to strangers, heroes feeling the call to start non-profit organizations and as is Las Vegas, heroes willing to risk their own lives running into a hail of gunfire to help strangers make it to safety. People think less about themselves. They're more patient, their empathy is stirred, and they work harder, faster and longer, pushing themselves through hours of work in grueling, dangerous conditions. Let's face it. Our race of beings behaves better during a catastrophic event then we do on a beautiful Sunday afternoon when our lives seem perfect, or when we're waiting in line at a grocery store or at a sporting event. Maybe this is the reason disasters happen. Maybe it's one of the universe's closely guarded secrets that a single disaster is that seed needed to grow countless acts of human kindness and love. We act out of love and no longer look at race, religion, creed, gender or status. All I know is that it truly happens, and I've witnessed it happening all around the globe. I sometimes feel I have a dual identity. I juggle Hollywood and humanity. But the more Hollywood encounters I have with stars like Kyle that lead to a bonding over humanity, a chance to inspire and an opportunity to pass along knowledge, the more I understand why the universe chose this path for me!

ABOUT THE AUTHOR

KEVIN BALL found his way in the humanitarian world because he felt the need for change. Hollywood's materialistic temperament was wearing on him. His career as a professional stuntman spanned over thirty years and it helped to prepare his mind and body for the hurdles of filming NGOs in developing nations, as well as giving him years of experience both in front of and behind the camera. Kevin decided to take his skills and advocate for those doing great things in the name of humanity. Since his first trip in 2007 to the K-5 minebelt in Cambodia with Freedom Fields USA and the international humanitarian demining group, The HALO Trust, he hasn't looked back. As of 2022, Kevin has had boots on the ground supporting NGOs in over thirty-five countries and has worked with the World Food Program, Operation Smile, The HALO Trust, International Health Emissaries, GUA Africa, Global Action for Children, and more. Acting as the personal film crew for Cindy McCain on her humanitarian missions, Kevin, with the assistance of his stunt buddy, John Evanko, accompanied her to Southeast Asia to document segments to be used during John McCain's run for Presidency of the United States in 2008. They then continued to travel with her, documenting her benevolent actions. Kevin's soapbox message, which he preaches often, is that "Humanity is simple one hand reaching out to help another hand in need, nothing more, nothing less." With this message as his guiding light, he continues to speak out in the darkness and to be a voice for those silenced by unfortunate worldly circumstance and for those that are just trying to do what is right.